Rebe

Clue

The unbelievable true story of Edward K. Reavie, a former grocery clerk, who created the greatest car show on earth and brought automotive royalty to a town with no traffic lights.

By

Sean E. Reavie

Rebel without a Clue-The unbelievable true story of Edward K. Reavie, a former grocery clerk who created the greatest car show on earth and brought automotive royalty to a town with no traffic lights.

Published by **Rich Pageant Media, LLC.**
www.richpageantmedia.com

And **Nostalgia Productions**, LLC
www.facebook.com/RebelWithoutAClue82
Book Design Copyright 2022 by Sean E. Reavie. All rights reserved.
Cover Design Copyright 2022 by Sean E. Reavie. All rights reserved.
Cover Photos Copyright The Ed Reavie Collection.
Internal Photos Copyright 2022 The Ed Reavie Collection unless stated otherwise.
Internal Design Copyright 2022 by Sean E. Reavie
Editor: Jack Randy Martin and Rich Pageant Media
Layout, Production and Printing: Rich Pageant Media

Published in the United States of America

ISBN: 9798423732356

Cover Photos- (top) a 15-year-old Ed dreaming about his heroes. (Left) Ed riding in the BATMOBILE with its creator, George Barris. (Right) Ed with automotive royalty Zora-Arkus Duntov and Carroll Shelby.

Table of Contents

Foreword

A passion for cars is something I believe you are born with.

It evolves from childhood with discoveries through experience, observation, movies, magazines like Hot Rod and Motor Trend, building model cars, and, in my case, the inspiration to draw!

Not being of driving age, it was a great outlet for horsepower-inspired artistic expression. The mid to late sixties was an incredible time to a car crazy kid. Fashion, music, Jimi Hendrix lighting guitars on fire, Stingrays, (cars and bikes), Cobras, Hemis. Jets with names like "Starfighter," "Voodoo," and "Phantom," how cool is that?

Fast forward, I was fortunate enough to draw upon this inspiration to energize and to add timeless soul to modern performance vehicles. These experiences had a huge impact on this modern era of seamlessly incorporating advanced technology and processes, which enable sending design and performance to the stratosphere.

My automotive infatuation continued to grow as I received my driver's license. Incredible new adventures were on the horizon that gave me first-hand experience working with real vehicles, mechanically and artistically. For instance, the movie "California Kid" inspired my first paint job that included flames on my first car, a 1968 Galaxie 500.

After graduating from Art Center College of Design, in Pasadena, California, I accepted a position at General Motors and went on to design everything from Corvettes to trucks. Adventures as a designer and enthusiast, with my lovely wife Carolyn and family, have shaped my life in ways I never could have imagined.

I have come to realize the love for cars is a timeless, universal phenomena that crosses families, careers, and culture with infinite variation.

Embodying this unique magic is the St. Ignace Car Show. I love the fact that it brings such an incredible mix of machines and people together in an unexpected, picturesque location right here in Michigan!

The year was 1991, and it was my first visit to the Upper Peninsula and this car extravaganza!!! As a young designer working in the Corvette and Camaro Studio for Design Chief, Jerry Palmer, and Vice President, Chuck Jordan, I was overwhelmed with pride to represent as a professional and a high-performance enthusiast. Wow!!!

The impact of my first St. Ignace visit still resonates with me to this day. Imagine the contrast of Norm Grobowski's '77 Sunset Strip T-Bucket alongside GM's latest concept, the futuristic mid-engine Corvette Indy, and everything else in between!

In 2020, Murray Pfaff, designer extraordinaire and event coordinator, kindly invited me to the show as Guest of Honor, where I had the distinguished pleasure of meeting Ed and Sean Reavie, the father who founded and promoted the St. Ignace Car Show for 40 years, and the son who is documenting it for history.

After fun and insightful conversation, the Reavies extended a gracious invitation to visit Ed's home. I had no idea what was in store...the mid-century ranch, in a classic U.P. neighborhood revealed an expansive collection of colorful car culture memorabilia!

The dedicated room was a giant "perm-a-grin" time machine of books, magazines and video, artwork, models, signed photos of industry, entertainment, leadership, celebrities, spanning 60-plus years.

To be honest, it was a bit overwhelming! As Ed and Sean guided me through this amazing space, I smiled as the powerful memories of my own experiences as a kid and throughout my life came rushing forward.

This was the culmination of a storybook weekend....an unforgettable adventure that felt just right with friends you have known for years or recently met. These are the experiences car enthusiasts are wired for.

I will always look forward to returning "home" in a car crazy way. Ed and Sean are excited to share their fabulous automotive journey with everyone! So, jump in and enjoy the ride!

Tom Peters
Chief of Design, General Motors Performance Car Studio (retired)
Designer C5-C9 Corvette
Corvette Hall of Fame

Editor's Note

I was already a snowmobile-racing gear head at the age of 13 when Ed Reavie created and organized the very first Straits Area Antique Auto Show, aka "St. Ignace." If its beginnings were humble, I sure didn't notice. I snapped seven rolls of film through my trusty Kodak Instamatic, then waited the customary ten days to see them, post-development. I had just left the drug store, prints in hand, when I walked past the First National Bank and saw Ed Reavie in his sidewalk-facing "fishbowl" office. It never occurred to me that he might be busy (ha ha!), so I just walked right in and asked him if he wanted to see my pictures. We sat there for a good fifteen minutes, looking at pictures, talking about cars, and talking about next year. There were a couple pics that he particularly liked, and he asked if he could use them for the 1977 show placard. Dang, I felt like a rock star. Ed indulged these spontaneous visits over the course of my high school years, and never once brushed me away. It was during this period that my parents were separated and my own dad was in Texas, so Ed was one of the few adult men with whom I had anything in common (cars) and it gave me great pleasure to spend a few minutes talking about them with someone who knew the topic. The thing that stuck with me all these years was that Ed indulged me, sincerely and earnestly, even though he had nothing to gain from it. I was just a kid with nothing to offer. I never forgot that.

When Sean approached me about contributing to this book, I jumped all over it. It was my chance, my one way to say Thank You to Ed Reavie for your kindness and your friendship during a time when it meant so much. Thank You, Ed.

Jack Randy Martin

Dedication

This book is dedicated to my sister, Danielle Sawyers. Without her relentless advocacy concerning my father's health, dad would have died years ago. Danielle gave up so much of her own life to give my father more of his.

Danielle traveled more than two hours round trip to see him and organized his life in a way he organized his shows. She cracked the whip on an often ungrateful, stubborn, and downright obstinate father to keep him healthy and living, demonstrating the same fierceness of her brother and father.

While I lived my life 2,000 miles away, my sister struggled with both our parents. Thank you, Danielle. Generations of car nuts and gear heads could not read these stories without the love and care you gave our father. Love you sis.

Autographs

Preface

Imagine a faraway place and a street named Memory Lane. Where Carroll Shelby, Father Viper, Zora Arkus-Duntov, George Barris, Bill Mitchel, Gordon Buehrig, and Big Daddy Ed Roth gather to share stories.

Where Gary US Bonds, The Shirelles, Little Eva, Danny and the Juniors, Herman's Hermits, Leslie Gore, The Crystals, Freddy "Boom Boom" Cannon, and Jerry Lee Lewis perform their hits.

Where Dick Biondi spins the hits of music's greatest era as muscle cars, street machines, and hot rods light it up, leaving clouds of nitrous and rubber behind. Where 100,000 people jam into a town of 2,000 residents and no traffic lights.

A place where Shelby Cobras snarl, the C8 Corvette shares the stage with the Hirohata Mercury Clone, The Swamp Rat, Brass Era cars, The Munster Coach, Rat Rods, a six-million-dollar Bugatti Royale, and a 1953 Corvette serial #003.

Cars of all eras and generations of gearheads share space under crystal blue skies, light breezes, and a perfect 72 degrees during a car show that occupies two miles of shoreline on one of the Majestic Great Lakes.

A place where legends meet their heroes and everyone feels at home during one incredible event.

Is this heaven?

No, it's St. Ignace.

Read on and join us at this magical event that, according to automotive royalty, is not only one of the greatest car shows in the world, but part of the tapestry of automotive history.

Words of Wisdom

When asked "Why St. Ignace, why here, in this little town?" Edward Reavie calmly stated, "Growing up, I was a gear head. All my heroes were car builders, designers, engineers, drivers. They were in California, the East Coast, all over the country. There was no way I could ever get to see and meet all of them so I decided to create such a spectacular event, all my heroes would come here to meet me. And that is exactly what happened."

Acknowledgements

So many people helped in this sprawling epic, it is hard to thank them all.

My wife, Melissa. For nearly a year she heard, "not now" and "sorry, I can't" and took it in stride. She knew the sacrifice needed.

Jack Randy Martin. Thank you for taking the time to mold and shape this book into something readable. Thank you for talking me off the ledge when I legitimately freaked out putting all this together, praising when worthy, correcting when needed. I owe you big time. Let's do a shot together sometime.

The General Motors Team invested 25 years into this show and community from specialty cars and their huge display, to their philanthropy to help build the Public Library. Their Friday night party, and their golf tournament on Mackinac Island, gave so much to St. Ignace and local charities. Thank you, Mr. Jon Moss, for the stories and for helping me fill in the blanks. Thank you to Craig Shantz for being such an ambassador to our small town.

The Chrysler Corporation for bringing an incredible display of cars and support for this show and community. Thank you, Mr. Tom Gale and Roy Sjoberg, for all you did for my father, and me.

Brian Baker, thank you for challenging me and reading this manuscript prior to publishing. Also, for the tip that a book this big needs more photos.

Tom "TJ" Tardy who, when my antique thumb drive containing every word of this book malfunctioned and "died", used his skills and company "GingerSec" to retrieve it. GingerSec techs also colorized the greyscale photos to add even more to this book. If you are in Arizona and need any IT help, look up Tom's company.

Judy Gross collaborated (with my father) on "St. Ignace Car Culture" from where I took a lot of the smaller details of the cars dad owned and what he did to customize them. Judy sent me a dozen handwritten pages of "Ed Stories" he told during that book process. Several appear in this book. Also Eileen Evers for your support with the book and you smile to every person who walked into the Chamber of Commerce.

Paul Ryerse, thank you for being such a great friend to my father. Paul faithfully drove dad around in his Chevy and took him to coffee and lunch with his friends.

Lisa Massey, Cathy Hamel, and Rene Halberg came to the house to take care of my father and keep him on track. Being a caregiver is not easy work, made harder by someone who lost his independence and mobility. Thank you.

To Judi Sved, lifelong friend to my mother, Mary Ellen, for standing by her with your giving heart through many difficult years.

Gary Engle, the "G-Man" behind the microphone for so many years. Remember when I worked for you in 1985? Friends for nearly 40 years.

Ed and Donna Ryan who worked with dad to raffle cars and as directors of vending and all the trouble shooting you did. I love you both.

All the heroes and legends who made themselves available to me for an interview and a quick story.

John "Top Hat" Jenza offered his insights and motivation to keep this project going, reading the first 50 pages and telling me I was on the right track. Calling me, helping with historical accuracy, and keeping me between the lines.

Quincy Ranville and the Visitors and Convention Bureau and the City of St. Ignace who helped market and promote this book.

Murray Pfaff who took the reins and continues to make this show great.

Wes Mauer Jr., a lifelong friend, who gave me all manner of publicity in the promotion of this book, scanned 35 hard copies of the photos in this book and sent them to me as digital files. Wes also gave me access to the archives of The St. Ignace News to help with my research. And, he gave me my first job in journalism when I was still in high school. The entire city mourned when your soul mate and wife, Mary died. Thank you for more than 40 years of support in my endeavors and for being family to me.

Scott Sefranka and his service dog Detective Bigby Wolf. Scott was shot and killed, brought back to life, and showed people what a real Superman is. Scott broke the 4th wall talking about his acute Post Traumatic Stress and his stand cost him his career. Scott inspired me, albeit years later, to finally face my demons and get help. I love you Scott.

Build It and They Will Come

Ed Reavie (left) shares a moment with two of his heroes. Zora Arkus-Duntov (center) and Carroll Shelby. Both men, who changed the face of automotive history, came to St. Ignace multiple times and called my father a friend.

Prologue

Standing on the airport tarmac of a remote city with barely two thousand residents, a town so small it contained no traffic lights,

44-year-old Ed Reavie prepared for the greatest moment of his life.

A one-time greaser with duck tailed hair and leather jacket, a shelf stocker, bag boy, and produce clerk in a grocery store, Ed was about to earn legendary status in a world he'd lived and breathed since he was a child.

A gear head, car nerd, possessing a ferocious work ethic and unbending will, the 6' 3" 220-pound Reavie trembled like a small child about to meet Santa Claus.

When the plane door opened, another legend, with a martini in one hand and an unfiltered Camel in the other, walked down the stairs, followed by the man in the cowboy hat, boots, blue jeans, and a leather jacket. Ed's heart stopped beating and he uttered under his breath, "Holy shit."

The coolest man on the planet made eye contact with Ed, strode over to him, his aura crackling with energy. Standing before him he looked up at Ed and extended his hand.

"I finally get to meet the most persistent son-of-a bitch I've ever known."

Carroll Shelby had arrived in St. Ignace.

The sleepy little town, and the Straits Area Antique Auto Show, would never be the same.

For that day, the legend of "St. Ignace" was born.

Introduction

A seed planted

Sunday, June 30, 1946, was no different for the impetuous six-year-old Edward Reavie than any Sunday previous or subsequent during his formative years.

It was 60 minutes wasted, every Sunday, for the young man whose mind did not allow anything to lock it into one singular place like the stuffy, ice-cold Methodist Church in which he was forced to toil.

His parent's only son, Edward felt the scowl of his perpetually angry mother, Elaine, and father Kress's feigned look of disappointment followed by a head shake.

His parents were pillars in the small community. Elaine was a small, joyless woman in a pill box hat, white gloves, and disdain for anyone not in her socio-economic class.

Kress was tall and lanky, a stern taskmaster with a presence felt by anyone around him. His Sunday best consisted of a collar so starched and stiff, it left marks on his neck when he turned his head.

Edward hated everything about church. The piety, the formality, the stark coldness, and the judgmental nature of its people. He wanted to be anywhere else but there.

He dreamed of being home, on the beach, playing with his toy cars, customizing his little red wagon, turning discarded orange crates into bitchin' customized orange crates, reading car magazines and dreaming of the day he could have one. Working at that beachfront cabin formed his personality which, later in life, became an astonishing force of nature that enabled him to succeed on sheer force of will alone.

His parents, in a constant state of befuddlement over their squirming, non-conformist young son, wanted nothing more for young Edward than to receive the gift of faith during a Sunday morning altar call.

Instead, on this day in history, Edward received a gift of another kind. One he would give back for nearly a half century and put St. Ignace, Michigan on the global map.

For on this day, a man named Raymond McLachlan, uncle of Edward's future brother-in-law Lester, gave him something other than the good tidings of the holy spirit.

Raymond was a car dealer and he gave Edward new car brochures as a means of keeping him out of the attention of church goers and the further scorn of his parents, with his antics of kicking the pew in front of him, sighing heavily, and asking if it was time to go home yet before stating that he needed to get to the little boy's room. Again.

The moment the brochures slipped into his hands, Edward immediately understood his purpose in life; cars. Everything about cars. The sights, the smells, the styles, the lines, and the designs.

That fascination didn't stop with the cars but the men who designed, built, and drove them.

The first thing that tingled his senses about the brochures, his new bible, was their smell; like a car showroom. From that point on, it was all about the car culture.

With the 1950s just around the corner, young Edward saw the rise of a new generation of music, clothing, attitude, and above all else, the love of the automobile.

The story you are about to read is the words of Edward Reavie as told to his son Sean. They are the words of a rebel, an agent of change, a dreamer, a doer, and an endless advocate for all things related to the car culture. A man of fierce, single-minded purpose that came off as engaging, sincere, and passionate to all who met him.

While faith was a gift Edward never received, he created his own place of worship that impacted five generations of gear heads and put him in Halls of Fame around the country and inclusion into the "Who's Who" Worldwide of Automotive Culture.

Raised in endless family dysfunction he carried on into his own family, Edward found his normalcy in another place.

A place where the music of his youth played endlessly, a place where poodle skirts, chopped, channeled, slammed, nosed, and decked cars cruised endless ribbons of asphalt with a guttural roar that vibrated his soul, and where the automobile reigned supreme.

Unlike many who were content with simply dreaming of this place, Edward not only dreamt it, he created that place, so others could escape with him and leave the struggles of life; if only for a few hours.

So, "roll down the windows and let the wind blow back your hair. The night's busting open, these two lanes can take us anywhere."

Author's Introduction

I am my father's son.

In 1976, I stood on Dock 2 in St. Ignace as an eight-year-old. I followed dad around as he worked the crowd and organized an event three times the size expected. If he was nervous, nobody could tell.

Standing an imposing 6' 3" and weighing 220 pounds with a large Fu Man Chu style mustache, my father commanded any space he occupied. There was no doubt as to who was in charge that day.

The small dock was full of show cars and dad stood among them, knowing for the first time he was onto something great. His only son was so much like his dad, except for one glaring difference; car shows were things I grew to hate as a small child.

My father dragged me all over the state of Michigan to shows that were, to me, the same as his experience with the church.

I was confined and taken from what I wanted to do most in life; read comic books, clip on a towel as a cape, and pretend I was a hero, running with arms extended, soaring above the clouds, saving innocents from harm.

Sitting in a dusty fairground, curled up in the back of his '48 Chevy, or on a broken lawn chair, time moved backward for me. Seeing this, dad always made sure to bring comic books. My heroes all wore capes. That led to something incredible for me, but that is another book.

I didn't share dad's love of the cars or the people, and it was arduous for me instead of intoxicating. No doubt he wanted me to share his passion but the word "obstinate" does not come close to describing me as a young man.

I am sure he then understood how his father felt seeing him rebel against his norm. Dealing with me, he apologized to his own laughing father when I went off on my little "Sean" tangents.

As the years went on, I was in awe of his ability to multitask. Though he worked full-time as a banker at the First National Bank in St. Ignace, he devoted all his free time to make the event he saw in his head a reality. An event with superstars of the car world; his heroes in his hometown. One that brought thousands of cars to a city with only 2,000 people.

One full of music, fun, and the excitement of the mid-1950s when he first heard Bill Haley and His Comets on the radio, and then Elvis and Buddy Holly and on the day that changed his life again, when he heard The Beatles for the first time. Music that changed his generation and caused his parents to opine on what would happen if you continued playing the Devil's music and refusing to grow up.

His bleach blonde duck tail and leather jackets made his mother blanch with fury that we later learned she drowned with Vodka and cigarettes that she'd hid from grandpa.

One that shook up the status quo. One that would make the same generation who hated his music, cars, and clothes, love his choice of events and love the cars and music played and now opine, it wasn't that bad afterall.

One that turned him into the duck tail wearing, leather jacket sporting, brill cream smooth, glass pack blasting, 396 Big Block engine growling anti-hero of the new generation of gear head.

One making the world take notice. The world took notice.

In June of 2022, the Straits Area Antique Auto Show, known for decades as simply, "St. Ignace" celebrates 46 years of excellence.

Two significant events occurred after the 2021 show. On Sunday, June 27th, Top Hat John, his lovely partner Victoria, and my father's son holding onto his arm to steady him, sat down and had ice cream together.

Dad struggled with his movements. Enfeebled by heart disease, declining vision, and serious cognitive issues, simply sitting down was a chore. Eating the ice cream cone was also a chore so I went inside to get a dish and spoon so that he might enjoy it with dignity.

As we finished, Top Hat John, an automotive historian with no equal, asked dad to tell him how on earth he was able to convince Carroll Shelby, the most iconic person in automotive history, to come to a town that was literally in the middle of nowhere, with 2,000 residents and no stop lights.

The question, normally delivered rhetorically, was direct, and dad perked up. Instead of just smiling and letting the asker form his own story, dad did something he never did.

This question lit dad's fuse. He had an instant recall of everything to do with Mr. Shelby coming to St. Ignace including the four years of persistence it took to convince him to do so.

"When he finally met me, he shook my hand hard and told me I was the most persistent son of a bitch he ever met," dad said with a chuckle. "I looked him in the eye and told him it must have worked because here you are."

We all sat completely enraptured with the story, to include Carroll and him getting pulled over by police, and a stubborn waitress who did not know, or care, about the man in the cowboy hat who made a simple request of getting a hamburger.

Told with humor, clarity, pride, and conviction, dad was animated in a way I missed. His mind is unique. I have not met another man like him anywhere. Spontaneously funny with incredible storytelling skill and with as close to a photographic memory one can ever have, dad held court as he told us the story.

At my father's side for 44 of the 45 car shows, the stories he told I had yet to hear. It was incredible. This is what we call a teaser as that story and many others appear later in this book.

John told dad his show was part of the tapestry of automotive history and how he built what he did, where he did, was beyond the scope of suspending disbelief.

Dad's struggles with his health were years long and a few weeks prior, he'd been taken in for another round of tests. The Monday after our ice cream, I was waiting in the Grand Rapids airport to fly back to the sweltering Phoenix heat, I received a message from my sister. The results of dad's latest CAT scan were in and showed significant dementia progression.

Sadness washed over me. For the next 6 hours on the plane, it struck me that the stories of Carroll Shelby in St. Ignace were going to be lost forever. Dad's mind held so much history and all that history was going to be systematically erased by this evil disease, gone forever.

My mind raced. How do I make those stories heard? Podcast? No. Magazine story? No. Newspaper story? No. Nobody had the knowledge of Ed Reavie to know what to ask.

Except for one person. Me.

I have a degree in journalism. I decided before I got into my car to drive home, I needed to write a book about Ed Reavie.

I wanted to interview my father and tell his stories to the world. I inherited a bit of his wit and storytelling skill, so I could not think of a better way to chronicle this amazing man and his show.

I wanted to tell the story about a one-time grocery clerk for the A & P store who changed careers when mom was pregnant with me. He went to work as an errand boy for the First National Bank and rose to the first Vice President in a legendary 40-year career, serving generations of St. Ignace families.

Outlining my plan for the book on a yellow legal pad (learned behavior), I called dad and told him to pull out his yellow legal pad and focus on the genesis of what became the car show of legend.

I heard a spark in his voice. I felt a renewed energy from him as he scrambled to get his yellow legal pad and Sharpie. I told him we were going to break this down in parts; His history, the show, the heroes, the concerts, the parade, and all the other shows he created and the memories to go with them. Oh, and the stories; the incredible stories.

The seed for this idea was planted in 1973 when dad saw his formative years so brilliantly told on the big screen in the legendary movie, "American Graffiti."

The foundation started in 1975 during a meeting of the minds with representatives of the City of St. Ignace when he, a lifelong car nut, volunteered to organize a one-time car show event to celebrate America's bicentennial.

He knew then what he had to do. I don't think he ever imagined opening dialogue with George Lucas and having Bo Hopkins, Candy Clark, and Paul LeMat in his living room, but the spark was there.

I interviewed my father twice a week (sometimes three) for six weeks and recorded our conversations. I sat at my computer, plugged in the headset, closed the blinds and began to write.

That gave me the core of the book. As summer changed to winter and then to spring, I interviewed automotive legends, recording stars, actors, actresses, and learned the impact that my father had on the world that had impacted him so much as a child.

We talked constantly, new memories, new stories and I went from worrying that I wouldn't have enough for a book at all, to crossing 500 pages and hoping reader fatigue doesn't set in.

As Dad told me the stories, I interjected out of pure joy, "I remember that."

One of the coolest things dad told me, "I never started this to make money. To me, it was about the quality of the show presented and promoted. That is what made it work."

Join me for a trip through automotive history, told by the man who created it from a void in his life. A history he lived. Edward Kress Reavie, entrepreneur, philanthropist, historian, creative genius, and my father.

Here's hoping you remember that too.

Introducing the 2022 Guest of Honor

Mr. Ken Lingenfelter

Starting the book with the last interview conducted, I wanted to introduce the man who takes center stage for St. Ignace, 2022.

Mr. Ken Lingenfelter is the son of a General Motors executive and purchased his first Corvette in 1977. After a successful career in real estate, he purchased the assets of Lingenfelter Performance Engineering from distant cousin, and NHRA racing legend, John Lingenfelter.

The "Lingenfelter Collection" of automobiles is world renowned and contains the 1954 EX-87 Corvette, the personal test car of Zora Arkus-Duntov known as the "Duntov Mule" which, in 1955 was driven to 163 MPH on the Arizona Proving Grounds by Smokey Yunick. It is the world's first V8 Corvette.

Mr. Lingenfelter called while on the road and we had a fun conversation. He later sent me photos of him driving the EX-87. Like all the great car guys I interviewed over the last 11 months, I felt as if I knew Mr. Lingenfelter my entire life, such was the ease of our conversation.

Upon learning that I live in Arizona, Mr. Lingenfelter mentioned his love of the area and its incredible car culture. Murray Pfaff asked him to be Guest of Honor at St. Ignace 2022, and Mr. Lingenfelter told me, "The stars aligned, and I was able to do it, and I am looking forward to it."

Mr. Lingenfelter fell in love with the '63 split window Corvette as a child and told me he had virtually every Hot Wheels car ever made. Ironically, during our conversation, my call waiting chimed and it was none other than Mr. Hot Wheel himself, Larry Wood, returning my call.

Mr. Lingenfelter was stunned by the astonishing list of past guests of honor. Because he is a lover of Corvettes, I told him the story (printed later in this book) about Mrs. Arkus-Duntov to which he replied, "Knowing her, that doesn't surprise me."

Mr. Lingenfelter is friends with virtually everyone in this book and is pleased to join such a list of dignitaries.

"What made the impression on me is that the St. Ignace car show has everything under the sun," he said. "It's a long drive to get there but the show brings in everything for the car enthusiast. High end, low end, and it attracts people from everywhere."

I explained my reverence for the car culture, the people within, how they treat everyone with respect and as a friend, and Mr. Lingenfelter told me he feels the same way.

"Spending time with car people, whether you are a Chevy guy, Ford guy, or Mopar guy, is the best," he told me. "The fact is, enthusiasts are enthusiasts to the core."

He explained the fascinating history of the "Duntov Mule Car.". He spoke of Zora blasting around the Arizona Proving Ground track at 164 MPH, and said, "You have to have nerves of steel or may have a few screws loose to go that fast in that car. Wow."

Mr. Lingenfelter and Top Hat John, one of my fathers and mine's dearest friends, are longtime friends. This made me love the culture even more.

Mr. Lingenfelter owns several of Carroll Shelby's cars, and said he was at an auto show in Detroit where Mr. Shelby was speaking. On stage in a tuxedo, Mr. Shelby was clearly uncomfortable.

"Can you imagine Carroll Shelby in a tuxedo?" he said with a laugh. "It was black tie night and Carroll, out of the clear blue sky, looked at me and said 'That's Ken Lingenfelter! Get your (edited for the family nature of this book) up here. If I have to be uncomfortable in this zoot-suit, so do you, my man."

Saying the moment was wonderful, Mr. Lingenfelter said with a laugh, "My god the language."

I shared a story that Linda Vaughn told me about Carroll Shelby in relation to her attending the St. Ignace event and it was along the same lines of editing. That story is later in this book.

I told Mr. Lingenfelter how lucky I am to be involved in writing this book as I spoke to so many incredible people in this genre, and he thanked me for including him.

Before we closed the interview, he asked me a question.

"Am I going to get a chance to meet your father?"

That really filled my heart. Thank you, Mr. Lingenfelter.

What is it about this show, so remote, so far away, that attracted incredible people like Ken Lingenfelter, Linda Vaughn, Carroll Shelby, Zora Arkus-Duntov, Bill Mitchell, George Barris, and others?

Turn the pages and read about the one common denominator regarding the success of this show. My father, Edward K. Reavie.

In the subsequent pages of this book, everyone is getting the chance to meet Ed Reavie; the six-year-old hellion turned promoter who created his own world and then shared it with everyone.

PART ONE

Growing Up

The six-year-old hellion Edward Reavie with his "customized" little red wagon - that he painted white. That smile confounded family, friends, and teachers as the young rebel did things his way.

Chapter 1: Small Town Boy

"Well, my feet they finally took root in the earth. But I got me a nice place in the stars; and I swear I found the keys to the universe, in the engine of an old, parked car."

Bruce Springsteen, Growin' Up

St. Ignace, Michigan is the city on the North end of the majestic Mackinac Bridge and is rich in history. At the boundary of Lake Michigan and Lake Huron, St. Ignace is joined to Michigan's lower peninsula by the Mackinac Bridge. Spanning nearly five miles, it is the world's longest suspension bridge. Its towers extend like the arms of God from the deep water, up 552 feet into the bright blue sky.

Founded in 1671, St. Ignace was the hub of the fur trading industry in the 17th century and was the site of a battle in the war of 1812. In 2021, the town celebrated its 350th year. Older than the nation in which it resides.

The U.P contains 29 percent of Michigan's land mass (16,377 square miles), but only 3 percent of its population (301,608). And, owing to its size, contains two separate time zones.

The U.P contains the only county in the country to be sued by a sitting President (Teddy Rosevelt) and has 84 percent of its land covered by forest. Lake Superior is the size of South Carolina, and the first Michigan-versus-Ohio battle came over the strip of land that is now Toledo.

Michigan lost and got the consolation prize known as the Upper Peninsula. You like apples, Ohio? How do you like them apples?

Off its Lake Huron shores sits historic Mackinac Island, home of the iconic Grand Hotel. The island itself is a world-wide tourist destination for those who want to wrap themselves in the blanket of history, showcased in a place that does not allow motor vehicles and where the clip clop of horse hooves echoes down the street. The aroma of sugar and chocolate permeate the air.

To the geographically confused, Mackinaw City is the only Mackinac to have a "W," while the county, city, and bridge, all have the "C".

The summer population endures a massive increase, owing to the Island and the now legendary St. Ignace Car Show which celebrates its 46th year in 2022.

At its peak, the car show brought 100,000 persons to the tiny Northern Michigan town with a population of 2,200 and more show cars than that population.

Edward K. Reavie was born May 4, 1940, to Kress and Elaine Reavie. Edward A. Reavie, Ed's grandfather, was an entrepreneur ahead of his time.

He, like all subsequent Reavie men, was a big, surly, persistent, relentless entrepreneur, (or depending on the person describing Reavie men, an asshole).

Edward A. Reavie built a home on the shores of Lake Michigan off the old US Highway 2 (US2) on the west side of town. For modern reference, it is across the road from the Deer Ranch on the shoreline.

His large family loved to visit and spend time on the lake. A situation Edward A. found less than delightful. He had a plan to handle such a thing.

The Reavie men, to put it honestly, can be real pricks about simple things like phone calls after 6 p.m., (or phone calls that could have been text messages and meetings that needed to be emails) putting vegetables on pizza, or having family drop in unannounced and mess with the schedule we have in our heads as to how the day needs to unwind.

To thwart their constant intrusion, the intimidating Edward A., standing 6' 6" and tipping the scales at more than 250 pounds, built cabins on his property to house his relatives simply to do away with their presence.

Instead of sipping his bourbon-infused coffee to drown out their chatter, he would sit on his porch in silence, knowing the cabins he'd built for them were far enough away as to not cause him concern.

For him, it was less work to build a series of cabins than to spend energy talking or spending quality time with your kinfolk. A very normal thing in my family. Edward A, on my paternal side, is considered a genius. On the maternal side? That asshole designation for sure.

As the years passed, Edward A. grew weary of his kinfolk enjoying his views and beach when he felt others would pay for the privilege. It occurred to him that those cabins could generate a nice cash flow and thus, Silver Sands Resort came to be. No word on the members of his family who were evicted. He also built a convenience store with two gas pumps to attract passersby to spend their money, the first such store in Upper Michigan. It was located on the North side of the highway.

A man ahead of his time and master of the alchemy of turning bright yellow citrus fruits into a tasty, thirst quenching drink, Edward A. became a successful entrepreneur at the expense of alienating his family. A fair trade, in his mind.

It was on those Lake Michigan shores that Edward Reavie II spent his summers, concocting an entire new world and ways to confound his family.

With Kress, arms folded, and stare fixed, my rascally father was stunned to learn that his time at this postcard-like setting would not be all frolic and fun. Not by a long shot.

Instead, the horrified young man found himself cutting grass, whitewashing the rocks throughout the property, staining and varnishing all 14 cabins, and, wait for it, making sure the outhouses were clean and orderly at all times.

This steady diet of horrific chores no doubt instilled the work ethic my father was known for later in life and that led him to spend his free time creating, shaping, and executing the plans to create the St. Ignace Car Show.

A family friend, and Edward K's future relative by marriage, saw how unsettled he was during church service and gave the hyper six-year-old some automotive brochures to limit the distractions coming from the pew each Sunday morning.

In his itchy church clothes, he flopped around the wooden pews, moaning, groaning, whimpering, relentlessly moving. His spontaneous outbursts and outright disdain for the subject matter embarrassed Elaine to the point of asking the pastor to inject young Edward with the holy spirit while praying away whatever it was that inhabited his body.

When I asked him about the church experience, dad blanched immediately. "I did not like it at all," he said. That is when Ray McLachlan intervened.

Ray was a car dealer who sold Buicks, Chevrolets, and Frigidaire appliances out of his dealership where the current Ace Hardware stands on main street.

Ray saw the irritation in the young lad and gave him a handful of new Chevy brochures he used as dealership sales tools.

Still enraptured by the moment, dad had one clear memory of how the brochures smelled as he lifted them to his nose and drew in a breath.

"It was a new beginning for me. I kept them all but, stupid me, I cut them up and put them into scrapbooks."

Dad recalled a story during the 40th Annual St. Ignace Car Show (his last as promoter), of giving a brochure for a 1955 Suburban to

Craig Shantz (head of General Motors Performance Line) and the first thing Craig did was smell them, smiling the entire time.

I do the same thing with books. I still buy tangible books simply so I can smell the pages. It is relaxing and nostalgic.

Dad was already hooked, thanks to a relative by marriage I never knew. The seed was planted. Insert hackneyed metaphor here.

My father absorbed everything about cars and, by the time he was seven, could tell you the year, make, and model of any car he saw. Later in life, he could tell the manufacturer of an exhaust system simply hearing it. My father is said to have a photographic memory. To hear the instant recall of events, people, and cars, I don't doubt it. My friends always marveled at how I could recite the backs of baseball cards and tell you how many RBIs Lou Gerigh had without even thinking. I still recite, word-for-word, "Rise of the Jabberwocky", a poem we learned in 5th grade. I can't explain it. I was also accused of memorizing all the answers in the Trivial Pursuit game. Accusations with some merit.

Kress Reavie, my grandfather, was another in the long line of intimidating Reavie men. He was President of the School Board and ran his household with an iron fist. He graduated with honors from the "Old School" and was a stereotypical depression-era man.

He worked for everything he had and did not suffer foolishness lightly. Or, at all. From anyone. Even his squirrely grandson with the long, platinum blonde hair that so infuriated Elaine, she put barrettes in it, dressed me in a skirt, and sent me home this way, along with parenting books for my horrified mother. Yes, I am in therapy. I still remember that day. A bad byproduct of the memory skills.

Kress stood over six feet, with a tight crew cut, horned rimmed glasses. and a scowl that shut down any displays of discontent from my father and, years later, me. "One thing you never did," dad said from experiencing it, "Was play grab ass around Kress Reavie."

Growing up with such rigid, conservative parents was just okay for dad. Not Ozzie and Harriet by any means, dad did his own things in life and stayed below the radar while his father worked two jobs. His main income from the State Highway Department, and secondary as owner and manager of the seasonal Silver Sands Resort.

It was at that resort, on Cabin #7 porch, at age nine, dad and a friend found old orange crates they pretended were cars. He still refers to this hunk of wooden planks as his "Orange Crate car."

He was not satisfied pretending the benign orange crate was what it was and immediately set about customizing it.

With a cup for a mirror and a coat hanger for an antenna, he modified the crate into what he envisioned. In a very prophetic statement he told me, "I changed it because I didn't like the way it was." He did the same with his second car, changing it from basic white to a stunning Peacock Blue. His reason? So, he wouldn't see another one just like it.

Dad was nine when he stood in front of the comic books and candy at LaRocque's Drug Store and saw a magazine that changed the course of his life.

More on that later.

As a teenager, having his own money was a good thing, as it paid for car parts and magazines. So, on a whim, he went into the old A & P Store in St. Ignace, applied for a job, and was hired on the spot.

He spent 12 years rising from bag boy to store manager, when he heard the Beatles for the first time ("what the hell is this?") and was still actively cruising into the wee hours of the morning in the bevy of incredible cars he owned through the years.

Acquiring that job bore consequences and responsibility. Living under Kress Reavie's roof was not a right; it was a privilege.

Now with cash in his pocket, it was not to be spent on fruitless endeavors such as a full tank of gas, shoehorns to customize his car's rims, or the latest "bee bop" record.

Upon receiving his first cash payment as a bag boy, Kress met dad at the door and handed him a payment book.

Dad asked what this strange looking booklet was all about and was given a rather blunt explanation on economics and his new role in a free market economy.

Payday Wednesday had an entirely new meaning. Dad got paid and, to his ever living horror, so did Kress. He was told he had to pay rent and help with food purchases, and quickly saw his dreams of the new car magazine on the drug store shelf evaporate.

When he balked and pushed back, Kress helpfully gave him several options. The first was a one-time, three-day grace period for dad to do some checking on other situations and roofs under which he could goof off, listen to music, and not listen to the homeowner.

He recalls exactly what he was told; "He glared at me with those steely eyes of his and said, Son, if you find a better deal, take it and I will open the door for you to leave."

After two days of searching, looking for something, anything, to allow him to not be $10 light every week, dad was astonished to find out no such deal existed. On the third day, he handed Kress the rent.

Dad was upset at the sudden onset of adult responsibilities, but soon became aware of the power that came with them. As a paying tenant, he no longer had to abide by the constricting house rules and iron fisted accountability of Kress Reavie.

The rent payment meant, "an unbelievable amount of freedom" and allowed him to come and go as he pleased. If he kept paying rent, then he moved about on his own time and did things he deemed important without resorting to the cloak and dagger stylings of "taking food to orphans." (actually, an all-night cruise with his friends)

And he did not have to explain to his mother why he woke up in the driveway after being dragged through a cornfield by the hellions he counted as friends. Did not have to explain coming home in the throes of a malted hops frenzy, wandering through the living room into a horrified Elaine's weekly game of Bridge with other well healed socialites, burping and smelling like a wet dog. Allegedly.

All was not bad being the son of Kress Reavie, who groomed his rebellious son to understand what hard work brings in life.

Kress's perspective regarding working hard and creating something of your own eventually rubbed off on Edward, which rubbed off on me. Living at Silver Sands was a utopia for dad. Growing up and spending his summers there formed his early dreams in life.

The $40 a week income taught him that, by paying his dues, he could get things in life he wanted. Things that his friends, living at home for free, never understood.

Dad says that to this day, when he tells this story, people are astounded he had to pay rent to live at home with his parents. Not when he turned 18, but the day he earned his first paycheck at 16.

People think I am kidding when I tell the story of him giving me a payment book for my first car after he introduced me to the First National Bank loan specialist.

I asked for his help in securing my ride, so he took me to the bank, sat me at the loan officer's desk, helped me fill out the loan application, and even more helpfully, took the check and made sure the car was purchased. He handed me the payment book with a sly grin straight out of the Kress Reavie handbook; it must have made him feel great.

This early life lesson prepared him for the obstacles and sacrifice of building an event to reach all his automotive heroes. And it served him well.

Once he was paying his dues and was no longer under the rules of the stiff, unyielding Methodists Kress and Elaine, he pulled the plug on going to church. He only returned years later, when Kress had died, to take Elaine to church in his 1955 Chevy, every Mother's Day until her death.

The relentless call for a cool car was not new to the Reavie family. Kress had a dream car, and it wasn't a Rolls, a Cadillac, or a customized creation. It was a Buick Roadmaster.

"That was his absolute dream," car dad said. "He wanted to see the four holes in the hood signifying the Road Master." Sadly, this was a dream his father never achieved.

Kress came home one day in a brand new 1956 Ford Fairlane Town Sedan with green interior, white walls, and a four-barrel-equipped engine. It also had power seats, and Kress held court with townsfolk showing how cool it was for his seats to slide back and forth with the touch of a button. It's one of the few times dad remembered Kress smiling.

He told me Kress got all his cars from Mackinac Sales in St. Ignace, the Ford Dealership still owned by the same family.

Kress had a sister who married a Ford Motor Company executive and got a new car yearly so when Kress was in the market for a new car, he purchased the car his sister had been driving. Years later, dad said Kress came home from picking up his new used car and, oddly, for Kress, he seemed downright jolly.

Why? He was pulled over and ticketed for speeding. The man in his late 70's, with a heart condition, was practically dancing for joy at having been clocked going 81 mph in a 55 zone.

I often wonder which trooper (or city officer) gave Kress a ticket. He was a highly respected member of the community who loved St. Ignace High School sports.

After his first heart attack, Kress, my "Papa", and my father started to build a relationship for the first time. They talked, they took drives, Kress came to see the car show and also came to all of my basketball games.

Kress never missed a St. Ignace football game in 50 years. The city rewarded him with a "Golden Ticket," allowing him free admission to any La Salle High School sporting event.

I still remember seeing him in the stands every time I ran out of the locker room. The one year I also played football, he was always on the sidelines, never in the stands, in his flannel jacket and orange hunting cap.

Coach Barry Pierson led the La Salle High School Saints to the 1983 Michigan State Football Championship. Kress was very proud of that accomplishment. I was still growing, injured my Achilles tendon, and never took the field that year. Coach Pierson, another fearsome man, asked me to keep players stats during the game. He was another staple in town. When I came back home in 2019, I saw him in the Northern Lights Restaurant as he was walking out. He stopped at the door, looked across the restaurant, saw me, smiled and waved. I got up, walked to him and gave him a hug. He was pleased to see me after all those years. Small towns are great.

Kress's position of President of the School Board helped my father the most. The highly intelligent Edward just had no interest in high school, was a "push out" and barely made it through. Without Kress's intervention, dad would have had to repeat his senior year. Using the veiled threat, "Do you really want to deal with him another year?" to the school administration, Kress pushed for dad's diploma to be signed and avoid the shame of his only son failing high school.

His only daughter, my Aunt Kay, was a straight A student, went on to earn a Master's degree, and had an incredible tenure as a high school teacher. It was sad for all of us that Kay succumbed to Alzheimer's disease, her brilliant mind erased. She died with my uncle Tom at her side in December of 2020. Aunt Kay was my education inspiration and, later in life, I earned my Master's degree with a 4.0 GPA.

Chapter 2: Cars Are Life

"If you don't look back at your car after you park it, you own the wrong car."
Edward Reavie

Dad was fond of telling me if he ever turned into the thing he thought of all the time, then he firmly believed he would be a hot blonde driving a red convertible.

On his own and having risen to store manager, with money in his pocket and a dream in his heart, it was time to get the car of his dreams. He'd learned to drive at age 12 in the 1940 Chevy Truck used at Silver Sands Resort. His love for cars grew to imagining what he could do once he got one. The treatment he and his best friend gave to Kress's Chevy Truck is a story of legend best told by both. And it will be.

Dad did not embrace tradition and wanted to give cars a special flavor. Now it was time to get just that car. Though he was still paying rent to Kress and Elaine, Kress insisted dad adhere to one house rule; eat one meal a day together at the dining room table. The older sister Kay was away at college, so it was just the three of them.

He always took the measure of Kress's mood when they sat together. He told me that you simply did not drop anything onto his lap, you had to strike when the mood was one of embrace, and that only seemed to happen during the magical family dinner.

I've come to learn and appreciate that the Reavie men's leadership style was a velvet glove over an iron fist; delicate, but steely in resolve and conviction. People saw strength and confidence with an underlying, unbreakable will in the way they carried themselves.

Dad was 8 years old when the love of custom cars began. It started when he first heard that "sound." The sound from dual pipes and echo cans hung on a lowered, maize yellow 1947 Ford with skirts, spotlights, spinner caps, and a flathead V8.

Don Clark, from downstate near Ann Arbor and a resident of Silver Sands, owned the first car dad remembered running out the door to see and hear when it started.

Years later, one of dad's A & P co-workers, Duane Sorenson, had a car dad desperately wanted to get and customize with his own images of coolness. Duane approached him about buying it, and dad knew he needed funds from Kress to make it happen.

But when was the time to ask? Much like Ralphie and his want of the Red Ryder BB Gun, dad needed to wait for the exact moment to strike and not F*** it up by metaphorically shooting his eye out.

Between mouthfuls of meatloaf, mashed potatoes, and swigs of thick butter milk favored by Elaine, dad thought he detected the hint of a smile on the stone-faced Kress. Now was the moment, he thought. Time to strike. With Perry Como crooning in the background, my 16-year-old dad casually brought up the topic of the new car to his authoritative father.

Dad, with his voice shaking and up one octave, tiptoed around springing the flamboyant car purchase on the buttoned-down, conservative Kress. Much like Ralphie, dad croaked out a fast "IWANNAGETANEWCAR", drew a breath, and started to sculpt his mashed potatoes into a perfect likeness of a Buick Roadmaster hood.

Fluent in "desperate speak", Kress responded, "What is it? A nice sedan?" Dad took a shot of buttermilk to calm his nerves, wiped his mouth with his sleeve, slammed down the empty glass and answered...

"Not exactly."

Upon being told the car was not a dark, four-door sedan in all original condition, Kress blanched in high octave discontent at my father's choice of conveyance. He waved his hands around and tilted his head back as he groaned. Dad poured himself another glass of delicious buttermilk, pressed his desire for the car and finally, to his shock, instead of being kicked out of the dining room, Kress agreed to go see the car.

"At that moment, I knew I was in," dad exclaimed at the first chink in Kress's armor known in his lifetime.

Instead of hearing the normal, "Hell no, you are not buying that G Damn thing" Kress wiped his mouth from his own shot of buttermilk and told dad to take him to see it.

The gunslinger and his prodigy walked side-by-side to where the car was parked; dad smiled and Kress raised his eyebrows, rubbed his chin, and wondered if dad was secretly adopted.

It was a carnival red 1953 Ford Convertible with a black top and black interior. The price, a remarkable $800, meant that Kress had to front the purchase. With the pink slip, dad received another payment book. This one for the car. (The book remains in dad's collection.) The payment was $50 a month, forcing dad to tighten his belt a bit. The financial shock of car ownership really hit him the day he received a notice for insurance from Cheeseman Insurance Agency.

The Cheeseman Insurance Agency is presently in its third generation with Henry, then Greg and finally Greg Jr. writing the policies my father had on the 53 cars he owned throughout his lifetime.

Dad got his first insurance bill from Henry Cheeseman and presented it to Kress, unsure what it was. Kress looked at him with a half snarl, half humorous smile and asked him what on earth he expected him to do about it. Dad explained that he didn't understand what to do with it, either, and didn't have the money to pay anymore bills on top of the cost of gasoline, cokes, dates, hair cream, and being the coolest 16-year-old in town. Without missing a beat, Kress pointed to the garage at the back of the property and told my father to park his "pretty little red car" in there until he figured out a way to pay his own bill. Dad parked the car as his mind reeled from yet another Kress Reavie life lesson. He finally did save the money to pay Henry for insurance. To this day, he proudly says he never again missed a payment to Greg Sr. and Greg Jr. since 1956.

When I bought my first car, a 1983 Dodge 300ES, that insurance policy was written by Greg Sr. The first thing I did was get a car catalog of aftermarket parts and purchased a Hurst Grip shifter for the four-speed manual.

The '53 Ford was a hit and dad had the only convertible in school. "Here I was in the 10th grade, and I not only had a better car than the other students, but the teachers," dad recalled with a laugh.

True to his nature, he changed a lot of things to make his cool kid convertible even cooler. He rolled up his buttermilk-stained sleeves and set about nosing, decking, and frenching in Oldsmobile tail lights. He removed the bumper guard, modified the grill, added Oldsmobile spinners and dual spotlights. He also removed the Coronado Deck (fake continental kit), added the "Bermuda Ding Dong Bell" (which he still has) and made an electric trunk release; the first in town. But before he could enjoy the fruits of his newly insured car, Kress made an out-of-the-blue request.

"He asked to borrow the car," dad said, still sounding shocked. "He never did that. Kress was a man you just did not say no to for anything, so I said yes more for self-preservation of myself than the car."

He went to work in his father's boring sedan and hoped no one would see him. He parked behind the store, covered his face, slid along the wall, hunched over, lest his cool cat image be tarnished being seen with a four-wheeled yawner.

He returned home from work, saw his car parked near the garage and went to give it a hug and kiss and welcome it home. Then he noticed something that shocks him to this day.

"There was another tail pipe sticking out of the car" dad exclaimed, the disbelief still in his voice.

When asked, Kress told my father it was his birthday present. He'd taken it to Mackinac Sales Ford and had a new exhaust and glass pack installed. Dad now had a beast of a car and cruised endlessly with his own fixes.

He once again took it to a body shop, had it lowered, the chrome removed, and added spinner hubcaps and bubble skirts.

"It was a fine, fine ride and I was only 16. Life was good. I had this car and always a cute girl sitting next to me." Dad spent countless days and nights driving the same loop that thousands of kids, just like him, drove during every one of his car shows.

All good things must come to an end and so did this fine American motorcar. Dad was its 5th owner, and the car simply wore out from use. Vern Erskine had originally owned it (years later I attended school with Vern's son, Brad), but his pregnant wife made him take the car back. Four owners later, dad drove it until the wheels fell off.

Dad's friend, Don Vallier, became a massive early influence. He had moved to California in 1953 but returned in 1958 to graduate. Their family sedan, a 1953 Chevy, returned with some California cool changes, including being raked, nosed, decked, and painted bronze. It had screw-on Moon disks, Lake side pipes, the first-ever furry Angola dice in St. Ignace, dual exhaust, and a split manifold.

But that wasn't the only car Don had to blow back dad's greased hair. It was an insanely bitchin' 1955 Chevy that opened his eyes to the possibilities of customizing.

The white convertible was scalloped in turquoise with Tijuana tuck-and-roll interior and completed with a turquoise diamond patterned, tonneau-covered backseat.

It was powered by a Corvette engine mated to a stick-shift, overdrive combo, full length Lake pipes, a modified grill and Corvette wheel covers. "When Don drove into town in that car, it blew us all away," dad said, his voice accented with wonderment, 60 years later.

His next car was a Peacock Blue and Colonial Ivory 1956 Ford Crown Victoria two-door hardtop that he called "Little Star." It had a stick shift transmission with overdrive. His friend Larry Pelone owned it and dad followed him out to Mackinac Sales, down payment in hand.

The '56 Ford went immediately into the body shop so dad could customize it. He de-chromed it, dropped it to the ground and painted it solid blue. Stanley Yantz, a brilliant painter, assisted with the customization that included new exhaust, modified grill, and 1959 Buick tail lights.

Dad cruised with his life-long friend Calvin "Bucky" McPhee and drove the wheels off his new ride. Such was their love for driving that they decided they wanted a hamburger in Ypsilanti, Michigan (some 300 miles away) at a local cruising drive-in. They ate, cruised the streets of the big city, and drove home.

Whether working, sleeping, or cruising, dad practically lived in the car, and nearly wore a trench in the asphalt as he drove around town, the township, and the county. Never one to get complacent, he set his sights on another cool ride.

Through the years cruising with Bucky, one constant remained concerning his cars and Bucky. No matter the car, the make, or the modifications.

"He could never beat me racing. Never," Bucky told me.

The shenanigans truly started at one place, Silver Sands Resort. Bucky told me a story that had me in stitches and dad never mentioned it to me or simply forgot as time passed.

"Your grandfather had a 1939 Chevy Pickup that Ed and I bombed around the beach all summer," Bucky said. "At that time, there was a two-track road all the way down the shoreline."

On a weekend when Kress and Elaine were not at the resort, the two friends had either a brilliant idea or the 10th bad one of their young lives. Either way, it only added to the legend of Kress Reavie's disdain for my father.

"We decided to make a hot rod out of your grandfather's pickup truck," Bucky said with a laugh.

Yeah, it was a bad one.

Taking a chisel and a hammer, the wannabe car designers removed the truck's fenders. When Kress came home, things escalated in a hurry. Upon seeing the truck, he leveled both dad and Bucky with his signature scowl and Bucky reacted quickly.

"I jumped on my bike, took off, and pedaled home, not giving Kress a chance to say anything," he laughed. "And that is when it all started."

Speaking of the debacle when next we spoke, dad said flatly, "First thing, that pinhead was wrong; it was a 1940 Chevy, and we also hand painted white walls on the tires with white paint," he told me. "The car looked great, from 20 feet away, any closer that is when problems started."

As Bucky recounted his many cars, he also recalled the two friends getting their first cars; Bucky, a 1947 Chevy Coupe and dad a 1950 Chevy slant back.

They were best friends from a young age and remain so to this day. When they meet, they are both quick with a story, hilarious, pin-point insults (dad famously left a handful of his just cut hair in a baggie in Buckey's mailbox in reference to Bucky's thinning hair line) but as always, they revert to talking about cars. The many years, months, days, hours, and minutes of their friendship gave lasting memories.

Though great friends, they always competed for the cooler cars. They drove everywhere together but, in the end, there was only one way to settle who had the baddest car in town and no, it wasn't a wicked black '55 Chevy or a yellow deuce coupe. To my father's mounting dismay when they would drag race, Bucky blew him away. Every time.

As they aged, each tried to one up the other. When dad had a flat head engine, Bucky got one with overhead valves. And beat him again.

I can just picture my father in Buckey's dust cloud, waving his fist and coloring the air with a string of expletives that would bring down Kress's hammer. Some of those expletives were no doubt uttered in future years with dad's constant befuddlement over his only son's life decisions.

One that comes to mind is when I told him I wanted to be a ventriloquist. As a father, there is no way to untwist your horrified, contorted face in time to be supportive. Still, he did get me a ventriloquist doll for Christmas and, to my horror, it sits in his museum in silent judgment of the worst decision I made as a kid.

But I digress. Back to dad and his endless string of failures trying to cross the line ahead of his lifelong friend.

Given dad's competitive spirit, the failures could not stand. At some point, he would prevail. Somehow. I envision the two of them in tricked out mobility scooters, dad's candy apple red, ghost flamed, and chrome wheels. Bucky's Lake Placid Blue with pipes, Thrush muffler, white tuck-and-roll leather upholstered seat, bombing down the hallway, sidewalk, or parking. Bermuda Bells peeling.

Walkers? We don't need no stinking walkers!

As the years went on, dad's futility did as well, owing to a level of losing consistency on par with my beloved Detroit Lions (even losing can be consistent). He purchased a beautiful 1956 Crown Victoria. Bucky got a 1957 Olds Rocket '88.

"Needless to say," Bucky started recounting another crushing defeat of my father. "He could never beat me with any car we got."

Bucky told me that, as early as Kindergarten, dad always doodled cars on his papers and books. His restless energy, blonde hair, and creativity made him stand out from the crowd. Remaining friends in such a small town was easy, as they always had the same teachers. St. Ignace is cool that way. James McDonald taught both my parents, my sister, and me, in his American History class. That doesn't happen much. The four of us also had the same driver's education teacher if you can believe such a thing.

Buckey and dad graduated high school and spent summers together at Silver Sands. They ordered brand new 1961 Chevy Impala "bubbletops" hardtops on the same day from Jerry Mahony motors on West US2. Bucky's was fawn beige, and dad's dark blue. Both had power pack engines and stick shift transmissions with overdrive.

Once obtained, each did their own custom work with dual glasspacks, long scavenger pipes, complete de-chrome, new taillights, and four-bar spinners for dad. Bucky nosed and decked his, rerouted the tailpipes, and added spinners and glasspacks.

Dad was beyond excited when he got the call from Bucky (who worked at the body shop, which only led to dad's paranoia about his losing streak) that his car was done, and he was delivering it. It had only seven miles on it and Bucky swears none were on account of him taking his best friend's car for a "test" drive. That would never happen. Ever.

Ten minutes later, dad stood outside, looking down the road like a small child looking out the window at Christmas. He saw it roaring down the highway and his heart skipped; he was filled with joy.

It was so close. So close. Then he heard a sickening grind and crunch. He ran to see his brand-new car smoking in the middle of the road.

"I was driving to the resort, and I saw your dad standing on the road to see his car," Bucky said.

Suddenly, calamity ensued.

"The car came to a screeching stop, the rear wheels locked up, and the car skidded sideways to a dead stop in the middle of the highway.

In their excitement to see the car, they (or he, depending on whom you asked) neglected to put grease in the Posi-traction rear axle

Shocked at the turn of events in front of him, dad refunded his lunch, twice. Looking to the heaven's, hands extended, he screamed, "NOOOOOOOOO!" (Ok, I made that up, but I would not be surprised as this is a man who once threw up after his '73 Type 3 VW FastBack got hit with a rock, causing a massive dent in the body.)

That story, and the slippery slope it soon descended, is the first story in the "Being Ed Reavie" section of this book. Don't flip ahead. Trust me, you will be horrified if you laugh.

Where was I? Right, dad's rear axle on his new car blew up. Here we go.

The car got towed back to the body shop and fixed with all new parts. Once returned, with only seven miles and the paper still on the windows, it fell to the cutting torch as he installed the aforementioned customizations.

A shocked Silver Sands guest saw the brand-new car getting the blow torch treatment from a tall, skinny, bespectacled, greaser, and just had to ask what was happening.

Dad stood, beaming with pride, and said, "Making this ride my own. Sir." The pipes gave the car a radical, savage sound, perfect for making a statement on the cruising circuit but not for the purpose he needed.

Scavenger pipes be damned, Bucky was his nemesis on the street, always had the fastest car and dad never was able to outrun him on the road. After years of chasing Bucky's tail lights, he was finally going to get him. This time, his customizations and his right foot were going to be the difference.

The two squared off once again. This time, with all his modifications, dad knew he had Bucky cold. Certainly, with the identical car, it came down to the skill of the driver.

I can only imagine, after all the volcanic explosions of anger I've seen from my dad, how he reacted when, once again, a laughing Bucky crossed the line first.

Not good. Not good at all.

Clearly, shenanigans were afoot! Dad was beyond pissed as he stomped around, screaming, waving his hands in the air as Bucky laughed hysterically, unable to contain himself. I imagine if Bucky smoked victory cigars, this is when it started. Remind me to ask Bucky's son, Kyle. (author's note, I forgot to ask Kyle.)

Dad screamed at Bucky, "You work there, you had to do something to this car to beat me!" With rolling laughter, Bucky denied the allegation. "He was so frustrated at that point he would say anything," Bucky said.

Things got serious. Dad let the gears grind in his head, trying to figure out how to finally cross the finish line first.

How did he accomplish this?

It took a while. A long while. We fast forward a few years (with Bucky getting there first no doubt) to the time both had married and had a child.

"It was some years later," Bucky said. "It was a nice day; I was out in my yard. And I heard him coming. There was a loud roar coming up the road."

Talking to Bucky's son, and my lifelong friend, Kyle, he said his father was "strutting around like a peacock" with his constant victories and endless bragging rights on his butt-whooping of my dad. Until the moment Bucky saw the car attached to the loud exhaust system and the driver behind the wheel.

Dad had done it.

"When I heard that engine, I wondered who on earth was driving that car," Bucky said. "And who pulls up but Mr. Reavie in a brand-new GTO." The GTO was a beast of the street and dad picked up a midnight blue 1965 model. So excited was he to get his new car that my mother, Mary Ellen, had to drive him the 45 minutes to Sault Ste. Marie to take ownership. His stomach turned with anticipation, he was a hot mess and the ride seemed to take forever. You may be picking up on a trend here.

Dad recalled Bucky's reaction upon seeing him in The Goat. "He turned a whiter shade of pale when he saw that sinister grill and GTO nameplate," dad said of his Darth Vader-like ride.

Buckey's 1965 Chevy Super Sport with a 327 and a 4-speed was no slouch, so he picked up the gauntlet dad tossed at his feet and followed him to their version of Paradise Road.

"I couldn't even touch him. He finally got one he could beat me with," Bucky said. "It only took him 10 years, but he did it. Wow, that was a fast car."

Dad's GTO got an advantage immediately off the line, and he recounted its front end rising up from the power as he speed shifted from first through fourth gear, leaving Bucky in a cloud of rubber, asphalt, gravel, dust, and bewilderment.

The friends ran three heats, and dad smoked Bucky like a cheap cigar from a dead start, rolling start, and from 100 MPH.

"I kicked his ass," dad laughed. "Finally."

The era of the muscle car was upon them. The music was great. The Beatles, Roy Orbison, and the British invasion, changed music the way the GTO changed the muscle car.

Dad blasted the tunes via AM radio and the high-end rear speaker. "This was a really big time for us, we didn't have all the things we have now but to us, it was heaven."

Bucky reminisced of those great times when he and dad cruised together for nearly 20 years. Talking with Bucky was incredible for me. He told me stories about my dad that I had never heard, when he was young, full of ideas, creative, and just a touch crazy.

"Your dad was a typical teenager in that era," Bucky said. "He dyed his hair blonde, fashioned a duck tail, and wore a leather jacket. It was a big fad back then."

I was this-conversation-old when I found out my dad dyed his hair blonde. Who could imagine such a thing? When their mutual friend, Don Vallier, returned from California, he brought with him a 1955 Chevy Convertible and peroxide blonde hair.

"That is where it all began," Bucky said. "The California car culture came home." So when he was 16 years old, my father, conservative banker Edward Kress Reavie, doused his hair with a bottle of peroxide, combed the now-platinum-blonde tresses into a ducktail and sent Elaine into a Vodka-fueled therapy session.

It was during this era that he spent time with a cousin in Metro Detroit and rode in his first '55 Chevy. They cruised up and down packed streets, dragged between stop lights, and even had his first ever pizza.

His life was never the same.

Bucky said that, as teenagers in the 50's, they had wall-to-wall fun. There were no worries of drugs or bad influences, and Bucky said the worst thing they ever did was getting an adult to purchase them some beer.

One particular night, Bucky had two jumbos of beer in the back seat and was cruising to meet my dad. They got loose, smashed together, and 64 ounces of golden mead soaked the back seat and carpets.

"He didn't believe me, so I let him smell my backseat," Buckey said with a laugh.

Another great idea in this era turned out to be disastrous.

Bucky went to Silver Sands, used some of Kress's white latex paint and painted white walls on his tires, trying to impress the "Rod Benders," the cobbled together group of car cruisers. By the time he got into town and picked up some friends to cruise, they started laughing. He got out, looked at his tires and gasped.

"The paint did not dry, so it had spiderwebbed all over the tire. It was awful." I may have told Bucky a similar thing happened to me with a broken side mirror and Gorilla Glue.

While backing my 2014 Dodge Challenger Redline out of the garage, I hit the side of the garage door with the passenger side mirror and knocked it from its mooring. Horrified, I did the only logical thing a distressed person can do when facing a 45-minute drive. I used Gorilla Blue to put it back in place (please note, I did not throw up. Yet.) The 116-degree Phoenix heat did the rest, expanding the glue until it bubbled and flowed all down the side of my car and created a macabre etch o' sketch that made me throw up. Genetics are wonderful things.

Back to the story.

The group of teenagers lived far away from the customizers, so they learned to improvise, including Bucky's borrowing work items to accessorize his wheels.Bucky bolted four metal shoe horns on his hubcap, giving the illusion of spinners. So cool was the modification that a Hot Rod magazine writer noticed his car and wrote about it in the next issue. It caused a ruckus in the small town, as one of their own "Rod Benders" made waves in a real-life magazine.

I remember seeing this hubcap, their jackets, and car club plaque in dad's office. Not having access did not mean they couldn't make their cars cool, and they did.

"Your dad's legacy is that no matter where you go out of state and talk to somebody and they ask you where you are from and you tell them St. Ignace," Bucky said. "And they all immediately bring up the auto show. That's incredible."

Life gets in the way of fun. Bucky and Dad both assumed jobs that took them off the road for the most part. Bucky with the Mackinac Bridge Authority and dad at the bank

That '65 GTO became known all over Michigan, as dad was known to have the fastest car, unbeaten in drag races, even against motorcycles.

As stories spread of the family man blowing out cars on drag strips with a Nightwatch Blue GTO, it was only a matter of time before Johnny Law heard and needed to investigate.

But, not in the way one would think.

Cops were a bit cooler in the way-back era, or so I am told. Although I have been called a cool cop by the middle-school students in my current assignment as a School Resource Officer; so, I have that going for me. Allegedly.

While eating lunch in the old truck stop on the Westside of town, dad was approached by a Michigan State Police Trooper. He looked dad up and down, then the fully uniformed Trooper told dad he'd heard he had a "pretty hot car" to which dad replied,

"I think I do."

Undaunted, the Trooper removed his hat, sat near him, leaned in for effect with his creaking leathers and bristling crew cut. Then the Troop asked dad if he thought his "hot shot of a car" could outrun the beastly Mopar-powered Plymouth Police Cruisers that the State Troopers drove.

Dad wiped his mouth, scrunched his napkin, put down his buttermilk (kidding) , took a breath, steadied his nerves, leaned forward on his elbows and responded with confidence,

"Yes, I think it would."

Silence. A sly smile crossed the Trooper's face. He switched the toothpick in his mouth from one side to the other and asked what dad wanted to do about it.

Dad looked around to make sure none of my mother's friends were within earshot, then looked into the dead-eyed Trooper's face and, before answering, asked, "Is this off the record?"

The Trooper ensured dad it was not entrapment and he simply wanted to know who had the fastest car, my father with his beast of a Pontiac, or the state police.

With the ultimate challenge before him, dad tossed down a quarter to pay for the Trooper's coffee, ordered a piece of pie, and stuck out his hand. The arrangement was to meet on the unfinished portion of I-75, leading to Sault Ste. Marie. There were acres of concrete and asphalt, and no cars were using it. It would be just the two of them.

Just after sunrise on a Sunday morning, Dad lined up his GOAT against the Mopar-Powered, high performance, big, blue Plymouth patrol car of the Michigan State Police.

He got there early to warm the car and to check the clutch adjustment. The engine rumbled like a jungle cat ready to pounce on the Blue Goose. All systems were ready to go. The conditions were perfect.

The agreed upon contest was three heats: dead stop, rolling start, and 100 mph rolling start. The same contest that Bucky and dad had done with his 3/133 win/loss record against Bucky. The three wins, of course, came behind the wheel of his unbeaten GTO.

The Trooper said he was going to get him in all three heats, hands down. He laughed as he kicked a rock out of the way and flicked his toothpick. The Trooper looked at dad and saw only the shy, humble country boy dad always claimed to be, prior to doing the impossible.

Dad said nothing, just climbed into the GTO cockpit. Hand on shifter, foot on gas, engine roaring.

At the first heat "go" signal, dad slapped his Hurst shifter like he hated it, and blew big blue off the line from the dead stop, finishing well ahead. Such was the GTO's power, the Troop said he felt his badge vibrate against his uniform.

Less confident for the second contest, the Trooper failed again in the rolling start. The big Plymouth was beaten by the time dad hit second gear. The margin of victory was such that dad said he waited for the Trooper at the finish line, telling him, "Hurry up, I have things to do this morning."

The top end challenge started when both cars hit 100 mph. The trooper told dad he hit 130 mph in the police cruiser and still could not catch him. The brash 25-year-old youngster with the GTO crushed him each and every time.

What we are dealing with here is a complete lack of respect for the law.

The trooper shook dad's hand, congratulated him, but put him on notice. He gripped his hand tight and pulled him close. The Trooper, with his hot coffee-tainted breath billowing into dad's face, said if he ever heard about a punk kid in a street-legal car beating a high-powered blue goose, things would not go well for him, and he would drown him in a tidal wave of speeding tickets.

Dad told the Trooper that he would never tell a soul (except Bucky, I learned) his name. As he walked away with a smile of self-satisfaction, dad heard the trooper call out to him.

"By the way, that is one bad ass car."

It most certainly was.

My father told me the story more than 55 years after it happened, but he said he made a promise that day and would not even tell me the Trooper's name.

Always the great wingman, Bucky laughed and confirmed this event did happen exactly the way dad told me, lending credibility to a story as unbelievable as this one and pronouncing it true.

A police officer of 15 years myself, I cannot conceive of such a thing. Several times, while sitting at a light, I've had kids in tricked out cars rev their engines at me in hopes of doing the same thing my dad did to a Trooper. I always gave them credit for their brass, but alas, it would cost me my job.

In all, my father owned 53 cars in his life. Unknown to me, he bought salvaged cars, sold them for parts, and kept them under tarps on the side of the house. People came from around the state to take their pick for cars they were building.

I think he told mom that cordwood was stored under the blue tarp next to the home. The same theory I use when I tell my wife how much I paid for one of my guitars. It is my hope that if something happens to me, she doesn't sell them for what I told her I paid for them.

His proclivity for Chevy's was such that he had the handle, "Chevy Man" as his CB Radio call sign. It was given to him by another longtime friend, St. Ignace Mayor, Bruce Dodson.

His early love of cars and the cruising culture never left him even as he married the former Mary Ellen Martin and had my sister, Danielle, in 1965. Before selling the GTO, an event he still laments, dad drag raced with my sister in the car with him.

I could feel the smile on his face as he recounted my sister kicking her legs in her car seat screaming "FASTER! FASTER!" as he speed-shifted the gears down a ribbon of asphalt known as Rayco Speedway. He put down one challenge after another, even a motorcycle, which came the closest to beating him.

As time moved on, he saw the writing on the wall for career longevity at the A & P store and his days as a carefree street racer. Managers were being fired or sent off to other locations in the state, so he knew his time as store manager was ending.

My mother was now expecting me and suffered a terrible pregnancy wherein I was delivered breech six weeks early (something she never failed to tell me). Dad learned of a job opening at the First National Bank of St. Ignace. Knowing it was long past time to grow up, he called Warren Hagen to make himself available for the job. Any job, as long as it kept him employed and working in St. Ignace. A week later, without even putting in an application, he was called and asked when he wanted to start.

That began a 40-year career with the bank, and the former high school push out was ultimately elevated to First Vice President and Chief Loan Officer.

He traded an apron and a name tag for a suit and tie, and he likewise traded his cruising life for that of bread winner and father of two children. One of those children was nothing but unpleasant. Endless screams and stiffening like a board whenever people tried to hold me, I hit, kicked and bit just about everyone around me.

No doubt those friends who have known me for 50-plus years, are laughing, as I am pretty much still that way. Minus the physical hitting and biting. It is more metaphorical now.

Dad laughed about going from a GTO to a Dasher Station wagon and we both laughed about a vacation we took in said Dasher.

The best part about our bi-weekly phone call interviews in writing this book was talking about our family and a few great memories we had during some tumultuous periods in our lives.

He recounted a disaster of a family vacation that I still remember. He pulled the Dasher (purchased to accommodate my mother) out of a Shell Station in Berea, Kentucky. On our way to Myrtle Beach for the worst vacation in memory (to include booking a room in a hotel that charged by the hour), we stopped to get gas and pecan logs.

Mom told him she smelled a burning fuse and told him to go back to the station to get it checked. Dad said he didn't smell anything and continued onto the highway, only to lose all power. He was just able to pull it off the road.

It was Easter Sunday, traffic was heavy, and we were in the middle of nowhere on the heavily-trafficked I-75 Southbound. He got out of the car, noticed a farmer in the field, walked to the fence line, got his attention, and told him the plight.

As luck would have it, the man's brother owned a service station in the small town. It was an amazing coincidence. He had no choice but to agree to have the car towed to the small service station, even as he knew that the city boy in the fancy foreign car was going to take a bath in this transaction.

I recall riding in the big tow truck as we rolled into the little town of Berea. The driver had on a dirty ball cap, a dirty sleeveless shirt, dirty jeans, and work boots.

Country music, something new to me, boomed through his AM radio and scratchy speaker from an AM station somewhere in the hills of Kentucky. My father had seen Deliverance and was rightly concerned.

The blood drained from his face when he saw the station. Literally every inch was covered in grease. Broken cars were strewn about the backlot in various states of disrepair. Some had critters living within their rusted hulks.

The man scratched his face stubble and whistled as he tried to diagnose a car that was built with the metric system. He made more than one crack about the piece of crap foreign car as he located the fuse box, pulled it open, and saw the problem.

Sure enough, mom was right.

A burned-out fuse. There we were, with a dead German car needing a German-made fuse while sitting on grime-covered chairs that reeked of oil, in the waiting room of a broken-down shop in Berea, Kentucky. Stephen King writes books with this kind of lead-in.

No doubt dad was computing how much this little trip was going to cost. It just so happened that I had broken my arm the day before this trip. I was in pain and was being a royal pain in the ass. Just what he needed.

Suddenly, the mechanic had a light bulb pop over his head (metaphorically, this is not a cartoon, although it felt like one). He recalled a year or so ago, that a man with a "piece of crap foreign car like yours" ordered a fuse for his equally-fragile ride. The customer had never picked it up and the shop owner wondered if the fuse was still somewhere in his work area.

He waded into the mess that was his shop and I heard tools clatter, items moving, and I think even a rodent squeaked. Then, to my shock, even to this day, I remember the mechanic shouting, "WOW!" He came out with a box, opened it, and took out a fuse.

Now, this was but half the victory as it was "a" fuse and we didn't know if it was "the" fuse. He looked at us with a smile, walked past my gloating mother, paused and shivered and then pushed the fuse

REBEL WITHOUT A CLUE

into place. All the lights came on and it started right up. We cheered and a sense of relief washed over dad. Even the critters whistled in unison.

Now, the moment of truth. He faced the prospect of seeing all his American Express Travelers Checks being made out to Jimmy, or Skeeter. He swallowed deeply. Were the vacation plans he'd made about to be changed?

He asked the mechanic, "How much?"

The man removed his oil-stained cap, scratched and tousled his hair, said he'd paid $15 for the fuse and asked for only $20, total.

Such was his relief that Dad gave him a $50 traveler's check, vigorously shook his hand, and thanked him profusely. I recall Danielle and I waving to him from the back seat as we pulled away, got back on the highway, and headed to Myrtle Beach. You saved our vacation with your honest business practices and good heart, nice man. I wish we had gotten your name.

When we got home, dad sent the Berea Chamber of Commerce a letter attesting to the man's honesty and good work. He didn't know the man's name, but still thanks him to this day.

In a bizarre coincidence, Janet Peterson sent me a message in March of 2022. On vacation with her husband, Steve, they were telling an Ed Reavie story.

Steve told Janet he gave dad his "American Graffiti" cassette to use during the first cruise night. The message started this way:

"So, we are sitting in a Wendy's in Berea, Kentucky, eating lunch to take a break," she said.

You cannot make this stuff up. I told her this story and she was shocked. "There is only one Edward K." she replied.

Back to the big picture.

The former leather-jacket-wearing, Beatle-blasting, high-horsepower-driving rebel now, to his horror, had a family station wagon and a young son who was nothing but a problem from day one.

That would be me.

Dad sheepishly admitted that he had to cover my mouth with a rag to silence my cries and screams. He also rubbed whiskey on my gums when I was teething because, now, enough of the crying bald tiny creature with the beautiful blue eyes who farted nonstop and projectile vomited. Again, those that know me over all these years will say nothing has changed.

My parents put me to bed and let me cry myself to sleep as they drove around the neighborhood to get away from my ear-piercing screams. I was doing "the worm" before it was practical and culturally hip.

I bucked up and down the mattress and wedged myself between the bars of the crib as I hissed and sizzled like bacon in a skillet before falling asleep in bizarre postures.

I was a handful from the beginning. I could not be more different than my father other than I had his iron will to do what I wanted and fight the system of oppression that was mom and him. How dare they swaddle me and nurture me! The horror!

To me, he was Kress on steroids.

I grew up loving baseball, basketball, and football. My heroes were athletes, not car guys. Dad called himself an "athletic supporter" and when I blossomed as an athlete, he told me that he had no clue where I got that ability. I often looked for him, baseball glove in hand, only to find him busy with his car, going to a car show, or working. That relationship was strained from the beginning and grew more so during the car show years. The public and his growing list of automotive royalty saw his son by his side, all the while they had no idea how I disliked the show, cars, and him. It grew where we had nothing in common and rarely talked. If we did, it was strained and transparent.

It wasn't until I was 22 years old that I started a relationship with him, which I will cover in this book. This is not a surprise to him. He knew. We both did. We just didn't know how to fix it. We speak of the moment when we both reached a point of saying goodbye or to be men and work it out.

But first, his vision was to create something he lived in the 50's and saw come to life on the big screen, through the magic of Hollywood, when a movie with the subtitle "Where were you in '62" swept the nation.

PART TWO

Reborn

Chapter 3: "Where were you in '62?"

In the fall of 1973, dad went to see the most significant movie of his life "American Graffiti."

He saw his youth captured perfectly on the screen. Endless cruising, with the greatest music ever written playing throughout the movie, backed by the howling Wolfman Jack.

This movie made such an impact that he stayed in his seat and watched the next showing. He recounted that what he saw on the screen was the best era of his life from 1955 to 1970. He and his fellow gear heads and Rod Benders cruised the circuit with the best cars and listened to the best music of the era.

"Elvis had just released Heartbreak Hotel, all radio stations started playing this new thing called rock and roll. There was no blueprint. Nobody knew what to do with the lot of us. We lived and breathed cars and music and were the first generation to do it the way we did it; with style."

Chief's Drive-in on the North end of town was the prime spot for cruising shenanigans. Home of the city's first neon sign, Chief's was awash in bitchin' cars, poodle skirts, slicked back hair, leather jackets, rolled up Levi's, and the new, uplifting rhythm of rock and roll. Or as Kress put it, "The Devil's Music."

This was not a TV show or a movie. It was real life, played out at every drive-in across the country as the love affair with the automobile was in full-throated lust.

Bucky and dad's reputation as having the best cars and cutest girls cruising with them was such that they had their own parking spots. If people were in them when the duo arrived, they moved out in deference.

The pretty girls always gravitated toward the hottest cars; color coordinated to match their favorite sled. One girl, whom dad did not name because "her boyfriend and now husband hated me for always ending up with her in my car as I roared out of the parking lot" waited for his arrival through the years as he always had the hottest car.

Years later, watching American Graffiti, he recounted the feeling as being struck by lightning. He saw his era alive on the screen, 20 years after it started. It was now presented to an entire new generation of gear heads and cruisers.

"I was born again that night, watching that movie."

Fast forward, (unless Bucky figured out how to beat him again) dad started a pen pal relationship with George Lucas himself, and he gave dad his blessing for what he was building and sent him several props from the original movie.

"It doesn't get much better than that, I will say that much," dad gushed.

Or did it?

In the hyper growth of the show, Bo Hopkins (Joe the Pharaoh), Paul LeMat (John Milner) and Candy Clark (Debbie) all came to St. Ignace, sat in our living room while shooting the breeze about tuck-and-roll upholstery, the car scene, the movie, taking shots of Old Harper, eating beef jerky, and being in St. Ignace.

"It was like the goddamn Twilight Zone," dad said with a laugh. "I had to step back and look into the room and saw all these guys in my house. Just...wow."

The adage of "two out of three ain't bad" applies to that group as interviews with two of them appear later in this book.

His insatiable love of the automobile gave him an interesting sideline during this time. His reputation as a car guy was growing and townspeople used his gift of gab and love of cars to sell their vehicles for them. Through the years, there were always cars parked out front and when I got my license, dad let me drive them as visibility was the best sales tool he had. He sold more than 300 cars. I asked him during one of our cruises in the Chevy when, or how, he got his car dealer license.

When he said he never had one, I asked why.

"I was already selling them so why did I need a car license?"

Hard to argue with that logic. He applied the same logic to his brief stint in home sales. He recounted his best customer as Forest Evashevski, one time head football coach of the Iowa Hawkeyes. His son, Tom, is my father's attorney and next-door neighbor. Another son, John, was a wrestler at Iowa, wrestling coach at LaSalle High School, and one of my favorite teachers.

John was a fantastic man who did a lot for me and trusted me to babysit his children. I was heartbroken when he passed away in the spring of 2021. He served generations of St. Ignace kids with honor and passion, and I am a better person for his example.

With American Graffiti still in his head, cruising never left dad's mind. This leads us to February of 1975 when the last thing people wanted to do was cruise the streets in the U.P.

He recalled a meeting with local radio personality Don Angelo, St. Ignace News reporter Greg Means, Ruby Goudreau, City Manager Jack Gall, concerning a special event the city wanted to plan. Dad leaped at the chance.

The discussion revolved around the 1976 Bicentennial. Nobody had any solid ideas to commemorate it, so dad approached Bruce Dodson about the possibility of a car show. It would be a challenge to pull off the first one. Why not St. Ignace? A town with no stop lights. Five hours from the closest car culture in Detroit, and a world away from all his heroes.

He made a list of car owners he knew and started contacting them to gauge interest. When told of his idea for them to drive to tiny St. Ignace over the Mackinac Bridge, all the car owners requested payment to cover bridge fare and gas. He brought this request to the city, and was amazed when they voted on, and approved, cutting a check for five dollars to any car owner that registered for the event.

But when to hold it?

Talking with dad, I learned for the first time how he picked the last Saturday of June for the show.

"I polled the business owners in town and asked them to tell me the worst weekend they had leading up to summer."

The Fourth of July had always been the kickoff for summer with parades and events. The weekend before was dead and businesses struggled to break even. Thus, the Straits Area Antique Auto Show was set on the last Saturday in June which, over time, turned into the best weekends in the 350-year history of our town.

The former grocery store manager and current banker's rough vision began to form. He had no experience in marketing, but used his creative genius, drive, ambition, and unnatural ability to persuade people as to why they needed to come to St. Ignace.

Dad "promoted the hell out of it" with three mailings, reminder phone calls, and any means he could to get his town full of show cars.

Remember, emails did not exist. Text messages only happened on Star Trek, and a fax machine was so futuristic that to imagine such a thing could get you committed. It was all hustle and persistence. Handwritten letters, postcards, phone calls, messages left with the same secretary time and again.

It was in this era that my father, with the help of his in-house supporting cast including my mom, sister, and me, built the foundation for what became the show of legend.

Scheduled for June 25, 1976, the First Straits Area Antique Auto Show was a go.

He expected between 50 and 100 cars and was stunned when 136 cars came and filled Dock #2 in St. Ignace to the hilt and brought thousands of people to town.

Bruce, long time mortician and owner of the Davis-Dodson Funeral home, had a pristine 1934 Packard. Dad recalled that several of his friends, Bucky of course, Bob Blair, and many others often traveled to shows around the state.

Nothing truly great happens without a strong foundation of persons who believe in the mission. While dad was the face, the cornerstone, and the architect, his support cast within the city and state was incredible.

Bruce J. Dodson came to St. Ignace in 1970 as a mortician, a role he ultimately held for 50 years. He was a City of St. Ignace Councilman and for 22 years, Mayor of St. Ignace. The perfect "Man in the Chair" to get things done.

And he was another thing; a gear head like my father. His 1934 Packard was a magnificent work of art. An original staple of the car show, Bruce always vied to be the first entrant. And as the world turns, Bruce and Bucky are neighbors, but Bruce is quick to say he was not around for the shenanigans of the early days.

He remembers dad's purchase of the 1948 Chevy that I told dad "smelled like an old person's attic," to which he replied, "Well, it was." He was the son of a Chevrolet dealer with a knowledge of automotive history, thus it was not long before he and dad became friends.

Dad was Bruce's banker at first, but their mutual love of the automobile led to discussing the possibility of putting together the first Straits Area Antique Auto Show in 1976. Dad approached Bruce, told him he had a budget to "put on a car show", and asked him for ideas. Bruce was a member of Flat River Antique Car Club in Greenville, Michigan, and good friends with the guys. He told dad he could recruit them to come to the show as a group.

The first-year plan was a picnic for show goers in Bruce's backyard, and they anticipated maybe 50 attendees. But the show piqued the interest of more than Bruce's car club, so Bruce and his wife, Carolyn, realized their small backyard and single bathroom home would not contain the 136 entrants and families.

He enlisted my mom, who enlisted my sister and me, and we all went to the St. Ignace High School and made huge vats of potato salad. Bruce bagged it up and took it to the picnic's new location, the beachfront near the Chalet North Hotel.

I recall being an eight-year-old kid wanting to ride my bike, play baseball, and read my comic books. Instead, I spent hours, with my equally disinterested sister, peeling potatoes.

Bruce said after that first year the event took off and "went wild." The subsequent years were incredible to behold with top cars and top car people coming to town, bursting onto the Main Street and creating something never before seen in my sleepy little tourist town.

When Zora Arkus-Duntov came to town, Bruce laughed as he shared a story concerning Mrs. Arkus-Duntov. As Guest of Honor, there was a brunch in Zora's honor at The Flame Restaurant. The Brunch was invitation only and the movers and shakers of the automotive world attended.

Zora told dad and Bruce that his wife was driving up from Detroit, but said he was not concerned that it was close to the 11:00am start time, but she had yet to arrive. The concern was that she had departed Detroit just that morning, and it was a five-hour drive from St. Ignace- for people not driving a Corvette.

Mrs. Duntov walked into the restaurant, on time, and Bruce was shocked when she announced, "Well I made good time."

She'd made the drive in two hours and fifteen minutes.

Mrs. Arkus-Duntov told a shocked Bruce, "Well that car runs best around 110 miles an hour." Noting she could do 120 miles per hour, but "110 seemed to be comfortable." Clearly, Zora found his perfect match. Bruce was a big fan of Zora and mentioned that he once had the promotional photo of Zora's record Pike's Peak climb in his Corvette, but lost track of it through the years.

Bruce was still mayor when the Cruise Night switched to the Big Boy restaurant, and he was involved in all the discussions regarding taming that beast. "It was gridlock for miles, both ways," he recalled. "These were car people and car people cruised. It's what they did."

Such was the Cruise Night log jam that driving from the Big Boy to the airport was a two-hour slog. It normally took 10 minutes, tops. The safety planning was immense but when a certain banker made calls, people moved. "Your dad had a way of talking to people," Bruce said. "It was hard to say no to him."

When dad and Bruce first talked about the show, and who would take the lead, Bruce said he was at a disadvantage. He was on call 24 hours a day as the County Mortician. Plus, dad had an office and a passion, and Bruce had no problem with dad taking the lead. "People asked me if I was ever jealous of the success," he told me. "Jealous? I can never be jealous of anyone who takes the bull by the horns and just does it. And he did it."

Dad worked normal hours, so it gave him the advantage in contacting people, and he had the city's blessing.

One thing Bruce still marvels at is the amount of high caliber, legendary men and women of the automotive hobby who came to his town.

"It was unbelievable to see Carroll Shelby riding around with Zora Arkus-Duntov," Bruce said. "I was sitting at the Flame and Carroll Shelby was sitting next to me. It was incredible." Bruce asserted that the impact on the community can never be measured.

Bruce has had regular talks with bank President Jim North, and confidently estimates that the show brought more than 150 million dollars over the 40 years that dad promoted it.

"Absolutely, no doubt about it," Bruce said, confident in that number. With the show's new direction, Bruce misses one major component; the Guest of Honor brunch.

"Even when your dad was not well, he sat in a chair, grabbed the microphone, and took care of business," Bruce said. "That event was a chance for people to meet him and for the Guest of Honor to be recognized."

Blessed not only with wit and humor, but dad also had an incredible speaking voice that carried over the din of a crowd and glass packs, alike. Sitting, standing, it mattered not. Give the man a microphone and people listened.

His success, Bruce said, is that he is a man who did not back down nor could be ordered around when it came to his show.

As for dad's legacy?

"The town should be named after him for all he has done," Bruce said with conviction. "What he brought to this town; nobody has ever done. More than 150 million came into this town that never would have made it. He built every hotel here and in Mackinaw City. No question."

Dad used his experience with other local shows to form what he did in St. Ignace. Such was dad's reputation as a gearhead that, in the years before the show, he'd served as a judge at events around the area. He traveled to Boyne City, Traverse City, Rogers City, and others as both participant and judge. But he came to realize something that bothered him.

My father is the most meticulous man I know, and his judging of cars was no different. He knew his trade and he knew cars. God forbid I cut the grass in a line anything but straight, or left "holidays" of grass on their own, having to do it over after a lesson in mowing a proper pattern. Trust me when I tell you this.

He was baffled after handing in his judging sheets why the cars he picked lost and cars that were clearly substandard took home trophies. He was told that one winner had worked the concession stand and had therefore earned the award for her sacrifice of spending the day selling dogs and soda.

He also noticed something else that bothers him to this day. If the town had a car club, each member of that club took home a trophy and left the out-of-town cars vying for the farthest drive award to attend the event. This left a bad taste in his mouth and, to be totally transparent with his own show, he made the rule that local St. Ignace cars were not eligible for an award of any kind.

He wanted people excited to show their cars, to win awards they deserved and earned, with no hint of the "good old boy" network that ruined dad's experience in showing superior cars, only to see the same inferior cars win time and again.

The first Straits Area Antique Auto Show was in the books, a success, and on its way to becoming known by only, "St. Ignace". The speed in which that happened was astonishing.

As he stood on the dock, he felt it in the air and knew the show was going to be more than a one-off special event. As it was, there had been no plan to make this show an annual event. During the show, with his 8-year-old son at his side, he looked into the future and felt that he was onto something.

The event's energy was overwhelming. It was not held within a cold auditorium or on a dusty fairground with few attractions for car owners or families, it was on the shore of Lake Huron. Right in the center of the bustling town, within walking distance to stores and restaurants that overflowed with people.

He was encouraged by the feedback. Some told him the show was unlike any other that they'd attended. With crystal blue skies and sparkling water everywhere you looked, the town took on the same vibe as when dad cruised the streets with his friends in the 1950's and 60's.

Which, I believe, was the point.

After the event, dad knew he'd made an impact, as other cities followed his lead and scheduled their own shows. They were sparsely attended and not promoted well.

I recall a show in Grayling with three cars where it rained all day. It was terrible. If memory serves, it was near a 4H pavilion with a small store inside. The smell of wet manure notwithstanding, an event occurred that helped form my future.

I purchased a comic book called "Crossfire," the story of a police officer who ran into a house to save a child but ended up getting shot and killed. It was a Christian style book, with the officer ascending to Heaven.

Like my father, Faith is a gift I have yet to receive, but the desire to be a police officer burned brighter in me. I was eight or nine years old. I still have the comic book. I took that urge and hunger to serve with me everywhere having no idea that another 30 years would pass before I'd have my own badge pinned on my chest.

Dad saw a vision of what the show could be, not simply what it was. The overwhelming success of year one paved the way for him to move fast. During the recap meeting with city officials, it became clear as to who the director of future shows was going to be. His passion and fire for the event crackled like wildfire.

He was to take the lead. Bruce Dodson, in the process of becoming one of my father's closest confidants and friends, wanted him to take the lead. He had the knowledge, passion, and wisdom to make the show what he wanted, and he wanted it to reflect well on those endless summers of his youth. He became the head organizer, and he took all his knowledge into the promotion of subsequent years.

He recognized the potential for tremendous growth, so he began a media blitz and mailed information three times a year; October, January, and May. Everything was directly mailed which required that my mom, sister, and I spend hours on the living room floor stuffing and licking envelopes and affixing stamps. How one of us didn't invent the self-sticking envelopes is shocking.

I remember that mom had a bowl of water and a small sponge which we dipped and then rubbed on the sticky inner fold, so we didn't get sick from licking toxic glue. Poor Susan Ross. Serenity now! Keep in mind, this was the 1970's and we had no fax machines and no internet for email. It was tedious work that Danielle and I grew to hate.

Dad kept every contact on 3 x 5 index cards in a drawer, each with the name, address, and phone number of the potential attendee. He started with a dozen and ended with more than 20,000, all of which he kept. New people came each year and were met with the same energy and picturesque backdrop. They told their friends, their clubs, and each year, more and more cars flowed across the Mighty Mac into a little town with no streetlights.

Year two saw 210 show cars come to St. Ignace. Year three, 363. Year four, 425. During this tremendous growth, St. Ignace was landing on the radar of the top names in the business.

SEAN E. REAVIE

Chuck Miller, legendary car builder, Ridler Award winner and the 2010 Guest of Honor, had a cabin in Grayling. For years he noticed the large caravan of classic cars and street machines heading North on I-75 to the tiny town of St. Ignace. This annual migration prompted him to attend and changed his perception of auto shows forever. Chuck's interview is later in this book.

The top designers, engineers, race car drivers, and personalities came to our small town with low expectations and left amazed. They saw just how perfect a car show could be.

The dusty fairground was replaced with an immaculate backdrop and, instead of a 4H pavilion behind the show, Lake Huron sparkled and moved like poetry in motion, dancing to the blowing wind.

Dad knew that the show's early success meant more could be done. Bigger things needed to happen. To do this, he needed attractions beyond the finest show cars in the state and from Canada. He needed a legend in the genre to give his show credibility. After year three, he called his automotive idol, Gordon Beuhrig, left a message asking him to be his first Guest of Honor, and hoped to hear back.

But between year two and three, something magical happened; Hollywood called.

Chapter 4: Meeting Superman

The first show was a complete success and the second showed no signs of regressing, so word of the man with car connections paid off in ways nobody saw coming and opened up an entirely new world.

In the fall of 1977, a man claiming to be from Universal Studios called the house, and things changed again. Dad laughed and said, "Sure you are." The man on the phone told dad he could call him back and dad still had a raised eyebrow.

He confirmed that Britt Lomon was indeed the Transportation Director for Universal Studios. Dad realized something big was in the works and it included him. Mr. Lomond told him that the studio was preparing to shoot a movie on Mackinac Island called "Somewhere in Time" and they needed period-specific cars.

Other cars, such as the modern-day Fiat Spyder Christopher Reeves drove up to the Grand Hotel entrance, were far easier to obtain.

For the rest; a silver and gray 1970 Jaguar Saloon 420G, a 1911 black Cadillac with ivory wheels; a 1910 burgundy Oakland with black roof and interior; a black 1909 Packard, a 1913 Rambler, and a 1904 St. Louis. To which dad replied, "Sure, is that it?"

Mackinac Island is known worldwide and is home to the Grand Hotel where the 1947 Esther Williams movie "This Time for Keeps" was filmed. Mackinac Island has a hard and fast rule forbidding motorized vehicles. Working with the movie industry to break those rules was a blast for the lifelong rebel as he received many perks for locating the cars.

First, he received an official copy of the script, autographed by the cast. It resides in the museum that seconds as his office.

Second, he was invited to the wrap party and the World Premiere at the Grand, which I attended with mom and Danielle.

The biggest moment of my young life was a result of one of those perks; I got to watch part of the filming. I am a lifelong superhero nerd, and, like all small boys, Superman was the king of all superheroes.

"Superman" starring Christopher Reeve, was released the year prior, a movie I watched multiple times on the silver screen. Suddenly, there I was, on the very same soundstage as Christopher Reeve shot parts of the movie. I recall with great clarity the scene in his room, rehearsing his eventual meeting with Jane Seymour's character, Elise McKenna.

"Hello Miss McKenna, you don't know me yet, but you will." Likewise, the seminal moment in the film, when he is in the attic going through the old guest registry to discover he was, in fact, there during that time frame. I was amazed to see those specific moments on the screen when we saw the movie. The most incredible thing for me was after the attic scene was "wrapped," a stagehand approached Mr. Reeve, pointed to me, and I saw him smile.

He walked toward me, Superman himself, bent over and, with a huge smile on his face, offered me his hand and introduced himself as Chris. I think I said I was Sean, but who the hell knows? I was meeting Superman. His huge hand engulfed mine. I was in a state of shock and don't recall saying a single word. He met my parents and sister and thanked us for coming and was then whisked away, his metaphorical cape flowing behind him.

I am still in awe to this day. Writing this brought it back.

Meeting Jane Seymour and Christopher Plummer was incredible but paled in comparison to meeting the Man of Steel. The cars used in the movie were also at the fourth anniversary car show in a special display.

In the early years, mom hosted a VIP party from 1977 to 1981 until they outgrew the house.

I still remember Steve Hellerstein, the Universal Studios representative, in attendance at the party. I spilled wine on his wife's velvet coat during that party. I thought the world had ended but she was very kind and told me all was okay, and it was no big deal. Dad still has all the correspondence with the studio including the envelopes. I read through the script; I've seen the letter on his wall. It was a proud moment for him and I was "big man on campus" at my school with the story of meeting Superman.

Ed Reavie's involvement in "Somewhere in Time" is documented through the Internet Movie Database (IMDB) if you want to check out another of my father's cool accomplishments.

Letter from a Legend - Voices from History

Throughout this book, "Letters from a Legend" captures handwritten letters to my father. As some are very old, I did not want to remove them from their protective covers to photocopy so dad read them to me and I transcribed them.

Dear Ed,

First, I want to thank all of you for your tireless efforts on our behalf during the filming of Somewhere in Time on Mackinac Island.

You were a great help in locating all the outstanding cars from the vintage 1912 to the others that did a great deal to add the flavor of authenticity to the movie to add to the color of our film. We appreciate everything you did for us. I will make every effort to get a souvenir signed for you.

Thank you always,

Britt Lomon

Production Manager Universal Studios for the "Somewhere in Time" Motion Picture.

Author's Note- The signed souvenir of which Mr. Lomon speaks turned out to be an autographed, original script from the movie signed by all three stars. Dad still has it in his office.

Chapter 5: The First Legend Arrives

During year three, dad placed that call to his idol, the famed designer of the Auburn, Cord, and Duesenberg; Gordon M. Buehrig.

His goal? To have Mr. Buehrig as his first Guest of Honor and to draw an entirely different segment to the show; the legends that designed the cars.

One thing I learned from watching my father was that no harm came from asking or doing. During the building of my charitable foundation, (Put on the Cape a Foundation for Hope) I was known in our public affairs bureau as the person "who asked forgiveness and not permission." I learned that from someone.

Dad had nothing to lose and placed the call to Mr. Buehrig. He left a message, hoping for a call back. Weeks went to months with no response. To my father, Mr. Buehrig was the man, designing the most radical, revolutionary, and historical cars of his time.

During the first St. Ignace Show, dad displayed "the most beautiful car ever built" an all-black 1936 Cord 810 Beverly Sedan. Gordon Buehrig and a small team of stylists (including later automotive luminaries Vince Gardner and Alex Tremulis) had designed the 810, and dad wanted nothing more for him to be his first Guest of Honor.

He was at work in the bank one day and received a phone call. The voice on the other end of the phone said, "Hi Ed, Gordon Buehrig here. Tell me what is going on in your town, tell me about your show." He nearly fainted from excitement and fought to maintain his composure as he spoke with Mr. Buehrig about coming to the show to be the very first Guest of Honor. He was clear that he wanted his first Guest of Honor to be the top of the mountain in the automotive world. He pitched St. Ignace as a unique and vibrant show. He spoke from the heart and his passion was evident.

Mr. Buehrig barely paused before telling him, "Sounds great, I'm in." Knowing that one of Mr. Buehrig's passions was bridges, what better place for him to come than St. Ignace, home of the engineering marvel known as the Mighty Mac?

In all, Mr. Buehrig came to St. Ignace five times. After his death in 1990, his wife Kay came in his place until such time that her health did not allow it.

When he came, Mr. Buehrig only asked one favor; to tour the bridge and climb the 552' foot tower high above the Straits of Mackinac. Along with my father and host of Bridge dignitaries, he did just that. In total, the tower is 772' from bedrock to the sky. In contrast, the Washington Monument is 555' tall.

In later years, dad had the Annual Gordon M. Buehrig Bridge parade that started in Mackinaw City, crossed over the bridge, wound its way through St. Ignace, and stopped at the Senior Center so the residents could view cars of their era.

This was the first time the bridge had hosted such a rally. Now, summer weekends the Bridge commonly hosts rallies of everything from Mini Coopers, to Jeeps, to Tractors, to Semi Trucks driving across its expanse.

"He was an absolutely wonderful man and his wife, Kay, was delightful. She even invited me to her 90th birthday party," dad said with pride.

When I asked him to tell me about Gordon, he waxed poetic about his accomplishments. The Cord. The Auburn Boattail Speedster, and the Duesenberg.

"Gordon was spoken of in hushed tones in the car world. His designs were ahead of their time and so iconic. He was like your grandfather, your buddy. We became friends. I cherish those memories."

Mr. Beuhrig's visit is what made St. Ignace the go-to destination where enthusiasts can see cars they only saw in magazines, and meet their automotive heroes.

During his stay in St. Ignace, Mr. Buehrig contacted his friend, Richard Teague, Vice President of Design for American Motors Corporation and sold him on coming to St. Ignace. Mr. Teague agreed to be the second Guest of Honor for the 1981 St. Ignace show.

"Gordon Buehrig opened so many doors for me," dad said, his voice wavering. "When I contacted other famous car men, when they heard Gordon came to my show, they immediately agreed to come. I hit a home run right out of the gate.

Dad's legend grew after the movie and, after Gordon Beuhrig came to the show, the door opened and stayed open as unbelievable cars and automotive royalty came to St. Ignace.

Headlining Guest of Honor Richard Teague was part of the biggest show to date. The 1981 show had 510 display cars and 22,000 persons crammed into the small lakeside town to see a fantastic collection of automobiles. A 1956 Lincoln Mark II won Best in Show that year.

Dad first met Mr. Teague in Hershey Pennsylvania at the swap meet while digging through a display of antique toys. Dad struck up a conversation and he played the card of Gordon being in St. Ignace, when he asked him to the show.

Mr. Teague designed some of the most beautiful cars in history, including the 1956 Packard Caribbean, later fashioned into a model by Danbury Mint. However, "he also did the AMC Pacer, which is questionable," dad joked, sending me into a fit of laughter.

Like most people, dad could not pronounce Caribbean correctly and each time he introduced Mr. Teague he got it wrong, a running joke between the two for as long as Mr. Teague came to the show.

Mr. Teague also wanted to climb to the top of the Bridge. During his trip to the top of the tower, Mr. Teague told dad it was one of the best moments of his life and something not many others can claim.

Automotive journalist Pat Chappell, author of "The Hot One," ushered in a new era of nationwide coverage of the show.

"St. Ignace was astonishing, " Mrs. Chappell said. "We saw nothing like this on the East Coast outside of Hershey, but Hershey did not have all the attractions Ed brought to St. Ignace."

Seeing was believing for Mrs. Chappell, as she stood in the center of town seeing cars in every direction. The noted author of all things '55 Chevy was direct to the point when I asked her about dad's 1955; "It was magnificent."

Hot Rod legend Tex Smith was a special guest and bemused dad by requesting two pounds of fudge as part of his payment for him appearing.

The 1981 show also introduced one man band Vic Hyde to St. Ignace. For the first time, hostesses greeted and educated guests on the history of the area. With 22,000 souls coming to St. Ignace, they were much needed.

Dad hand-picked all the hostesses, all from St. Ignace to include Pam Larson, Debbie and Cheryl Schlehuber, Nancy Brown, Ruthie Visnaw, Carol Lorente (my kindergarten teacher), Judy St. Louis (with whom I played tennis and was trounced each time), Laura Greve (our neighbor), and Denise Winston, a young lady who worked at the bank and on whom I had a serious crush.

Vintage rock and roll from the 50's and 60's played live on the dock by "Trilogy" led by City Manager Bruce Wood.

"I decided I wanted to look into getting live music during the show to add a much-needed element," dad said. "And that led to the legends of rock and roll shows we did at the High School."

The show grew in numbers and mythology as participants brought savage American muscle cars, street machines, and hot rods, nudging aside the brass era and original cars of the first few years.

In a moment that shocked dad's soul, legendary Corvette engineer Zora Arkus-Duntov, "The Godfather of the Corvette," agreed to be guest of honor for the 1982 show.

"American Graffiti Night" happened for the first time and dad, a huge fan of John DeLorean, secured a DeLorean and displayed it in Feature Car Row. Another hero, Al Drake, writer of "The Big Little GTO" book, came to town for the first time.

Letter from a Legend – Dick Teague

Hi Ed,
I wanted to most heartily thank you for the amazing three days I can ever recall.
Your hospitality and thoughtfulness shown to Mary, Lisa, and me shall be remembered for the rest of our lives. Please pass on thanks to Randy Wilson and Larry Reuben and your most charming wife and children.
The Bridge climb was an ultimate thrill that happens to very few mortals. I am honored to count that opportunity in my memories. Thank you again.

Dick Teague

Author's Note- Richard Teague was Guest of Honor in 1981. Mr. Teague rose to Vice President of Design for American Motors Company, responsible for the Gremlin, Hornet, Ambassador, and AMX. After the buyout of AMC by Chrysler, he designed the Jeep Grand Cherokee. Mr. Teague came back numerous times to St. Ignace.

Chapter 6: A Change is Coming

"It's the World's Greatest Car Show!"
Le Bond Magazine, France 1991

Such was the volume of cars and people that came to St. Ignace in 1981 that, for the first time in the city's history, North State Street (the main street through town) had to be closed to accommodate the growth of the show. It prompted a Michigan Department of Transportation spokesperson to ask dad, "You want to do what now?"

Magazines caught wind of the show, and Hot Rod and Rod and Custom traveled to the picture-perfect Upper Peninsula to cover this growing phenomenon that was St. Ignace.

The very magazines that my teenage father had saved to purchase and pour through the pages were now in his hometown putting him on those pages for other eager, impressionable young kids to read.

People came out of the woodwork to help. Celebrities called the house, movie companies reached out to him. Legendary disc jockeys, notably Dick Biondi, walked right up and introduced himself.

"These were people I only read about, saw on television," dad said. "Now, they were calling me, coming to see me. It was pretty cool, man."

For the show to grow past the confines of Dock 2, dad needed something to happen that had not happened in the 300-year history of St. Ignace; street closure for a special event.

Hindsight being what it is, it is incredulous to think there was a time dad got pushback on this endeavor. The show is so ingrained into the city now that it is hard to imagine at one time that was not the case.

Dad set this trend, taking car shows out of fairgrounds, pavilions, and football fields and blending them seamlessly into their cities; opening the entire shopping district for thousands of spectators to walk right by their open door.

For his show to expand bringing more cars, more people, more celebrities, and more exposure, he needed that street closed. Not the entire town, (as eventually happened block-by-block), but simply the block between the Thunderbird Motel/Ace Hardware, and where the Gang Plank Restaurant sits. For you old timers, Pemble's Grocery store.

Dad credits Stanley Gierlaszynski, a long-time businessman and owner of the Galley Restaurant, as the driving force for the city council to finally approve the street closure. During a meeting, he told the council to stop playing games and pretending this show wasn't going to continue to grow. It was akin to telling Santa to lose weight and not just loosen the belt. He convinced the council that, by closing the street and giving three blocks of Main Street for the show, it would increase interest, visitors, and revenue. It was right in front of them.

The council passed the motion, and, for the first time, dad's vision drove the closure on those very streets so people could enjoy the display of cars bringing back memories of years past.

During the run of the first few shows, his car cruising days were not behind him, and he owned several quality cars outside of the loathed but necessary family trucksters.

The first show gave my father local and regional acclaim that grew to national acclaim with Gordon Buehrig, but he wanted more.

He had the vision in his head to re-create what he did as a teenager. He wanted to relive all those amazing days and nights when he cruised in his cherry cars, cute girls, and his best friends. He knew for his event to be successful he had to add one important thing.

He wanted to have a cruise night.

PART THREE

The Straits Area Antique Auto Show Transforms Into "St. Ignace"

Chapter 7: Cruisin' is King

Given the opportunity to recreate the best years of his life, dad started planning a cruise event. After year two's success, it was not as easy as it should have been.

The Chief Drive-In was sold and renamed "The Chalet North Kitchen" hosting the cruise. He deemed the event subpar. It didn't have the sizzle and bang. No matter what he tried, things just didn't generate the crackle of energy he sought.

Dad then went to the local "Bootsy's Drive-In" (a former A & W) and tried to catch lightning in a bottle, but to his continued befuddlement, he couldn't. The cruising was far from his vision and even farther from his memory.

That was a problem.

The root of that problem was that he did not have a secondary partner to share the passion. The drive, will, and ambition only multiply the frustration unless people buy into the vision and share a stake in its success. Dad was not one to be vague about his wants. He gave the manager explicit instructions to play the American Graffiti soundtrack.

The energy of the music and the cars creates the excitement. When we arrived to check on the event, he was horrified to hear

country music blasting over the speakers and only five cars in attendance.

When he asked, the manager told him he liked country music better. Never one to hold his tongue or temper, dad gave the young man a lesson on what the show was all about, and it included the music dad instructed him to play.

The Cruise Night got better when the right person took over and not only played the right music but did everything, he could to recreate the late 1950's.

To nobody's surprise, it worked.

Cars stuffed into the parking lot and the drive-in had the best two days in their short history. Sadly, two days of great revenue does not make a successful business, and Bootsy's closed the doors for good.

Dad sought a better situation and, working with Bob Goldthorpe, local entrepreneur and owner of the Big Boy Restaurant, came up with a plan. Whether or not their plan was meant to turn the town on its head, change the entire course of the show, cruising in Michigan, create a license to print money, see the crowds quadruple, and change the cruising culture in America, was unknown.

But they did just that.

After four marginal years of "Cruise Night", dad still held to the goal to cruise just like they did in American Graffiti during an endless summer night in 1962.

And that is exactly what happened. Cruise Night in the 80's changed everything. The Down Memory Lane Parade simultaneously grew to the point that it added another fantastic event to a growing list of unbelievable, genre shaking events.

Chapter 8: Down Memory Lane Parade

Always looking to add more attractions for his show, Dad needed a Thursday night event to lead into Friday's Cruise Night and Saturday's main show to create excitement for three straight days.

Ever more quality show cars were coming to St. Ignace, and dad's inner motor drove him to create more buzz, so he devised a large parade to showcase those cars, bring more people to town, and create a buzz in the automotive circuit.

Enter The Down Memory Lane Parade. It was 1981, the show was red hot, owing to Gordon Buerhig's appearance as the first Guest of Honor, and an entire new crowd coming to town.

One large problem existed in regard to having a parade kick off the show and be a draw. Dad hated parades. Intensely.

He felt the person to take over this ambitious project was fellow bank employee and friend Merv Wyse.

"We were looking at that time, as the car show was developing, looking at an event to bring people to town earlier," Merv told me. "That was the genesis."

Merv started work at the First National Bank in 1977. He didn't know many people in town so he rode with mom and dad to the annual bank dinner.

"I remember also sitting next to your dad when Janet and Steve (Peterson) got married," Merv said. "The maid of honor was Janet's sister and as soon as I saw her, I knew that was the woman God meant for me to be my wife."

He married Judy Foote less than a year later, he also shared a story about my father I never knew, and it really impacted me.

Premising the story by confirming what I did know; that my father was a rather hands off, unemotional person. Merv experienced dad's walled off business persona in the work environment. You just didn't walk up and be demonstrative with my father. It was akin to trying to ask Kress how he was feeling about something. The answer could hurt a bit.

Tragically, Merv and Judy's first-born child passed away in his crib. I remember this event profoundly because Brandon was born on May 12th, my birthday. Baby Brandon died July 6th, crushing the entire town and bringing heartbreak to all those who knew or worked with Merv.

With emotion in his voice, Merv told me, "The first person who came to my door that was not family, was your dad."

Standing on the porch, dad paused before stepping into the house. "He gave me a hug that was so genuine, to this day, I can feel his arms around me."

This was the most profound thing I learned during the entire process of writing this book. My father was a very cold and rigid man toward me, something he learned from his own parents. To learn that this emotional part of my dad existed then was a pleasant surprise. It shows the heart of the man.

A self-professed lover of parades, Merv walked around the car show and asked dad if he ever thought of having a parade to add to his calendar of events.

As with everything, dad took out the yellow legal pad and drew two columns; one pro and one con and filled in the blanks. He sent out a survey and gauged the interest of adding a parade to the show schedule.

The idea was "favorably embraced" by the car owners, he told me, and the "pro" side of the ledger far outweighed the con of the parade being part of the show. The con, of course, was dad hated parades.

Merv was given a budget for expenses and began planning the parade. Happy to have the diversion from his grief, Merv said Judy and he had not planned on another child and were still very distraught over their son's death. Merv got started on the "diversion" and ironically, during the planning stages, Merv and Judy learned she was expecting another child. Their son, Jonathan, was born in March of 1982.

Zora Arkus-Duntov was named guest of honor, so Merv had his hands full planning the first parade with the attention of the automotive world. He designated the St. Ignace Airport on the North side of town as staging grounds, with no clue how many cars would participate. The staging turned into a grand display of cars and people, talking, meeting, greeting, and starting to enjoy the weekend in earnest. This activity became a strong part of the pre-parade festivities.

A fond memory for Merv was every year, before anyone could get to the airport, a Corvair-driving gentleman always beat them there. No matter what. No matter how early Merv and his team arrived. Every year.

Merv assembled a team of local volunteers, including Steve Peterson, with the longest tenure. Wes Therrian, Jerry Fenlon, Ken and Josh Feldman, and Mike Wilkins also worked tirelessly, along with his entire family, to make the event so successful. Sadly, Mike Wilkins and Jerry Fenlon, longtime supporters of everything St. Ignace, passed away at a young age from cancer and heart failure, respectively. Both were great men who helped build "St. Ignace." Growing up with both, working side-by-side with them at the show, and getting to know them, it was a sad time in our town when they passed.

The parade, like the car show, is a year around venture. Like the car show, the parade started with no competition. Historically, the parade was spectacular and added so much depth to the show and the town, turning into one of the finest parades in the state.

The success of both prompted towns to the south to hold similar events, sometimes on the same weekend, and they lured away a lot of the bands and displays Merv was accustomed to having exclusively.

"We were the most unique commodity in the entire state of Michigan," Merv said. "There was nothing like it."

As the 1980's waned, Merv said show goers started drinking very early in the morning. By the time the parade started, people went from respectful show goers to hooligans of the highest order and insulted the young band members with torrid vulgarity as they passed. When Merv called to book the bands in subsequent years, the band leaders said no. They refused to bring their young children to St. Ignace and put into such a situation. The show started veering toward the absurd with a sea of drunkenness comparable to any major college campus during last call.

Recalling the Down Memory Lane Parade, when the entire two miles of North State Street were jammed bumper-to-bumper with cars, one of the most intimidating State Troopers in the area, Chris McGraw, got on the radio and asked, "Who is in charge of this cluster?"

St. Ignace Police Chief Tim Matelski looked out his windshield, saw Trooper McGraw on the side of the road. Glaring at him, Chris yelled at Tim, "It's you!"

The law enforcement entities in St. Ignace (State Police, City Police, County Sheriff, Tribal Police, and Immigration) met with Merv and coordinated the Down Memory Lane Parade. They broke bread and discussed the logistics of a massive parade through a small town.

"Merv was wrongly blamed for the huge gaps in the parade, "former Police Chief Tim Matelski said. "But he was down at the other end of town. It wasn't his fault cars were overheating,

Firemen were stopping to do skits with their clown (Dynamite), and bands stopped to play in the middle of the road. Merv took a lot of flak but he did a great job with a parade of that size in such a dinky town."

This prompted dad to approach Merv and tell him he was given an ultimatum by law enforcement and community leaders to end the lawlessness or see the show canceled. Merv caught on quickly and oversaw the parade as it skyrocketed to one of the state's premier events. Dad supplied high-end, must-see cars, and placed the show Guest of Honor in the front. Merv packed an incredible amount of attractions into the parade and electrified the throngs of people who'd gathered hours ahead of time to see it.

Keeping with dad's strength, he promoted the heck out of everything to include this now-legendary parade. Soon, lawn chairs lined the sides of the road for miles and people waited sometimes 12 hours for the parade to start. The electricity was palpable. Bands played, clowns clowned, cars sparkled, princesses and queens waved, marching bands marched, and people cheered wildly. It was a two-hour festival paying homage to what made America great. With fire trucks and law enforcement leading the way, the fire whistle blew and, because it was heard for miles, signaled the simultaneous start of the multi-stage parade.

Future Guest of Honor "Top Hat" John Jenza, started the tradition of the "man in the street" interviews during the parade when he saw singer Bobby Lewis of "Tossing and Turning" fame driving through the parade with no signs on his car.

John stepped into the street and interviewed Mr. Lewis, garnering a huge response from the crowd. Every year henceforth, John did just that; interviewing celebrities and talking about all the cars right down to the type of nuts and bolts used to construct them. It was a huge hit with the crowd.

Merv was a genius and perfected the chess match that organized marching bands with rolling cars without missing a beat.

For cars that had issues with overheating, like dad's 1955 Chevy, Merv started them up front, before the bands, so they could safely make it the three miles of the parade route without boiling over.

Since day one of the parade, by St. Ignace City Council Resolution, "State Street will be named Memory Lane for the Auto Show weekend."

With more than 300 cars (more than most dedicated car shows), Merv balanced them with other displays to make a two-hour flowing spectacle of sight and sound. He encountered some sentiments to change the route of the parade, but refused, as it worked 100 percent of the time and he did not want to risk changing anything for the sake of change. Dad also had people pitch him a new route for the cars to cruise through town, complete with drawn out models.

"They were an answer to a question I never asked," dad said, recalling that movement.

Second only to the Cherry Land Parade in Traverse City, The Down Memory Lane Parade was legendary in the state for what it offered. It was the opening act to one of the greatest shows in the country and served as the primer for Cruise Nights from 1982 to the mid-90's, and it was a must-see and must-participate. Such were the people and love of the parade that the City of St. Ignace made downtown a mandated tow-away zone after 5 p.m. to clear the way.

This was before "The Redneck Party Van", the hand-painted two-tone van (black and rust) with the viewing platform bolted to the roof, parked itself in front of the First National Bank and became a parade-goer staple.

St. Ignace is geographically unlike any other city in the State of Michigan. It borders two of Michigan's Great Lakes, with the Mackinac Bridge and Mackinac Island in the same hula-hoop.

"What your father started was emulated throughout the state, but they did not make it because they did not have the location," Merv said.

The Mackinac Bridge or Island Ferry boats appear in the background of countless photos of people and their cars. With 38 years of parades, Merv glowed that God was always faithful, before he paused and said, "Except for one year."

Ah yes, the biblical flash flood that crippled the parade and is spoken of in hushed whispers from everyone including Jon Moss, Top Hat John, and yours truly.

My fortune of driving a ZR1 Corvette convertible in the parade turned into misfortune as sheets of rain slammed into the parade with such force that cars with tops down were flooded, bands were knocked off their feet, winds took signs, knocked over anything not bolted down, and caused the parade to grind to a standstill. Floats were destroyed, cars stalled, and people were drenched. Driving in a group with the rest of GM Performance, we immediately drove back to the GM Performance Show area to take cover. When I opened the door to my car, water flowed out and took my shoe with it. Women in white scrambled for coverings as their clothing stuck to them. Food floated through the parking lot. Sad, wet dogs, waggled around town, not entirely sure what hit them. This was a first, as they had always been lucky. It had only ever rained PRIOR to the parade. Merv had a safety protocol if lightning flashed; he would cancel. It never came to that. But the rain of that day sent Noah scrambling.

The rain's severity was such that Merv considered it more than an interruption. "It was so bad," he lamented. "So bad."

"All I can say is I am so thankful I had on a long shirt and was wearing underwear," Merv laughed as the parade crew wore white pants. "When the rain came, there was nothing hiding under those pants and shorts."

One year, while working for Merv in those white pants, my fly broke and I had to wear my shirt untucked. I wasn't asked back the next year.

The rain in the middle of the parade was a "really bad thing, it came so quickly, those in convertibles had no chance."

The Glen Memorial Baptist had the final parade float and Merv was pulling it with his truck. He was resigned to the fact that, when he came through town, the soaked streets would be empty.

"WRONG!" Merv stated. "People stayed. They got drenched and accepted it. They stayed, the kids were playing in puddles and the people were soaked but they were there until the bitter end."

One of Merv's fond memories from his three-plus decades was being on the Church float, playing a pump organ. Ed Ryan, long-time show supporter and hot rodder, was pulling the float and didn't know how touchy the brakes were. He pumped them hard going down a little hill and flung Merv from the church bench his mother-in-law had loaned him for the parade.

"She gave it to me with the caveat that if anything happened to it, you are in trouble."

Laying on the float bed, he looked over and saw his mother-in-law's piano bench, "In smithereens." Not knowing if he needed to cry or be mad, members of the crowd gave him another chair to sit on for the parade's duration.

Ed Ryan, the offending driver, looks at first sight like he belongs in a biker gang. Big, muscular, full of tattoos and bald, (In reality, along with his wife Donna, are some of the nicest people you can meet) stayed hunkered down in the truck to avoid being verbally slapped by Merv.

Merv is presently hard at work to bring back his passion with the 39th Down Memory Lane Parade, scheduled for 2022. The previous two years were lost to Covid.

Working with dad was an interesting endeavor for Merv.

"Sometimes, your dad can be very frustrating to work with," he said, telling me something I didn't know.

"There are so many memories of working with your dad," Merv said. "We were family." Merv and I shared memories over the years and both concluded the same thing about one particular

Guests of Honor who we felt was the coolest person to come to town.

"John Schneider was incredible," Merv said. "His booth was by our church booth, and he never left. He was a people person. He stayed all day to sign autographs."

I reached out to Mr. Schneider's representatives for an interview and sadly, did not get a response.

When the show was sold to the Visitors Bureau, Merv was not approached to run the parade and was shocked to learn the parade was not part of the sale package.

"The talk was there was not going to be a parade and if there was, I was not to be in charge of it." He heard another director with more experience was replacing him and took it in stride.

"Ultimately, they came to me," Merv said. "I put my faith in God and things shook out the way it was supposed to be."

The City approached Merv for the 350th Anniversary Parade and, now, he is in charge of that.

I've known Merv for more than 40 years. He shares the same passionate approach to life and his vision as my dad. He is a kind man, a true servant and one of the cornerstones that made the St. Ignace Car Show so popular for so long.

Nowhere else in the state did you see a triple header with a parade of this magnitude, a cruise night so legendary that Japanese magazines covered it, and the car show. Dad knew his weakness and he knew Merv's strengths. It worked out just fine.

Mike Stowe, long-time supporter of the show and owner of Great Lakes Motor Works in Boyne City, Michigan, loved the parade and the opportunity to mingle with the greatest automotive minds on earth.

"It was where I met (Chrysler Chief of Design) Tom Gale, "Mr. Stowe told me. "We formed a lifelong friendship and traveled the world together."

A car collector and historian, Mr. Stowe provided Mr. Gale's number and enabled me to interview him. Mr. Stowe "may have" come to the first show and helped dad but neither can be sure.

"I parked cars for years, downtown at the ungodly hour of 4 a.m." Mr. Stowe told me. "Then I took over parking Feature Car Row and didn't have to start until 7 a.m. which I liked much better."

I cherish the memory of seeing Mr. Stowe, waiting for dad and me with cups of coffee, and his excitement to be part of the show. Another local hero, a man of great accomplishment, who dropped everything to be part of this magical show.

"One of the greatest things about the parade is it allowed us all to unplug, sit on a bench, eat ice cream, and watch all the cars go past," Mr. Gale said. "I sat there with some great people through the years, watching all the amazing cars ride past and it was something we all looked forward to every year."

Other automotive legends had different memories of the parade.

Jerry Palmer, retired Director of Design for the Corvette and long-time participant in St. Ignace, trailered up a concept car. It was a mid-engine Corvette with a twin-turbo, four-valve engine, ceramic brakes, and a state-of-the-art electronic system that used multiplexing, where the same wires are used for multiple functions of the car.

"Lotus helped us build out the engine," Mr. Palmer said. "It was a fabulous car and for the time, as state-of-the-art as you could get."

Mr. Palmer entered it in the "Down Memory Lane Parade" and drove it himself. Things went well. For a while. Then things went an entirely different direction. Literally.

"All of a sudden, with the Gull Wing doors up, the car went into reverse." Moving forward at parade speed, the car violently lurched and then immediately went back at parade speed.

"I am standing on the brake with both feet," Mr. Palmer said with a slight laugh. "We were trying so hard to not hit the car behind us."

They finally got the car off the road and then the high-capacity fuel pump burst and started squirting gasoline near a group of people attempting to light their cigarettes.

"That would have made headlines for all the wrong reasons," Mr. Palmer said. "Thankfully, we got them to stop before they lit those lighters."

Chapter 9: Talking Cars with Mr. Craig Shantz

"It was an awesome show, in an awesome setting, planned and executed in one of the most professional ways and that is all because of Ed Reavie."
Craig Shantz, *Engineering Group Manager of Performance Vehicles and Events for General Motors.*

Engineering Group Manager of Performance Vehicles and Events for General Motors

Craig Shantz, now retired, first came to St. Ignace in 2001 and now lives in Northern Michigan, right on the lake. After "40 years, 11 months, and four days" Craig said. "At retirement, GM rounded it off to 41 years."

A cornerstone of the show and the parades, Craig's last show was also dad's last show in 2015. "I miss seeing him and talking to him," Craig said. "He is a great man."

Craig had moved around the country for years and was happy to land in the Specialty Vehicle Group.

"I was relocated by GM nine times," Craig said. "In 2002 I was transferred to the Specialty Vehicle Group and I came every year after that."

I laughed as I told Craig how much I loved coming up for the show, knowing that GM Performance had many amazing production cars to drive. I told him I may have "Allegedly" burned out the clutch in the ZR1 Indy Pace Car one year.

Craig was unsure about that (I wasn't, sorry Craig) but did say there was a GM executive who certainly did just that. I remember not paying sufficient attention as I brought up the rear, so enraptured was I to be in the cockpit of that fabulous car. I hadn't noticed that the group had left.

The cars were in line, ready to go onto the street and into position. I noticed the cavalcade had left, leaving me alone.

I popped the clutch as one would do in an old, four-cylinder station wagon. I swore the nose lifted completely off the ground as the car roared and fired forward as if I'd been flung out of a Monty Python-style giant slingshot.

I would've undoubtedly landed on a car, had one been in front of me. Dear God. Don't even get me started on the first time I drove a Viper and did the same thing. I am still seeing a chiropractor.

Living in Northern Michigan, Craig was amazed when he first came to St. Ignace. "The show was much bigger than I ever expected," he said. "I've been to a lot of car shows, a lot of car shows, but this was one of the most thorough, planned, and executed shows I've ever been to."

Craig has attended shows from Maryland to California and Minnesota to Florida and was thoroughly impressed with the way the St. Ignace Car Show was put together.

"The show being right down the middle of main street, in that beautiful setting, the community in general, it took over the city and it was a great setting."

Most successful shows were purchased and used the foundation already built to improve it as the years went forward, Mr. Shantz said. Not St. Ignace.

"Your dad created this from the ground up, he built it and built it extremely well," Craig said. "The things he did, not charging admission for spectators, showed he cared about the participants and the spectators in relation to the revenue it generated for St. Ignace."

The "behind the curtain" work dad did to make it successful was the most amazing concept of the show, Craig said. From the show, to the Cruise Night, to the concerts, everything worked.

GM Performance brought as many as 26 cars to St. Ignace every year. Craig said the cars had dual purpose; Those parked in a static display and others specifically for the Down Memory Lane Parade.

Craig said he never saw such a relaxed show setting. "People just strolled around, looked at cars, went into a store, got ice cream, asked questions about cars, and really had a good time."

Craig saw the amazing organization of dad's shows, so he approached him about GM doing their own awards (which were astonishing) and he was more than open to the idea.

GM brought up crate engines for raffle and the proceeds built something great. "Your dad took the cash from those raffles and donated them to the library," Craig said. "There is a plaque inside the new library thanking the GM Performance Division."

Craig was amazed at the philanthropy dad showed to St. Ignace. I told Craig that dad had donated an ambulance to the hospital, a fact he did not know. I didn't either until someone told me.

"That is just his way," Craig said.

GM's strong commitment to St. Ignace shone brightest during the parade.

"The St. Ignace parade was really structured well," Craig said. "They just didn't have hot rods driving down the street. The town was involved. The parade was longer with more displays than most parades in the country."

Through the years, many great stories from the parade are part of show lore. Linda Vaughn's driver, on the way through the backroads to get back to the GM display, ran out of gas.

Craig laughed as he told me, "The driver told Linda they were out of gas and she said, "Oh, I've heard that story before."

The structure of the show was the most impressive quality of it, Craig said. Everything was planned so well, there was not the stress involved as there was in other shows.

"People came to St. Ignace from a distance," Craig said. "It had an amazing notoriety. People came from Florida to be part of the show with their cars. Your dad created that need."

The St. Ignace show had another quality. "Your dad made people feel important and appreciated, he was a mastermind of that."

Once dad retired, GM Performance worked with the new regime, found that the show just wasn't the same and ultimately ended their participation.

"It's a credit to your father how successful that show was for all those years," Craig said. "The show is always so much more than people anticipated and they end up coming back year-after-year."

Craig summed up his time in St. Ignace. "It was an awesome show, in an awesome setting, planned and executed in one of the most professional ways, "Craig said. "And that is all your father."

Thank you Craig.

PART FOUR

The Sting Ray, Cobra, and King of the Kustomizers

Chapter 10: Zora and the Vette

"I finally got to meet the most persistent son-of-a-bitch I've ever dealt with."

Carroll Shelby, *Famed Engineer, creator of the Shelby Cobra and Ford GT, and Guest of Honor 1984, upon meeting Ed Reavie.*

Once the car show grew beyond the perimeter of Dock Two and eventually took over two miles of St. Ignace's main street, it became "cool" for cities to shut down their streets and make the entire town part of the show.

Dad told me of the endless phone calls, letters, and faxes just to get someone to call him back. Then the courting process began and that could take months.

Getting Zora Arkus-Duntov to agree to come to St. Ignace was easier than dad had thought. It took one phone call. As the neighbor of Gordon Buehrig, Zora got an earful about St. Ignace when Mr. Buehrig returned from his Guest of Honor roll and was told in no uncertain terms that he needed to go when asked.

When dad called him, he had already made up his mind to come. A long-time car rebel, Zora famously contacted GM after the Corvette debuted in 1953 and said he wanted to be a part of working on such a remarkable car.

He loved the car, but he was less than impressed with what was under the hood. When Ford introduced the Thunderbird, Zora went on the offensive, writing a letter to the engineers and Harley Earle, telling them they needed to get going and up the ante on their six-cylinder, underpowered Corvette.

All the 1953 Vettes were white with red interior, and all were made in Flint, Michigan. The early design was far from the C8 Corvette and Zora wanted to start changing the look to a sleek, yet powerful, motor car.

By 1957, he got carte blanche to put some muscle in the Corvette. He was instrumental in getting the fuel-injected 283 four speed and "made the corvette what it is today," dad said.

While Harley Earle created the Corvette, Zora took his design into the stratosphere. Upon the news of Zora headlining the show, more than 20 Corvette publications covered his appearance and news of St. Ignace went worldwide.

Zora took his own plane to St. Ignace and dad met him on the tarmac. Zora got off the plane holding a Camel cigarette and a martini and "never put either one down all weekend," dad said with a laugh.

For Zora's first trip, dad wanted to impress him and boy, did he. On the showgrounds sat the top feature car; a 1953 Corvette serial number 003, roped off from the public.

Legions of Corvette clubs converged on the show to get a glimpse of their hero and the man who once held the stock car record for the fastest climb up Pikes Peak and was a four-time competitor in the 24 Hours of LeMans.

With Zora's thick Belgian accent, dad had a terrible time understanding him, but his legend preceded him, thus requiring little talking. I never saw Zora without a Camel cigarette burning in his hand. He was cool and knew how to work a crowd.

Zora's impact on the Corvette cannot be overstated, dad told me. The 1963 Split Window coupe is an icon, favored by Mr. Mitchell and despised by Zora, Chief Designer of the Corvette and future Guest of Honor.

When the dust settled on the 1982 show, 620 show cars made their way to town with 25,000 spectators. With Zora in the mix, nothing was ever the same.

Letter from a Legend - Zora

Dear Ed,
To your question, I don't have a favorite Corvette, I like them all. I have decided to fly to St. Ignace in my own plane and will have someone bring up the Duntov Turbo for display.
Best regards,

Zora

Author's Note: Mr. Arkus-Duntov was the Guest of Honor for the 3rd St. Ignace Show. He did fly, and came back a few years later with Carroll Shelby and the Duntov Turbo did find its way to St. Ignace

Chapter 11: Legend to the Legends

"I walked among the cars and instantly remembered the days I designed them. I remember the team that worked on them and all their personalities; it was like a dream world."

William Mitchell, Head of Design for General Motors and one of the most influential designers in history. Guest of Honor in 1983

On a serious roll, with the show making headlines, legends serving as Guests of Honor, and a postcard-like backdrop, dad felt it was time to reach out to one of the most influential designers in American Automotive History; William Mitchell.

Recruited by Harley Earle, Mr. Mitchell started with General Motors in 1935 and, during his tenure, was responsible for the design of more than 72 million cars sold by General Motors.

He rose to Vice President of Automotive Design and had a heavy hand in the designs of the Buick Riviera, the 1955-57 Chevy, The Cadillac de Ville, the Corvette Stingray, The Camaro, and the Cadillac Seville; all cars of legend.

He smoothed out the lines, then removed running boards and other objects that detracted from the appearance. Dad had read about him his entire life.

Seeking to impress him, dad located in Oklahoma a copy of the first car designed by Mr. Mitchell; a 1938 Cadillac Sixty Special. He personally paid for the car's transport and made sure the car's owner was seated next to Mr. Mitchell at the Guest of Honor luncheon.

Dad parked the '38 Caddy In front of the house so it was the first thing Mr. Mitchell saw. A photograph of Mr. Mitchell and my dad next to that 1938 Caddy is in this book's photo section.

The stage was set for another incredible show, and again, it met expectations. Mr. Mitchell drove into town in a cranberry and silver Seville Muscleback with chrome wheels and made a serious statement immediately upon driving through the Mackinac Bridge toll booth.

With a mentor like Harley Earle, Mr. Mitchell was a tough man to work with and the stories became stuff of legend. His dealings with dad, however, were nothing but pleasant.

I still remember the cranberry and silver car pulling up to our house and dad walking outside to meet yet another hero.

He took Mr. Mitchell for a three-hour tour of St. Ignace in Dick Crane's triple black 1976 Eldorado convertible. "He was a son-of-a-bitch to work for (so I was told)," dad told me. "But with me, he was relaxed, and we did nothing but talk about cars the entire time."

Dad wished he'd had a tape recorder, so blown away was he while talking to the legendary designer about his thinking and process of design. Heaven for a car nerd and gear head like my father. Dad said he sat back and, while listening, it was hard to not be emotional.

The greaser with the blonde ducktail, the nerd so uncoordinated who couldn't hit water if he fell out of a boat, the kid who paid to live in his own home, was driving Bill Mitchell around the same streets he cruised as a teenager, in the very cars designed by his passenger.

You like apples, Kress and Elaine? How do you like those apples?

As dad rustled all the papers in front of him to stay on point, he spontaneously uttered, "I simply cannot believe I got all these people to come here. All these cars. I don't know how I had any time to do anything other than this show. It was never easy. Each person took at least three calls to get them or their cars here, but they came."

That they did, dad, that they did.

To put peanut butter on that apple, the famed Alexander brothers made their first trip to St. Ignace. Mike and Larry Alexander redefined the custom car culture from their small shop in Detroit, attracting the attention of the greatest customizer of them all, George Barris.

Hot Rod magazine wrote the Alexander brothers were as important to car culture as Elvis, Chuck Berry, and Little Richard were to Rock and Roll.

Three-time winners of the prestigious Ridler Award, the Alexander Brothers styling radically changed how customizers approached their work. The brothers came to St. Ignace multiple times to show some of their amazing cars to the public.

The 1983 show was spectacular and set attendance and registration records with another off the hook cruise night, but it paled in comparison with what happened in 1984.

Letters from a Legend - Bill Mitchell

Dear Ed,

I cannot thank you enough for the wonderful hospitality Mary Ellen and your staff showered on me while I was in St. Ignace for the show. I certainly felt at home; what an experience. I walked upon the cars and instantly remembered the days I designed them. I remember the team that worked on them and all their personalities; it was like a dream world.

You certainly have put a tremendous amount of effort and work into making your car show such a success and deserve a lot of credit. I really enjoyed the Guest of Honor Luncheon and hope I said the right things. It was a great honor to be the lead car for your parade and to present the various awards.

Thank you for having the 1976 Eldorado at my disposal. It was a lovely car and I was afraid to drive it in fear of putting dents into it. Thank you to your lovely mayor for the cup and saucer and I am sorry I was unable to visit Mackinac Island but will make sure I do so on a future visit.

Everything was wonderful including the weather and I will treasure the memories. Let's keep in touch. If you ever get down this way, please contact me and I will arrange for us to get together.

Thank you again.

Bill Mitchell.

Author's Note. Bill Mitchell is one of the most iconic designers in history and was the 4th Guest of Honor at St. Ignace.

Letter from a Legend- Gordon Buehrig

Dear Ed,

Thank you for your invitation to the 1983 St. Ignace Auto Show. We plan to attend.

I have one request, as Bill Mitchell is the guest of honor, please keep Kay and me somewhere in the background so we do not diminish his appearance in any way.

Bill is an old friend and it will be nice to see him there. I have a great deal of respect for Bill for his designs. Kay and I look forward to this occasion.

Sincerely,

Gordon Buehrig

Author's Note: Class and elegance. Times have changed.

Chapter 12: King Cobra

"St. Ignace had a back home type atmosphere. It was genuine. The love, the passion, the fun, everyone smiled. I never had a bad time in all my years. I was passionately in love with y'alls show."

Linda Vaughn, *The First Lady of Motorsports and 1999 Guest of Honor who came to St. Ignace 20 years in a row.*

The Private plane landed at the tiny St.Ignace airport, containing two of the most legendary engineers in history. Dad stood on the tarmac, hands sweating, heart pounding, nearly sick to his stomach with excitement.

The door opened and Zora Arkus-Duntov emerged with his trademark unfiltered Camel and martini glass, Carroll Shelby was right behind him.

Carroll exuded coolness and class, he approached my father and shook his hand. Nearly five years after first reaching out, Carroll finally had an opening in his calendar and committed to St. Ignace.

"You didn't give up," Carroll told him.

During their introduction, dad's crowning moment was interrupted by the pilot demanding payment for the flight. Zora took a drag on his Camel, looking away as he blew out the smoke and made it clear he was paying for nothing. Carroll dug in his pockets before saying, "I have a friend's card for expenses. This should work."

When dad saw Lee Iacocca's name on the card, he shook his head in astonishment. This moment truly punched dad's front row ticket to what would become the greatest show on earth.

With Carroll Shelby headlining, Zora at his side, and Shelby Cobras roaring into town by the minute, more than 35,000 persons came to St. Ignace, and the town swelled to 920 show cars parked on both sides of the two-mile North State Street (Main Street).

For dad, having Carroll Shelby in St. Ignace was akin to a child having Santa Clause sit down and enjoy cookies and milk and telling them to take any gift they want out of the bag.

Adding to this legendary Guest of Honor and former Guest of Honor (Zora), Dick Teague returned, forming a holy trinity of automotive royalty in one small town.

An astonishing photo of Mr. Teague, Zora, and Carroll Shelby, seated with dad on the Colonial House porch must be seen to be believed.

The thing about St. Ignace is that, once these great men came, it wasn't a one-and-done. They returned. Watching the banter between Carroll and Zora was the highlight of dad's life.

Carroll Shelby, as parade Marshall for the Down Memory Lane Parade, was shown love and respect on such a level that dad worried about his safety. So many people rushed to shake his hand, take a photo with him, and some women tried to give Carroll their room keys.

Mr. Shelby sat on the back of the triple-black Eldorado while dad drove. The day was a gloomy, rainy mess but before the parade began, the clouds parted and the sun emerged, prompting Mr. Shelby to tell dad, "Man, you really do control this town, don't you?"

I honestly cannot imagine how things like this impacted my father. I think of my love for Bruce Springsteen's music, (as such I have an identical butterscotch blonde Telecaster) and knowing how I would react if Bruce sat down next to me and complimented me on my playing.

The parade was a massive success and dad had to stop more than once so the thousands of Carroll Shelby fans could take his photo (selfies were not a thing yet) and attempt to get his autograph.

The parade route rolled past the State Bar (Now Village Inn). and Mr. Shelby told dad he was parched and needed a Budweiser. Dad knew the bar was packed with Carroll Shelby fans and told him he had concerns for his safety.

"No worries," the man in the black hat said. "Get me in there and I will get a Bud for you too."

When Carroll didn't come out for a long time, Dad went inside to check on him, only to find him drinking and having a blast with legions of his fans telling stories about cars. Dad waded in, reminded Mr. Shelby they were on a time constraint to get to the Cruise Night and, with traffic so thick, it would take about 30 minutes to get there. Carroll waved and shook hands with just about everyone as dad pulled him out. The two left and Carroll popped open the Bud as the new friends roared out for more adventures.

Laughing, listening to roaring cars all around them, and toasting to each other with their open Bud longnecks, dad was unaware of the two State Troopers on his tail.

"Red, white and blue means freedom unless they are flashing behind you," KSLX morning man Neanderpaul once said. Oh, how true that is.

Dad panicked when the red and blue lights illuminated behind them. Fearing local headlines such as "Bombed Banker Busted with Bud," dad banged his head on the steering wheel.

With a Bud in his pocket and Mr. Shelby holding a cold one in his hand, dad looked in the mirror and saw the two State Troopers walking toward the car. I always tell people to check the officer's headgear to get an idea how many tickets they will get.

No hat or a baseball hat? There exists a 90 percent chance you get a warning and go on your way. The Trooper Smokey Hat? Yeah, even off duty cops are getting a ticket at that point.

Dad made himself small in the seat and hoped he knew the two men who held his pocket book and reputation as tightly as Mr. Shelby held his Budweiser.

After standing by the car for a few seconds, the Troopers spoke, but not to dad.

"Mr. Shelby, welcome to St. Ignace," said one of the Troopers. "Can you autograph this photo for me?"

Exhaling and smiling, Carroll was happy to oblige, signing the photos and snapping a few more. Getting back in the car, Mr. Shelby looked at dad as he got back in the car and laughed, "Nice town you have here."

On the way to the Big Boy, traffic was thicker than dad predicted. Badass cars were lined up two-by-two. People sat in lawn chairs along the highway, in the backs of their cars, or stood waving and screaming at all the cars and at Mr. Shelby.

The closer they got to the Big Boy, the crazier the atmosphere. Dad was astonished at the sounds of turbochargers, big blocks, glass packs, monstrously horse powered customs squealing tires to a cheering crowd, and screaming punctuated with sirens.

I remember it sounding like an airport, such was the ambient noise in the air. "Good God," dad said looking into the sea of people and cars that occupied every inch of West US2.

Cruise Night was such a raucous party that he did not want to take Carroll to the Big Boy for dinner as a free Big Boy sandwich clearly was not enough of a draw to brave it.

He opted instead to go across the street to the then Zodiac Restaurant and hoped the open parking space was not an optical illusion.

The timing was perfect as large tables of people were just leaving. He and Carroll snuck around the line and grabbed a table in the packed house. Carroll and dad craved the same thing and asked the young waitress for two burgers, two orders of French fries, and two Buds. Carroll winked at dad knowing this meal was on Mr. Iacocca.

The dead-tired waitress had no idea who the two men were and told Carroll Shelby the kitchen was closed, and only cold sandwiches and potato chips were available.

Undeterred, Dad told the waitress to find Wally Massaway (owner and lifelong friend of dad) and tell him Carroll Shelby was in his restaurant and he wanted a hamburger.

She was terrified to do such a thing on the busiest night in their history, but dad assured the young lady he would vouch for her with Wally. She agreed and walked into the back room to give Wally the message and returned minutes later, pad and pen at the ready.

"What would you like on your hamburger, Mr. Shelby?"

From there, the party was on. Clinking their Buds together, gobbling up their burgers, fans of Carroll everywhere, dad had never had a night like this one.

He had also never attended college and wondered if this was what it was like. The best of times. Almost in a dream state, laughing, sharing stories, and making toasts with one of your heroes in life.

Does it get better than that? Of course, it did.

Carroll saw a commotion in the corner of the restaurant, the thick Belgian accent catching his ear. Carroll and dad walked over to find Zora holding court with a Corvette Club whose members were rollicking with great stories from a slightly inebriated Zora, wine bottle in hand. Already on their third or fourth bottle of wine, the two joined Zora and their fans, talking, toasting, and laughing until the wee hours, the night turned to day.

"I had no idea how I got home that night," dad laughed. "I never drank wine, but with Carroll and Zora, I did that night." Pretty sure I myself drove dad home that night, but it's all a tad fuzzy as clearly, I was far too young to drink.

Word spread fast about this amazing little show in the far reaches of Northern Michigan. Finally, the spotlight shone on somewhere other than California or New York. St. Ignace became the place to be in the automotive world.

"This was the tipping point," dad said proudly. "We were right at the cusp with Gordon, Bill Mitchell, and Zora, and then Carroll came to town and rang the bell and the automotive world took notice."

With his fourth Guest of Honor, dad succeeded in bringing four of the most influential engineers and designers in automotive history to our town. Zora and Carroll's creations, the Corvette and the Shelby Mustang, were among the most prestigious cars to ever prowl the streets of the country.

Mr. Shelby was the real deal and it mattered not if you were a fellow legend or a local pilot, he treated you the same. Paul Fullerton of St. Ignace had the honor and joy of flying Mr. Shelby the next few times he came to St. Ignace.

"He was cool. He was a man's man," Paul said. "I gave him one of my cards and Mr. Shelby took it and told me he was into cornbread and chili and said he would send me some."

A few months later, a huge box arrived from UPS filled with cornbread and Carroll Shelby's Chili mix. "Being young and dumb, I gave most it it away and didn't think of keeping one for myself."

Through the years, Paul also flew Linda Vaughn into town and even worked with Merv Wyse to organize parking for the parade. Another local hero, Paul, was a vital part of the show.

The National automotive press heard rumblings of the goings on in St. Ignace and now were fully onboard as the place to be for anyone who's anyone.

It was a great summer and fall in Michigan as the Detroit Tigers won the World Series. St. Ignace was riding the momentum of the good tidings. Baseball, hamburgers, Budweiser, and Carroll Shelby.

Letter from a Legend - Carroll Shelby

Dear Ed,
Sorry it took a while to get back to you. I have been traveling and will head out to Europe again this weekend. My thanks to you for your card and best wishes, the photos are great and I enjoy looking at them as they remind me of the joyful time I spent with you in St. Ignace.
I want to tell you how crafty you are; did you know you could see a Cobra, a GT-350, and a Shelby Charger through the window of the restaurant during my Guest of Honor Brunch? Well done.
We hope to see you again soon.
Your friend,

Carroll Shelby

Author's Note: When dad read this to me, he proclaimed, "Does it get any better than this? For anybody?" No, dad. It doesn't. Dad also said the three cars outside the restaurant was not a planned thing but is glad it happened.

Mr. Shelby returned three more times to St. Ignace.

Chapter 13: King of the Kustomizers

How do you top the legendary Carroll Shelby? You don't, you simply keep riding the wave of the fantastical.

In 1949, dad stood in the local drug store with a quarter, trying to decide between two comic books and a pile of candy when something else caught his eye.

Issue number one of Motor Trend Magazine was on the shelf above the comic books he'd thought to purchase but he decided to change allegiance and purchase an automotive magazine (he still owns it).

He read with complete fascination the story of a car builder who took a 1941 Ford Coupe and lowered, modified, chopped, and transformed it into a spectacular hot rod. The man, George Barris, developed the California Kustom. The custom became the Hollywood look and, without George Barris, dad admits his life would not have gone the way it did to Kress's horror, a lover of modified cars. It changed the way he saw the world.

Flash forward to 1985. The 10th Annual St. Ignace Auto Show was headlined by George Barris. Dad held up that magazine and thanked Mr. Barris personally for what he did for the car world and him personally.

"My God. I got George Barris to come to town. My hero. How on earth did I do that?" George Barris' books are all over dad's home. Dad credited 1986 Guest of Honor Bob Larivee with getting George's number, getting it to dad with the marching orders of, "Now go get him here."

Dad was concerned that this moment was not going to happen. Mr. Barris did not understand St. Ignace's diminutive size and made demands on dad that he could not accommodate, forcing change after change to dad's promotional copy. This pushed him to the brink of his sanity and the St. Ignace News's deadline. Wes Mauer Jr. (longtime owner of the paper) and dad were forced to work late into the night, every night, to accommodate his demands.

"George wanted a book to showcase all his cars," Wes said. "He didn't want to pay for it, of course, so we had to make it for him."

Years away from digital technology, Wes recalled shooting photos of the cars, scaling them, printing them, and cutting and pasting them into the book. It was all tedious, long work made longer each time George sent new photos he wanted in the book. This meant the other photos had to literally be ripped out and the entire page rebuilt.

"It took forever," Wes said. "One night at three in the morning, I told your dad there was no way to do this. We were running out of time and energy."

The free book was at 50 pages, hundreds of hours, and still George Barris sent more and wanted it included. It meant, of course, that the 50 pages had to be ripped apart, resized, re-key lined, and re-designed.

"George Barris got pissed, but there was nothing we could do, and we threw in the towel," Wes said. "It felt good because I didn't care how much George Barris yelled at your dad and I don't think your dad cared very much either."

Dad agreed with Wes and was finally out of patience (of which dad had next to none anyway) and under constant fear of Mr. Barris pulling out of the show. So, he reached out to legendary show promoter Bob Larivee Sr. for help.

Known as the King of the Car Show, Mr. Larivee held indoor shows around the country; up to 106 shows in one calendar year. As such, Mr. Larivee was used to dealing with Mr. Barris and told dad he would call George to smarten him up as to the issues and stress he placed on dad and Wes.

"I didn't know what the hell to do with him," dad said of Mr. Barris. "Bob called me back and said George would be at the show and would be as charming and engaging as he always is at shows."

Bear in mind that my father was a small-town banker so far removed from the world in that town and George Barris was…freaking George Barris.

With the legendary builder and King of the Kustomizers fully in pocket, the 10th Annual show was spectacular.

Crowds went wild for George Barris as he rode through town in one of his creations, the 1966 Batmobile. Several of his builds, including the Munster Coach, were in town.

Mr. Larivee laughed when I told him about all this and said he truly didn't remember, but had no doubt that it happened, as George tended to be a bit difficult from time to time. (see Mr. Larivee's interview).

Building cars was a George Barris specialty and he constructed the Monkee Mobile (don't ask Dean Jefferies), the fabulous Torino for Starsky and Hutch several KITT Cars for Knight Rider, the Beverly Hillbilly Coach, and even NASA worked with George Barris on a car to be used on the moon and future trips to Mars.

Custom Barris Golf Carts went to clients Bob Hope, Bing Crosby, Glen Campbell, and Elton John. George even built a gold-plated Rolls Royce for Zsa Zsa Gabor and a "his and hers" set of 1966 Mustangs for Sonny and Cher.

Dad and George became good friends during their time together at the show, and dad traveled to California to visit George's shop. He also met Tommy the Greek, Dean Jeffries, and Joe Bailon during the same trip. That California odyssey is later in this book.

Landing George as Guest of Honor was achieved by sending him all the prints of the legends who came before him. When he called George, dad was amazed to hear that George was eager to attend the show and ride in the parade as Grand Marshal.

In all, more than 40,000 persons attended the 10th show with 1,214 show cars packed into the two-mile ribbon of main street, breaking records from Carroll Shelby's year.

Bob Stevens, editor of Cars and Parts, attended and St. Ignace received huge press across the country and was no longer a secret.

One of dad's proudest moments was during the guest of honor lunches when a tall, thin man with sunglasses came into the room and introduced himself.

Dick Biondi was a legendary disc jockey who rose to fame on WLS 890 AM where he became the first American DJ to play the Beatles, among the first to introduce Elvis, Jerry Lee Lewis, and Gene Vincent to the throng of teenagers hungry for the new, yet unnamed, rock and roll.

Such was his love for the new music, legend has it that he famously barricaded himself in his studio and endlessly played "That'll Be the Day" by Buddy Holly until studio executives broke down the door and stopped him. This scene is portrayed in the movie, "The Buddy Holly Story." So wild were his on-air antics, Dick was fired 23 times in his career.

Dick was master of ceremonies at an early-years appearance by Elvis, during which Dick asked the future King to autograph his shirt. Once done, Elvis fanatics swarmed Dick, grabbed him from the stage, and the fans tore the shirt from him with such violence he required hospitalization.

I cannot imagine what it was like for my father to be in the same room with George Barris and Dick Biondi. Two of his idols growing up, now in his hometown, and they wanted to meet him. Mind blowing.

To add even more history, dad had Tommy Durden, the man who wrote HeartBreak Hotel for Elvis, at the show. Mr. Durden wrote the first ever song for the car show entitled, "Wheels, Wheels,

Wheels," which could never be confused with Heartbreak Hotel, but was cool nonetheless.

Dick Biondi returned four times to lead the ever-growing Cruise Nights at the Big Boy. People hung out of the trees and got onto the roof of the building to see Dick on the grandstand doing what he did best as they drank, danced, drank, danced, and drank some more. The people and cars were so thick, you could not move.

Such was the out-of-this-universe atmosphere of Cruise Night that, even by itself, was regarded as one of the largest collections of automobiles in the country, condensed into a six-hour, free flowing stream of cars, consciousness, ridiculousness, and mind-altering antics.

Dad then created the first Gordon Buehrig Bridge Rally To pay respect to the man who opened the door for future automotive royalty. It featured brass era cars and cars that Gordon had personally designed.

For the first time, traffic lanes on the Mackinac Bridge were closed to accommodate the cars. Thirty years later, it is rare when there is not a summer rally of some kind on the bridge. Again, Ed Reavie set a standard by shifting the paradigm.

I graduated from high school in 1985. Now 18, a generation of show attendees watched me grow up standing next to my dad during 10 years of unprecedented growth and history. I went from being a bad haircut sporting thick-glasses-wearing, nerdy-looking eight-year-old, to a pimply bad haircut sporting thick-glasses-wearing, nerdy-looking 18 year old, albeit nearly a foot taller and with horrible fashion taste.

The Honey Radio Car Caravan began in 1985. They drove up together from Detroit in classic cars and brought a new element to a show that was constantly adding new elements.

Letter from a Legend – George and Shirley Barris

Dear Ed,

Shirley and I want to thank you for all your hospitality during the St. Ignace Car Show. We thoroughly enjoyed ourselves every day at the wonderful events you planned for us.

I cannot tell you how proud I was to be in the parade driving the Batmobile with you and driving through the Big Boy Cruise Night. I enjoyed meeting everyone in your great town and they treated us like royalty.

More so, I was happy to hear about the record breaking crowds. You deserve a lot of great recognition for all the hard work but at the end results should make you happy. Thank you again and again for your courtesy.

George and Shirley Barris

Author's Note- The King of the Kustomizers, Mr. Barris was Guest of Honor in 1985. His legendary works need no explanation.

Letter from a Legend - Dick Biondi

Dear Ed,

Thank you for the fantastic time in St. Ignace. Working with you is a great pleasure. I wish the people in my business had the opportunity to see what a great job you do. THANK YOU! Your show is fantastic and very well run. It should serve as a model to other events in the country, auto related or not.

I will be in touch with you soon so we can do a quick bit on WLS Radio in Chicago.

Please let me know if I can ever repay your kindness.

Best regards,

Dick Biondi

Author's Note- Dick Biondi is one of the most legendary voices of the American airways. Broadcasting from WLS in Chicago, Mr. Biondi's rapid-fire prose and promotion of the new "rock and roll" music across the Midwest are things of legend. Mr. Biondi served as MC of the Cruise Night four years in a row.

Chapter 14: The Best Car Show Ever?

"St. Ignace is the best car show ever."
Pat Ganahl, on the cover of **Rod and Custom Magazine**

Dad was never hard pressed to outdo himself and always looked for new ways to improve on the hit formula of cars, music, and memories.

With 1,410 show cars in '86, 1,840 in '87 and, for the first time, 50,000 spectators came to the '87 version, demonstrating that the show was only just starting to hit its stride.

The Down Memory Lane Parade grew to 350 cars, with an incredible number of floats, bands, and performers, and required more than two hours to snake its way through town as thousands of spectators lined the four-mile parade route and cheered their favorites under crystal blue skies, beside the sparkling waters of Lake Huron.

Robert Larivee Sr., show collaborator, promotor extraordinaire, and the man who talked sense into George Barris, was the '86 Guest of Honor, in homage for his role of the consummate car show promoter.

His company, Promotions Inc. set the standard for organizing auto shows nationwide. Promotions Inc. produced 100 car shows annually and worked with the most dominant specialty equipment manufacturers in the world.

Ford, General Motors, and Chrysler used the stages at Mr. Larivee's shows to debut their newest cars.

Detroit's Autorama was his signature show. The legendary show is home to the prestigious "Ridler Award" and is a can't-miss event for anyone with a love of the automobile.

For more than 35 years, Mr. Larivee set the standard for promoting, organizing, and shaping car shows around the country. I briefly worked with Mr. Larivee after he sold his company to his son, Bob "JR" Larivee.

The renamed company, Championship Auto Shows Inc, kept up the tradition of staging and promoting the top class of shows across the country.

At one event, the World of Wheels in Cincinnati, I was to assist Mr. Larivee with the show, logistics, and to take care of talent like the Texas Bikini Team, wrestlers such as Mic Foley, Jeff Jarret, Steve Austin, King Kong Bundy, Superfly Jimmy Snuka, and Captain Lou Albano.

I learned there is one way of doing things when working with Mr. Larivee. His way. Period. Tragically, I used one of his pencils and received a five-minute coaching session on what "mine and yours" was all about and at no time was I to ever confuse the two again. I knew he was not kidding as he gave me the same look when he saw "his" pencil in my hand as Kress no doubt gave my father just about every day of his life.

"Son, are you f*****g crazy?"

While interviewing him for this book, he did not deny the incident took place. Mr. Larivee laughed when he responded, "I remember being upset with you for something."

St. Ignace was an interesting show for Mr. Larivee, as he had tried to promote outdoor shows, but to no success. His vision went beyond showing cars in fairgrounds as was the case when he started his shows.

"I always loved St. Ignace and respected what your dad did up there in such a small place," Mr. Larivee said. "I often wondered, as the years went on, if your dad started his show so he could meet all of his heroes because that is what he ended up doing."

One of Mr. Larivee most impressive accomplishments, to me, was his forethought. He saw things others did not. Much like my father with his vision, Mr. Larivee knew that taking his shows on the road and adding elements never before attempted would somehow work.

The amazing thing about St.Ignace, Mr. Larivee told me, was that there was no event to match it in metro Detroit. That was what drove traffic north to the magical place they all thought had to be fiction.

Successful men are successful for a reason. I learned valuable lessons working with Mr. Larivee. The first and foremost being, staying in my lane with the No. 2 yellow pencil rationed to me.

Mr. Larivee was buttoned down, everything organized, everything had a purpose, everything was connected and if one thing is out of line, the entire show won't work.

He told me when Promotions Incorporated was at its height, he rewarded employees at his office by placing money on their desks if their workspace was organized.

Mr. Larivee still travels the country with new projects and new books.

Lesson learned. I carry that lesson with me in my Charitable Foundation.

But I digress (and not for the last time.)

Dad enjoyed the status of bringing legends to town and wanted St. Ignace to showcase rarities like a car manufactured by Sears and Roebuck called "The Allstate."

Only 797 "Allstates" were made in 1953 and it was a living commercial for the brand. Of the 797 in the world, one was on Main Street in St. Ignace.

Dad finally hit on another project that had been in the back of his mind from the beginning. And so, Ronnie Dove, hit maker of the 1950's and 1960's, appeared on the concert stage inside the Lasalle High School gymnasium. Ronnie's 23 consecutive Top 10 singles included "One Kiss for Old Time's Sake", "One more Mountain to Climb", and many others.

When Mr. Pat Ganahl came to St. Ignace it finally gave dad the connection to the West Coast. "Pat Ganahl is the man," dad said. "He was the West Coast, he saw them all, knew them all, when he came here to write the things he did, it validated everything I ever wanted to accomplish."

I was a fledgling journalist and wanted to see Mr. Ganahl work. Until I met him, I did not know he was 6' 9" and I could tell he was highly intelligent. Just a bit intimidating. I learned more about him, his engineering background, and especially his car building skills, so it was easy to share my father's view on Mr. Ganahl.

Some story excerpts he wrote are easy to find, as the issue from June 1989 is still prominently displayed in my dad's office. I will include them in quotes through this interview.

"If you are a car nut and are not on your way to St. Ignace this summer, you are just spinning your wheels."

In explaining St. Ignace, Mr. Ganahl wrote of a quiet, quaint place with 2,800 people, best known as a summer destination spot to visit Mackinac Island. For several years, St. Ignace was a well-kept secret but the "word of something this good was bound to get out."

The event Mr. Ganahl attended set the record for most Bridge traffic crossing in history (60,000 cars). Don Garlits was the Guest of Honor, The Rat Fink, Ed Roth, returned, Tom Monaghan brought to town one of six Bugatti Royales in existence. Joe Bailon, the Alexander Brothers, Bob Kaiser, Chuck Miller, Doug Thompson, and others made appearances.

"Gordon Beuhrig came back, the creator of Henry Highrise Dave Bell, Albert Drake, Dick Biondi, and Jack Scott. not a bad first show for a man who makes his living covering auto shows."

I spoke to Mr. Ganahl on the phone, but he was on deadline for another project, so we did not speak for long. I am including (in italics) parts of the story he wrote in 1989.

"I finally made it to the event I had heard so much about and they didn't disappoint. It was the best car show, cruise, or rod run I ever attended, and I've been to a few."

The validation of such a notable automotive journalist still makes dad swell with pride. "Having Mr. Ganahl come here, and write what he did about our show, was a big deal to me," Dad said. "He is a true California guy who saw all the big shows including Oakland."

"This show brought together all kinds of cars and people. At St. Ignace, you could see a horseless carriage or the most amazing hot rod. It was incredible. Where else can you see the Bugatti Royale parked next to Ed Roth's Outlaw and Don Garlits Swamp Rat? If you like cars of any kind, you will find one you like at this event. This is a must attend event. Once you go, you want to go back."

Dad has seven books written by Mr. Ganahl, and every issue of Rodder's Journal. Another legend came to our small town and his words painted such a glorious picture that others followed. Lots of them. Thank you, Mr. Ganahl.

PART FIVE

The Soundtrack of your Life

Chapter 15: Suddenly, It's 1958 Again

"You forget most places and certain people. Some places are etched in your memory. Certain people are worth remembering and Ed Reavie is worth remembering." **Dee Dee Kenniebrew**, *Founder of "The Crystals" who dedicated "He's a Rebel" to Ed Reavie during a concert.*

"Suddenly it is 1958 Again " made its debut with Ronnie Dove and the "Deacons of Do Op," The Laredos. Playing to a packed house, the first concert added to the list of amazing events during St. Ignace.

Dad picked the name because he graduated from high school (barely) in 1958 and wanted others to relive the fondest memories of his life.

Through Honey Radio contact, Fred "Boogie" Brian, Dad reached talent agent Jerry Patlow who booked 23 years of live concerts during the Saturday evening of the show.

Starting his radio career in 1966, Fred "Boogie" Brian retired in April of 2020. Serving as MC of both the concerts and the Cruise

Night "Sock Hop" Boogie told me getting to St. Ignace was half the fun.

"The Honey Radio listeners were coming up anyway, so we decided to make a caravan out of it," he said. "We had a bunch of classic cars rolling up the highway to St. Ignace."

Driving the '57 Chevy he called "Little Darling" Boogie led the way as "Little Darling" became the Honey Radio mascot during their five-year run-in St. Ignace.

Patlow is a high energy man who got the job done. Dad always told me if his own phone rang at midnight, he always answered, "Hello Jerry."

Jerry first arrived in St. Ignace in 1985 with Bob Larivee and spoke with dad about the potential of having concerts during the show.

"He loved the idea," Jerry told me. "He gave me a list of his favorites and, after he secured his sponsors, we started in 1986 and kept going until 2000." Jerry worked within dad's budget and secured four to five acts every year as opposed to booking one major act who commanded up to $25,000.

"Your dad was fun to work with, he was so eager to get people in town who he wanted to meet, people he listened to and enjoyed," Jerry said. "Your dad was like a kid playing with toys. He was responsible for bringing all those people to the sleepy little town of St. Ignace."

I was sad to hear all the "Hermits" had passed, but Peter Noone bought the name back and still makes appearances. "Some of the groups were so outrageously priced (Chubby Checker's fee was the entire budget) and others were so notoriously hard to work with (Chuck Berry), he knew to stay away and keep great acts like Gary Lewis and the Playboys, Sonny Geraci, The Crystals, Danny and the Juniors, and other Hall of Famers, coming to town every year.

St. Ignace, so far from the mainstream, required long drives from the airport just to even get there. It made booking groups harder, but many were happy to come.

In total, 16 of the Billboard Top 200 acts of the 1960's made their way to St. Ignace.

Jerry told me that the most difficult act to come to St. Ignace was Leslie Gore. "She was a very difficult diva," he said, laughing. "But she did great once there."

Boogie Brian, who served as MC of the concerts from 1990 to 1995, shared a funny story with me. He thought Leslie was doing an encore, but alas, she did not share that thought.

"I came on stage and waved her back, telling the crowd she was coming out to sing another number," he said. "She stood off in the wings and just raised her arms in the air with this look on her face that said 'why'?"

Boogie said he realized his mistake, hugged her, and prompted the crowd to give her a big hand for her performance.

Freddy Cannon, on the other hand, was a pleasure. "Freddy was a piece of cake," Jerry said. "I met him in 1966 when he came to Detroit to perform after Tom Shannon introduced us."

They hit it off immediately, and Jerry said he asked Freddy to let him know if he ever wanted work in Michigan, to give him a call.

"He gave me his phone number right away," Jerry said. "And I've been calling him ever since." Jerry also told me a great story about Bobby Lewis thatI had forgotten; he was legally blind, but still knocked them dead on the stage.

Dad had a reason with everything he did. One thing always connected to the next. A seamless flow of fun, connecting dots, creating a once-in-a-lifetime show each and every year.

Regarding the concerts, they were an obvious next step in the show's evolution. One simply cannot cruise without music. How can you dance with your best girl, in silence?

He wanted the complete experience of his youth. Sharing it with 100,000 people just needed a few more steps. How did the music get to us? Records. Who plays the records, but the DJ's through the radio stations? Then you contact the station and find the guy who gets the people who make the records. And you get those people to come to town and sing those songs. It's not like calling George Lucas asking for red drapes to show a Tucker. Oh, wait. Yeah, it is kind of like that. Enter the man who knew everyone in Jerry Patlow and then the perfect MC, Boogie Bryan.

Boogie led the parade in "Little Darling," and said Honey Radio folks pedaled around the car on vintage bicycles (including Bob Larivee Sr.) to add flavor.

In discussing his favorite performer, it didn't take Boogie long to say, "Freddy Cannon brought down the house every time. He was amazing."

I asked Boogie, in all his travels and all the shows, if he ever saw a show like St. Ignace. "No. The environment alone made it special," he said. "I have every award your dad gave me for coming. Your dad made everyone feel special. He made everyone happy. It's the hallmark of a great man. What an event. What an event."

In totality, with all the events covering the three days in St. Ignace, Boogie is 100 percent certain of one thing. "The St. Ignace Cruise is the best in the nation. No doubt. It even beats the Woodward Dream Cruise, in my estimation."

Boogie's biggest memory of the show made him laugh. As a childhood fan of "Howdy Doody," Boogie saw Buffalo Bob. However, instead of approaching him, he froze.

"I said, wow, that is Buffalo Bob," he laughed. "And it was like I turned into a seven-year-old kid again. Holy smokes, I was afraid to talk to him. I kicked myself for years. I was a grown man for heaven's sake."

Dad saw the success of a car show that not only shook the genre, but recreated it, so he decided to do the same with the musical guests that came to town for 23 consecutive summers. The concert was another event that, alone, was a successful show.

The St. Ignace school system, like the rest of the town, is small. For my school life, the school was designated both Class C and Class D, the two smallest designations, with "D" being the smallest. My High School class had less than 70 students. The gym did not hold a lot but was standing room only for 23 years of outstanding shows.

I grew up listening to Elvis, Buddy Holly, the Beatles, The Beach Boys, the Rolling Stones and the rest of the British Invasion. Seeing many of these stars on the stage, singing those songs, was a rush. It spanned 23 years and added to the rest of the attractions. It made St. Ignace the most complete show in history.

"You put the car show guest of honor lists side-by-side with the list of artists who came to St. Ignace and it is astonishing to behold," dad said both proudly and accurately.

"I wanted to do that. Nobody else did this anywhere near here. With Cruise Night, the parade, the VIP Cruises, and the main show? There was nothing like it in the country."

In talking to Boogie, I told him I spoke to Jerry Patlow. Boogie said that, on his retirement show, he took only calls from listeners who shared stories and well wishes with him. The last person to call Boogie as a DJ? That would be Jerry Patlow.

In 1975, my mom dropped the needle on the album "Born to Run" and it changed my life. The thundering cascade from Boom Carter's drums to open "Born to Run" nearly knocked me over.

And, I want to thank Phoenix DJ Mark Devine of 100.7 KSLX for correcting me when I told him the same story and said it was Max Weinberg. That would have been embarrassing.

My love of all things Bruce is well known to my friends and family. In 2002, I had tickets for "The Rising" concert at The Palace of Auburn Hills.

The music of Bruce is one thing over which mom and I bonded. It's the one time we talked about mutual love. Whenever he dropped a new album, I bought it and sent it to her.

I called my sister and arranged for her to take mom to West Branch where I would pick her up and drive her down to Auburn Hills, have her stay with me, and then drive her back. She called me the morning she was supposed to be in West Branch and informed me that she woke up with a sore foot and didn't want to risk having someone step on it in the jam-packed Palace.So, I took my friend, Fred Stock, with me (Fred and I traveled the Midwest and East Coast going to Major League Baseball games). We sat on stage left, second level, with a great view.

After you read the chapter on the relationship with my mom, you will understand how hard I tried to please her. I decided to keep trying. So when Bruce came on stage, I called mom on the old flip phone I had and held it out for her. She told me she could hear it perfectly, so I kept it open for her to listen as long as the battery held out.

The battery held out for the entire show.

When Bruce played "Thunder Road," it was akin to the first real bonding experience between us as that is our favorite song.

Where am I going with this?

Well, dad secured Gary "U.S." Bonds for one of the concerts. This was several years after his mammoth comeback hit, "This Little Girl" was released, which catapulted him back into the limelight.

What many casual fans did not know, I did. "This Little Girl" was written by Bruce Springsteen.

Well, by golly, I happened to arrive early for the show and found Gary backstage going over his set with the house band, Tommy C and the Gamut Band.

I waited patiently. The crowd parted and he was left standing near the percussion section of the LaSalle High School band room. I looked around. Nobody was coming to him. Nobody, but me.

Nervously, I walked toward him and extended my hand, introducing myself as the son of the promoter and a big fan.

He was such a nice man. I prefaced by saying "I know you get this a lot," and proceeded to ask him about how The Boss wrote "This Little Girl" for him.

Laughing and smiling he said, "Oh man, I am dealing with a hard-core Boss fan." We sat down and he told me he met Bruce after he simply jumped on stage with him at a club and played "Quarter to Three". The two became friends and Gary said he talked to The Boss about his own career, as he was stalled as far as creativity. It was then, Gary received the ultimate gift of an original Bruce Springsteen song. Bruce's newest album sessions for "The River" were joyful and upbeat but Bruce had so many songs, he didn't plan on using "This Little Girl" on the album so he asked Gary to come to the studio with him.

With the full might of the E Street Band backing him, Gary recorded "This Little Girl." When the song was released, "This Little Girl" put Gary U.S. Bonds into the stratosphere again as the song went to #5. When he performed it that night, he pointed in my direction and it was one of the coolest moments of my life.

The concerts always amazed me. I heard all the songs on vinyl and now, here they were, on the stage of my high school. Older, but man alive, they sounded great! The electricity was insane. Dick Biondi opened the concerts four years in a row, introduced the artists, talked with the crowd, and got the crowd roaring as only he could.

Dad sought out artists he loved and all of them hit a home run. I still get chills thinking of Leslie Gore hitting the notes from "You don't own me" as the crowd roared. Lou Christie going six octaves high for "Lightning Strikes" while doing Karate Katas. "Soldier Boy" gave us all chills as the Shirelle's hit every note in harmony rolling seamlessly into `Dedicated to the One I Love,' 'Will You Still Love Me Tomorrow,' and 'Tonight's the Night.'

One of dad's favorite girl bands (The Crystals) sang one of his favorite songs (He's a Rebel) and performed at the top of their craft. Years later, while attending one of their concerts at the Kewadin Casino in Sault Ste. Marie, dad was shocked when Dolores "Dee Dee" Kinnebrew spotted him sitting in the audience.

She called him out, pointed at him and introduced him to the crowd. "I want to take a minute and dedicate the next song to a real Rebel, Mr. Ed Reavie." When they belted out, He's a Rebel, dad was in all his glory.

"That was the highlight of my life," dad beamed. "I loved those girls. They had so many hits. Dolores introduced herself to me and said, "My friends call me Dee Dee, and you can call me Dee Dee." So, I said, "thank you Dee Dee, I will do that."

I called dad for clarity regarding the concerts. He is proud of the talent he brought to our town and is most proud today when listening to the 60's on 6 because there is not an hour that goes by when he doesn't hear a song from one of the groups he had in St. Ignace.

"Sometimes it's multiple, the other day, I heard four straight," he said. "All of them performed here. All of them were in my home. Wow."

During the entire run of shows, I can only remember a few hiccups along the way. Bobby Lewis, of Tossing and Turning fame, had to be constantly eating peanut butter to deal with a lower GI issue. My kindergarten teacher, Carol Lorente, a long-time friend of my father, was given the task of locating said peanut butter and making sure Mr. Lewis had enough.

He scooped it out with his fingers while he prepared for the show. When I shared this story with Jerry Patlow, he said, "I didn't know that, but his nickname was "mumbles," so maybe that is why."

the first major issue we had was the year Herman's Hermits came to town. During the parade, I received a call on dad's phone. Someone with a British accent asked for "The governor," and I thought I was being pranked. Turns out, it was their manager wondering where their shuttle was to take them from Pellston Regional Airport to St. Ignace. I had no answer and asked him to hold the phone. On another line, I called the van driver and asked if he was close to the airport for the pickup.

"I have them on my schedule for tomorrow night."

I reminded him that the concert was tomorrow night and they were in the airport waiting for him. His reaction was immediate. Since this is intended to be a family-oriented book, I shall leave out his actual response. To compound the issue, the drive time to the airport was close to two hours. I got back on the line with the manager and told them I would rent them a car and take care of it.

Now that I knew what the term "Governor" meant, I told him I was the assistant governor and would take full responsibility.

I saw him Saturday and he paid me a compliment (I think), called me "A nice bloke," and slapped me on the back. Jerry confirmed this after telling me the Hermits were legendary for their kindness and gentle manner. "He called you a classy gentleman," Jerry said with a laugh. "And, you must have taken care of it because I never heard anything about it."

One of dad's most chilling moments came when Johnny Tillotson took the stage. Dad was unsure if Mr. Tillotson was going to come. Three days before his scheduled appearance, dad received a call telling him Mr. Tillotson's 19-year-old daughter was killed in a car wreck and they were unsure if he would appear. Johnny had never missed a show since he started in 1957, and he called dad the next day to confirm he was coming. Johnny took the stage, performed flawlessly, and sang his 14 top 40 hits including his top song, Poetry in Motion. As he closed his set, Johnny told the crowd that his daughter had been killed, shared memories of her, and dedicated his last song to her. It keeps on hurting since you've Gone stunned the crowd into a respectful silence. When he was finished, the crowd erupted, tears flowed everywhere, chills went up and down my spine. My father, never one to be emotional, had tears in his eyes.

Someone had to follow that incredible performance and Leslie Gore matched the emotion with You Don't Own Me and blew the roof off the place.

The talent that Jerry Patlow and dad brought to St. Ignace still astonishes me. Jerry was as hard driving as my dad and was relentless in finding the acts dad wanted.

Chuck Berry was the one-person dad wanted that was just too far out of his price range. He asked Jerry to check with Chuck, but Jerry immediately put on the brakes.

"Some guys, you look forward to calling," Jerry said. "Some, not so much."

When Jerry called Chuck, he was immediately asked how much. When told, Chuck hung up on him without a word. "He never talked small. How much, where, and when. No amount of money was ever enough for him."

Chuck Berry was the hardest person to work with, period, Jerry said. His way of doing business was to ask for a deposit in the form of a money order. On the show day, he'd meet with the promoter, refuse to sign the contract and demand that the promoter buy back the money order (which he never cashed) in cash.

If the promoter demanded that he sign the contract, Chuck added to his price. With a screaming crowd chanting his name through the next door and a full purse, the promoter had no real option but to pay all cash without a signed contract.

"There was never any record of him being paid, ever," Jerry said. "I told your dad he was trouble and to expect trouble and to have extra money on hand if he decided to do it." He didn't.

Dad remembered that conversation, but later in his life, he had front row seats to see Chuck Berry. "I just looked up on the stage and there he was in his duck walking splendor," Dad said. "Chuck Berry. Wow."

Like everything else with his shows, there was one person making decisions. I fondly remember when a car owner asked him how a car got picked to be a Feature Car.

Without missing a beat, dad said, "Simple. I have to like them and if I do, I pick them."

It was the same for the concerts. If dad loved them, he told Jerry to find them. However, sometimes getting acts to town was just dumb luck.

He landed Bobby Vee by pure accident. Thrust into the national spotlight as a 15-year-old, a young Bobby Vee, already a budding local star, was rushed to a show as a fill-in for Buddy Holly, The Big Bopper, and Richie Valens after "The Day the Music Died" in February of 1959.

That moment in time catapulted him to a successful career with 38 Hot 100 hits including The Night Has a Thousand Eyes, Rubber Ball, Take Good Care of My Baby, and Devil or Angel?

Dad was sitting in a dentist office, picked up a Grit newspaper and read an article on Bobby Vee. He thought of all the great hits Bobby had back in the day. When dad got home, he called Bobby's marketing office.

He spoke to Bobby's secretary, used his smooth operator vernacular and finessed her to the point that she gave him Bobby's home phone number.

Well, not exactly.

To stay true to her boss, she did not give dad Bobby Vee's phone number; she gave him the home number of Robert Velline, which dad knew was Bobby Vee's real name.

During his stay in St. Ignace, Bobby autographed a rubber ball (one of his biggest hits) and gave it to dad. It sits proudly in his office. Dad's home museum is a must see for any fan of not only the automotive genre, but Rock and Roll.

Freddy Cannon appeared four times and gave dad a trophy for being a sensational promotor. St. Ignace was just another stop on the road for Freddy; until he got there.

"I remember asking your dad from the stage to please bring me back again," Freddy reminisced. "It was a sensational show and I never wanted to leave."

Freddy's love for St. Ignace was such that he gave that award to my father. Dad spoke to Freddy's manager and learned that Freddy never gave praise to promoters, let alone awards.

"He is my rock and roll buddy," dad said of Freddy, "He loved it here and when I told him in year three we had no sponsor money to support bringing him back, he came back on his own dime."

Freddy loved St. Ignace and my father so much that he agreed to stand up as my best man (Linda Vaughn was matron of honor) when I got married during the sunset Mackinac Island cruise on June 24, 1993. Tommy C and the Gamut Band sang In the Still of the Night after the vows, and Freddy became a permanent member of our family.

"I got to meet all these superstars," dad said. "I loved working with all these bands. I never had a problem with any of them. They did their job, and they did it well."

The coolest thing about interviewing my father for this book is how sincere he was about everything he accomplished.

Decades later, his voice still rises with emotions unhidden as he talks about meeting his musical heroes. Sitting there listening to Bryan Hyland sing Sealed with a Kiss and just saying "WOW".

When the man putting it all together is the biggest fan in the room is when you know things are going to work out.

With all these great groups, there was one thing missing to make it a perfect party; a great house band. The band leader and front man of the "House Band" for nearly 20 of those years, Tommy Clusetos, known as "Tommy C" brought high energy and phenomenal musicianship to the stage, flawlessly backing the Hall of Fame acts.

"Not only was Tommy a great house band, he could back up anyone, he was a fantastic opening act to get the show started," Jerry said. "So, when I realized I needed one I could count on, Tommy was the first person I called."

When last I saw Tommy, his son was playing the drums for his Gamut Band at the age of 13. That son, now 42, went on to have a fantastic career playing drums for Mitch Ryder, Ted Nugent, Alice Cooper, Rob Zombie, Ozzy Osborn, Black Sabbath, and many others.

Tommy came to St. Ignace the second year and played for 21 years. "The memories of St. Ignace were always the joy of it," Tommy said. "There was no pressure, be it Freddy Cannon, The Shirelles, Herman's Hermits, Gary US Bonds, they were all there. Man, it was cool, and I wish it was still going on."

Tommy spent 10 years as Chubby Checker's musical director and is still touring and rocking. I reminded him of my wedding and he interjected, "I sang for you! The event, all those events, were the highlights of my career."

Tommy told me that crossing the Mackinac Bridge on those pre-show Thursdays was akin to entering another world. The energy, the feel, the atmosphere. There was nothing like it at any other stop he made.

"The cars, the stars, going to Ronica's restaurant, (the old Chief's Drive-in) the show, the parade, all of it. I loved all of it," he told me. "There was no pressure like other gigs. You got to hang out with friends and really enjoy the experience."

Now 66, Tommy started professionally at the age of 13. "I was not a car guy and really don't know a lot about cars, but wow, I loved the event."

I told Tommy that the concert was the only time in the week my father was able to sit and relax and just take it all in. "That was his fun time right there," Tommy said with pride.

He presently tours as Tommy C with the "Black Widow Grease Band." He still performs the classic hits but has added more to the catalog, but all rock in and roll.

I play blues guitar and asked him if he ever plays the blues. "Ain't no money in the blues," he laughed. "But I love the blues. Lightnin Hopkins, Howling Wolf, man listen to those guys, that is how you learn."

This led to the conversation about Jimmy Vaughn being on the boat during my wedding. I did not recall that, but Tommy assured me that was the case. Tommy and I spoke for nearly 30 minutes and he shared two stories of which I'd never heard. The first was about teaching "Dee Dee" Kinniebrew, the lead singer for the Crystals, how to drive a stick shift.

"I am pretty sure it was Jerry (Patlow)'s car," Tommy said with a laugh. "But that was fun, I had her drive up and down the street by the airport."

When I asked Dee Dee about this, she laughed. "I remember Tommy teaching me how to drive, but I don't remember actually learning how to drive."

the highlight of the call was talking about the time Jerry, Dee Dee, the other Crystals, the Contours, my father, and he were all eating together at the old Chief's Restaurant.

"Everytime someone fired up the microwave, the fuse blew, and all the lights went out," Jerry told me.

During the many blackouts, something magical happened, and is truly an "Only in St. Ignace" moment.

"The Contours stood up and sang Happy Birthday in perfect harmony," Tommy said with a laugh. "Everytime."

"We even sang when we were in the parking lot getting into our cars when everything went dark again," dad said when I reminded him of this little piece of history. "Show me anywhere in the world where the Crystals, The Contours, and Tommy C and his band all sang together in a parking lot during a blackout."

After telling me the story, Tommy sighed and said, "God, what a great time we all had. You know what?" Tommy asked me. "I think I need to drive up with Jerry to see the show and to see your dad and you again."

Before we ended the call, Tommy had a question for me.

"Rhythm and Blues had a baby. Do you know what they named it?"

To which I replied: "Rock and Roll."

"You got it!" he said.

Rock and Roll is here to stay, it will never die.

Chapter 16: Talking Rebels with Dee Dee Kenniebrew

Founder of "The Crystals"

On March 25, I told my father I was done interviewing as this book's publication deadline was just days away. He was a little upset, as there were several people who never got back to me for an interview, but he understood the situation.

On March 26, at 6 a.m., I started work on the final table of contents and prepping for final edit. I was tired, aching, needing a shot of Wild Turkey, and ready to watch the NCAA.

At 5 p.m. my phone rang, and I decided to answer.

"Hello, the friendly voice on the other end of the call said. "My name is Dee Dee Kenniebrew and I understand you've been trying to reach me."

I guess I wasn't done. This is why this entry has no chapter title by the way. At the end of our 30-minute call, I felt like I'd known Ms. Kenniebrew my entire life. She knew the names and ages of my bonus children, my dogs, and what my life was like. She was the kindest, sweetest person I've ever interviewed, and her memory and instant recall of events astonished me.

She told me (without my asking) that she not only remembered her appearance in St. Ignace, but fondly remembered my father.

"You forget most places and certain people," Ms. Kenniebrew said. "Some places are etched in your memory. Certain people are worth remembering and your dad is worth remembering."

Ms. Kenneibrew was astonished by the size of this project and asked me about dad and how he was doing and if the show is still going forward. I caught her up on the history of the show and the story of my dad and told her how much dad loved her and asked her what she remembered most about the show.

"There was this very sexy lady on the bill," she said with a laugh. "Blonde with beautiful layered hair. She was so nice."

Her mind began to roll back in time, asking me if there was a place called Mackinac Island where there are no cars allowed. When I told her yes, she said, "I loved the ice cream over there. I remember having a great time."

She also remembered when the power went out at the restaurant and singing "happy birthday" with the Contours and Tommy C and the Gamut band."

"Some things make you remember places and people and that was definitely one of those things that made me remember."

One of dad's favorite stories is seeing Dee Dee in concert, at a later date, and her dedicating "He's a Rebel" to him.

"Hold on, hold on, let me think, yes, some place called Kewadin? I saw your dad out in the crowd and called him the original Rebel and then we sang the song."

Astonished that she'd remembered, I told her, indeed, it was during a show at Kewadin Casino in Sault Ste. Marie. She reminded me of something after I told her that. It is a rare thing to be in the presence of someone with a photographic memory. After our interview, I called dad and told him what Dee Dee said to me. Without hesitation, he answered.

"It was so cold, so cold," Ms. Kenneibrew said. "I remember I parked my car and it got snowed in for four days. We couldn't leave. I am pretty sure it was around Christmas because I remember seeing decorations."

Dee Dee said the snow was such that she could not find the car as it was buried under snow drifts. It took days to get it and, when she did, she couldn't find the road. Everything was snowed under.

She finally made her way out of the Sault and remembered the name of the airport; Pellston. But she said that she drove past the entrance twice because of the snow.

Here is what dad told me. Keep in mind I didn't tell him anything she said, I simply asked him details on that show.

"It was during December and it was freezing cold," he said. "After the show, we heard the weather report of a huge storm coming in and decided to try and beat it home. I am glad we did because it shut down the Sault for four days, stranding everyone at the casino."

Simply amazing.

I did some research and found that the record snowstorm to which they referred hit the area on December 9th, 1995. Nineteen inches of snow fell, followed by twenty-seven inches on December 10th, and paralyzed the area. The National Guard was called up to help with snow removal and to assist the County Sheriff's office reach those in dire need. In total, the storm dumped 65 inches of snow during a three-day span. The entire region shut down for four days.

Ms. Kenniebrew recalled her time in St. Ignace, remembered Jerry Patlow, called him her favorite agent and asked me for his number so they could catch up.

To the ultimate Rebel, Ed Reavie, Ms. Kenniebrew said; "I thank him so much for having us. We've traveled the world. We've been to so many places and met so many people and it takes something special to remember every interaction you have with a person. Your father is special. Him I remember very, very well."

Before we ended the call, Ms. Kenniebrew thanked me by my full name, and pronounced it correctly as "Rayvee". She told me she had a gift with names and could normally tell ancestry by name, I asked her to do that with mine.

"I am guessing your name is derived from something else and was not always Reavie. So, based on that, I am going to say Scottish."

Nailed it. Wow.

I thanked her profusely for calling me back and told her how important she is to my dad. She was very happy to hear that and told me to make sure he knows how much she cares for and remembers her time with him in St. Ignace.

I did tell him, and I heard him become emotional. He was speechless for a while before saying, "How does all this happen? My god this is amazing."

Yes, it really is.

Chapter 17: Talking Cars with Mr. Robert Larivee Sr.

"King of the Car Show," Promotions Inc Founder and 1986 Guest of Honor (Only show promoter in the SEMA Hall of Fame)

It was a bit of nostalgia for me, talking to Mr. Larivee.

In 1999 I went to work with Championship Auto Shows and worked with Bob Jr. to help promote some of their series of car shows and had the pleasure of working with Mr. Larivee at their Cincinnati show.

Bob Larivee Sr. earned the moniker "The King of the Car Shows" after hosting 99 shows in one calendar year. He controlled five semi-trucks and brought such show cars as the Batmobile, General Lee, and the Knight Rider to an audience of at least 10,000 people during the three–day show.

Mr. Larivee figured out early on how to market his brand and, at one time, sold 300,000 to 400,000 show programs a year, which made his publication second to only Hot Rod Magazine for total sales in a year.

"It was a mind-blowing thing for me," Mr. Larivee said. "In the late 80's, things took a turn and I sold the business to my son a few years before I was guest of honor at your dad's show."

Mr. Larivee became a great fan of dad's show and gave high praise to what dad was able to do in such a small town. "Your dad really accomplished some great things up there, " he told me. "People still talk about it. I admire him for what he accomplished, and I think it was great."

Mr. Larivee didn't initially understand the power of St. Ignace, given his own resume for national show promotion. Until his first time.

"I thought it was just a little rinky dink show," he said. "I was wrong. What he accomplished with getting all those big companies up there was remarkable."

I asked him about dad's frustration with George Barris and how he reached out to him to get Barris in line with what was needed. He chuckled a bit.

"George was always difficult and a guy who always wanted everything," he said. Recounting the first time he heard from George, Mr. Larivee said he was flabbergasted when he picked up the phone and was told who was on the other end.

Turns out, George Barris wanted to meet the "King of the Car Shows" and the two had lunch which was served with a very one-sided offer from George.

"He wanted to be partners," Mr. Larivee said with a laugh. "He wanted to let me use his car collection to put in my trucks and transport all over the country."

George was prone to using the word "we" in the narrative, Mr. Larivee laughed again and said he told George his vision was not going to be a reality. "First, I am doing all the work," he told him. "And I am not really looking for a partner, but if I were, he would be someone with a lot of money. That was typical George."

Through the years, the two became very close friends with George Barris, including living and traveling with him. "He was the only guy in the world who called me Roberto."

When George arrived in St. Ignace, Mr. Larivee, George, and my father, all went up the Bridge tower. "That was a fabulous experience. Your father pulled off so many amazing things in a city so remote, and so small."

Meeting Gordon Buehrig and his wife was also an amazing experience and Mr. Larivee recounted all the years Mrs. Buehrig came back after Gordon's passing.

Mr. Larivee made several return trips to town when his friends were honored or when dad brought something new and different. He marveled at the amazing cars and people constantly on stage in St. Ignace. "To see Don Garlits, Chuck Miller, Bill Couch, Jack Walker, and men like Zora (Arkus-Duntov), and all the incredible cars was a treat."

Mr. Larivee is a man who has traveled the country and promoted shows, so I asked why he thought that some of the biggest, most legendary names in the industry came back time and again to St. Ignace.

"Because it was fun, it was amazing, it was great," Mr. Larivee said. "You got to see your friends, which is what life was all about. You knew the great people who were going to be there. We all sat and watched the parade, ate dinner together, caught up, and it was so exciting."

When dad added the Rock and Roll shows, Mr. Larivee, who famously rode an antique bicycle in the parade, said that added another amazing element to a lot of amazing elements.

St. Ignace is historical for the total package of what it offered with a backdrop never seen before for an outdoor car show and it changed how outdoor shows were presented, Mr. Larivee told me.

"Overall, the greatest thing was, it was a lot of fun," Mr. Larivee said. "Most shows you sat in a field, took out a chair, and drank beer. St. Ignace was different. The parade, Mackinac Island, the downtown, great local people who understood the culture, and something for wives, girlfriends, and kids to do all day long."

St. Ignace, for Mr. Larivee, was a get together of friends who could go to the show, head to Mackinac Island in the afternoon, and go see Freddie Cannon sing at night at the high school. Last year, Freddie Cannon called Mr. Larivee on his 90th birthday.

"The camaraderie is what made that show so great and you didn't get that in any other show," Mr. Larivee said. "St. Ignace was way different than that. You looked forward to going, seeing your friends, and knowing the quality of the people and the fun things you could do."

Mr. Larivee recalled that the year he was Guest of Honor, his daughter, Tracy, took my dad's call. She told my dad that, for her father to be Guest of Honor, she must be allowed to climb the bridge tower, even though she was only 12.

To Mr. Larivee shock, dad made that happen and Tracy became the youngest person to ever climb the tower (after Mr. Larivee signed a waiver). The year previous, Tracy rode with George Barris and dad in the Batmobile during the parade.

"What your dad accomplished was major league," Mr. Larivee said. "I think everyone would love to accomplish what your dad did in that small city. It put St. Ignace on the map, literally."

I asked him to rank my father as a promoter and he told me, "Not everyone has the drive, the gumption, or the ability to do what he did and do whatever it took to succeed. Your dad had that vision, different from everyone else, in what he did. That is what is needed to succeed. We all had that passion for what we did and that is how he accomplished that in a city that small."

To Mr. Larivee, St. Ignace was not boring, it was fun and it was a neat place with something for everyone. It was a beautiful area and you did stuff you never thought you were going to do. However, there is one burning question on his mind after all these years.

"How on earth Ed got Zora Arkus-Duntov, Gordon Buehrig, and Carroll Shelby to come there, I have no idea," he said laughing. "But, he did it. He got the biggest names right away and was able to leverage those names to get anybody he wanted."

As accomplished as Mr. Larivee was, it was in St.Ignace where he first met Zora, Gordon and many others. "If your dad needed anything from me, I was always ready to help. These were legendary people, the top men ever."

Before I let him go, I reminded him how mad he got at me for using his pencils and phone during the one time we worked together at the Cincinnati show.

I vividly remember the at-least five minute "pep talk" I received from him regarding what was his and what was mine and to make sure I did not cross that line. As previously stated, he didn't recall the details, but remembered being mad at me.

I thanked him for helping me understand organization in that regard which produced a long chuckle from him.

PART SIX

Big Daddy, Candy Apple Red, and the Pizza Tiger

Chapter 18: Legend after Legend

Eugene "Gene" Bordinat II, legendary Vice President of Design for Ford Motor Company (1961-1980) headlined the show in 1987.

Mr. Bordinat was responsible for the design of nearly 70 million vehicles in the 19 years he sat in the big chair.

"Gene was a big-time guy," dad said. "I sure could pick the legends, one after the other, and nobody ever turned me down after I called and asked him."

His designs or direct supervision of designs include the revolutionary Mark III, the Ford Racing Program, and the complete Mustang Regime. The GT-40 was created with only one purpose in mind; win LeMans and the car did just that in 1966.

"He was a flashy dresser, high class, both his wife and him were impeccable and really looked the part," dad said. "He was to Ford what Bill Mitchell was to General Motors."

The morning of the Guest of Honor brunch, dad said Mr. Bordinat and he were talking about what Ford cars would be represented during the event. Mr. Bordinat approved but said something was missing that he wanted there and told dad to give him a minute.

"He picked up a phone and called headquarters," dad said, still in amazement. "He said he wanted the Mustang II on a trailer and into St. Ignace by morning. He got off the call and asked if there was anything else I wanted. I told him the Mustang II would do just fine."

Arriving in St. Ignace, the Mustang II, (The concept car from 1963), drew huge crowds and made the front page of the St. Ignace News.

I remember meeting Mr. Bordinat and his wife, Teresa, as they both Exuded class with Teresa in glorious gowns and perfectly appointed and Mr. Bordinat with an open collar dress shirt with an ascot, silk sport coats, and perfect silver hair.

Dad had a collection of cars designed by Mr. Bordinat lining Feature Car Row. Mr. Bordinat enjoyed all the trappings of being Guest of Honor and was blown away by the size of the event, the fervor of the crowd, the electricity of cruise night, and the incredible visuals only St. Ignace offered.

Tragically, upon returning home, Mr. Bodinat passed away on August 11, becoming the first of the legendary Guests of Honor at the St. Ignace shows to leave us.

Even though dad met him only once, Teresa invited dad and Gary Engel, long time voice of the show, to the funeral which dad said was more of a celebration of his life than a funeral.

"It was a beautiful event, like a Hollywood set with violin players, champagne, beautiful cars, art, and the grounds were immaculate. He lived his life right. He did things right and it was a thrill for me when he agreed to come here."

Chapter 19: Big Daddy

"Ed Reavie has the most organized mind of anyone I've ever met."

Thomas Monahan, *Founder Domino's Pizza and former owner of the Detroit Tigers*

Dad reached out to another of his heroes, the legendary Don "Big Daddy" Garlits and secured his attendance for the 1988 show.

With more than 57,000 spectators and 2,155 show cars, the event was a wild party extending to Sunday with an invitation-only party at the resort of CEO and Founder of Domino's Pizza, Tom Monaghan.

The Godfather of Drag Racing, Mr. Garlits was the pioneer of the rear-engine top fuel dragster. He developed the design after losing his foot in an explosion early in his career. At that time, the massive engine and all the components were in front of the driver. He was also an early promoter of the full body fire suit. Ripping down the quarter-mile strip in his legendary and innovative "Swamp Rat" Top Fuel Dragster, Mr. Garlits was the first driver to exceed every speed from 170 to 270 miles per hour.

Winner of 17 National Championships and 144 national events, he finally retired at age 54 in part to a detached retina caused by the parachute's G-force when slowing down his 300 MPH dragster.

An icon in NHRA, Mr. Garlits told my dad he was honored to be the guest of honor but wondered if the car show circuit participants would know who he was as the NHRA was a different animal altogether. Not only did Big Daddy downplay his popularity, he found out how wrong he was about this group of car enthusiasts knowing who he was. During an autograph session, he called dad, fearing for his safety, as he was surrounded by thousands of die-hard NHRA fans in addition to the car culture fans during his autograph session and he did not know how he could get out of the tent. We pulled up the back of the tent enough for him to duck under. It was a scene not to be believed.

If having Big Daddy was not enough, Tom Monaghan landed his corporate Domino's Pizza helicopter on the beach at the old Dettmans Hotel (now Harbor Pointe) to serve as the Down Memory Lane Parade Grand Marshal.

Never before had such a display of awesome happened in St. Ignace. A billionaire and pro sports team owner landed his corporate aircraft on one of our beaches? Only during the Car Show.

To top it off, Mr. Monaghan and his wife, Marge, walked hand-in-hand down the street, waved at throngs of people, took photos, and signed autographs. I remember his bodyguards scrambling wildly to cover him as he waded into the deep well of humanity laid out before him.

Mr. Monaghan purchased the Detroit Tigers in 1983 after he'd built Domino's Pizza into a billion-dollar empire. His helicopter had the Olde English "D" on the side of the Tiger Blue whirlybird. He owned a resort on Drummond Island in the Eastern Upper Peninsula. On the first ever Sunday event, a caravan of cars made the trek through the beautiful Eastern Upper Peninsula, took the ferry boat to the Island, and were led to the resort for endless pizza, soda, and entertainment.

Mr. Monaghan had his car collection team clandestinely bring up his Bugatti Royale Speedster, one of only six ever produced, and that he had purchased for nationally-reported 8.1 million dollars. The mammoth car's body and wheels were constructed from mahogany. At his event, surrounded by water, blue skies, and car world superstars sat my father and me; we were completely awestruck now.

During a break in the band's performance, in a lame attempt at humor, the band leader announced the car was on display and encouraged people to take photos with the "8-million-dollar bucket of Bondo".

The man was summarily escorted from the resort by security. Perhaps he was tossed into "Pepperoni Pond" or "Lake Marge" for saying something so ridiculously stupid as he did. One never can tell as the Eastern U.P holds many secrets: it's lakes and ponds full of such charlatans.

As guests left, Mr. Monaghan, dad, and I went into the resort's rustic dining room. Varnished logs were everywhere, and it had a huge stone fireplace. We were the only ones in there other than workers hustling to make sure we all had everything we needed.

"Yes, more of everything!"

The pizza kitchen operated 24/7, allowing the VIP guests, of which dad and I were two, pizza at our leisure. I was then a junior at Central Michigan University. My friends and I (one with whom I am still close friends and as a successful author, helped me with this book. Thanks Cliff) ate Domino's Pizza nightly.

We kept the box tops and used them to decorate room 711 in Carey Hall, covering the walls. When I learned that Mr. Monaghan was to be at dad's show, I had photos taken of the gang; Scott, Steve, Mike, Chris, Jim, Cliff, and I posed in the middle of the room, now carpeted and wall papered with Domino's pizza boxes, with us holding the remaining box tops like cards. When I presented the photos to Mr. Monaghan, he audibly laughed, smiled brightly and signed a photo, using our names, for each of us. I still remember him kneeling on the floor wearing blue jeans and a flannel shirt, smiling as he signed them. An inattentive worker (cell phones hadn't been invented yet) kicked Mr. Monaghan's feet as he passed and knocked him over to the hardwood floor.

The look of sheer horror on that young man's face would have looked great on a movie poster. I helped Mr. Monaghan up and he smiled as he slapped the young man on the shoulder asked him if his foot was alright. Pretty classy move. Of course, he may have ended up in the same trunk and pond as the band leader, but at that point, he ran back to the kitchen thankful he still had a job.

I spent the night in Tiger Manager Sparky Anderson's cabin and dad in the cabin of legendary Michigan Football coach Bo

Schembechler. The cabin was nicer than any home I'd seen in my life, with heated, cedar-planked floors.

It was a fabulous trip and dad and I were actually starting to get a bit closer as father and son. Just a bit. The real moment happened the following year.

Mr. Monaghan was a very nice man and a devout Catholic who later divested himself of his holdings to support his causes with hundreds of millions of dollars. To meet a billionaire, owner of my favorite team and pizza store, and with the sense of morality as Mr. Monaghan was an amazing life lesson for me.

Dad had an idea for Mr. Monaghan to make a grand exit in his corporate helicopter named, "Pizza Tiger", after the parade. He mentioned how cool it would be to buzz the shore line, tilting the helicopter to show the Domino's logo to the tens of thousands of persons on the street. To dad's shock. Mr. Monaghan liked it and instructed his pilot to do just that.

Bigger, better, badass. St. Ignace was fast approaching legendary status and dad, the King of the (outdoor) Car Show. The show broke all molds, introducing one genre after another to St. Ignace and the world. Nowhere else could you see men like Tom Monaghan, Don Garlits, 2,000 show cars, and 50,000 people all happening and smiling at a postcard perfect show sight. No one was more shocked at the outcome of the show than the Guest of Honor himself. Happy to be wrong, Don Garlits said to my father before leaving, "I can't believe that so many people showed up to see a drag racer."

Letter from a Legend - Don Garlits

Dear Ed,

I want to clarify with you I will not be bringing a race car or a truck; just my little hot rod. I crashed my dragster "Swamp Rat 31" in August and It will not be replaced in time for your show. It sounds like a great, exciting event there and I am honored to be your guest of honor in 1988.

Sincerely,

Don Garlits

Author's Note: Mr. Garlits was a widely popular guest of honor for the 13th anniversary show with lines so long to see him that dad and I had to rescue him from his tent as he could not get out of the front. Dad lifted the back, and I walked Mr. Garlits out and we made our escape.

Chapter 20: Interview with Big Daddy Don Garlitts

"I've never seen anything like it (St. Ignace)"
Don "Big Daddy" Garlits, *legendary NHRA drag racer and 1988 Guest of Honor*

St. Ignace News, July 2, 1988 By Sean E. Reavie

St. Ignace, MI- The Guest of Honor for the 13th Annual Straits Area Antique Auto Show, "Big Daddy" Don Garlits, Show Director Ed Reavie said, was everything he had hoped for.

"Don was everything I had read about for the past 30 years and more," he said. "I was a fan then, I am a fan now."

"This show is awesome. I have never seen anything like it. Nothing compares to this." Mr. Garlits said. Mr. Garlits said he had no preconceived ideas about the St. Ignace Auto Show. "I knew it was a big show," he said. "And I will tell you what's going to happen; When Hot Rod Magazine writes about this event, hold on."

Mr. Garlits said when people read the story, it could conceivably double cars and spectators. "When people read this, it will stir up more interest and people will come from the Midwest and the Southern parts of the country".

When Mr. Garlits first heard of the show, he thought it only included antique cars and a swap meet but soon learned it was so much more.

Switching topics to talk about his future endeavors, Mr. Garlit's said that, although he hasn't raced much in 1988, and "I don't intend to" he also said, "I actually feel more comfortable going down the drag strip at 200 miles per hour in a modern dragster than I do going 170 in the Swamp Rat 1." He said it is because modern cars are built to survive a high-speed crash and "The Swamp Rat 1 is not made to crash at any speed."

With the technology available, Mr. Garlits said it would not surprise him to see Top Fuel cars reaching 300 miles per hour in the near feature. "It may open the door to someone hitting 350," he said. "These guys are fearless."

Mr. Garlits said if he did go back into racing, he could visualize 300 miles per hour flashing on the screen as he crossed the finish line. "Never let the negative side of yourself tell you what to do," he told me. "Always go out into the world with a positive outlook as that is how you get things accomplished."

Author's Note: Mr. Garlits predicted the 300 MPH pass which is now pretty standard with the record for Top Fuel Dragsters 338 mph from Courtney Force (who I met when she was a child) and the overall record holder is Robert Hight (Funny Car) at 339 mph. One of the great things about working for Wes Maurer Jr. was that he trusted me to write stories with the biggest names like Big Daddy Don Garlits. Wes first hired me when I was 16 and was fast to remind me the only reason he did was as a favor to dad. I think we were 11 cans into a 12 pack of Strohs at the time, so it was pretty funny.

Chapter 21: Richard Crane Memorial Truck Show

Big Rigs Take the Bridge by Storm

One summer day in 1976, shortly after the first car show, dad was out for a drive, taking in the beauty that is Northern Michigan summertime. He saw a 1976 triple-black Cadillac El Dorado off in the distance with the top down. He did what most hardcore car guys would do; chased it to talk to the driver about his ride.

"It was a strange sight for such a car to be in Moran, especially with the vanity plate CRANE."

He caught up to the black-on-black car near downtown Moran, just north of St. Ignace. The driver pulled over to find out what the crazy man behind him wanted as dad was blowing his horn and flipping his lights. Once they were stopped, a tall man stepped out of the car, looked at dad and said, "What the hell do you want?"

Once dad made his reasonings known, the man laughed and introduced himself as Dick Crane. Unknown to dad, Dick Crane was the president of The American Truck Driving School in Garland, Texas and a major gearhead. That same car later carried both Bill Mitchell and Carroll Shelby through town in their Guest of Honor years. Mr. Crane was in town for a boat show in St.

Ignace, and they stood on the side of the road and talked about their cars and mutual passions.

Mr. Crane had a cottage in Brevort Lake and told dad he wanted to get involved in the car show anyway he could. Simplicity is always the best route. Simply flashing his lights, honking his horn and getting a cool car to pull over, dad planted the seed for 25 years of one of the most amazing truck shows in the country.

For the 2nd Straits Area Antique Auto Show, Mr. Crane brought a show truck called "First Choice" to St. Ignace and parked it on Dock Two downtown. "It was the first time a truck of this magnitude was brought to St. Ignace," Dad said. "It was a showstopper."

Dad noticed something in the driver's compartment that he did not recognize, so he asked Mr. Crane what it was. Told it was a device called a "Fax machine," dad asked what that was.

"I had never heard of it and he had one in his truck," dad said. "He had the best of everything. He helped his truckers over the years with insurance and truck repairs. He was a very giving man."

The car show continued to set records for entries and attendance through the years and Mr. Crane brought a few of his finest 18-wheelers each year. As he and dad continued to work together, they got to know and respect each other. As the car show neared its 20th year, and with interest being shown by show goers in the big, beautiful 18-wheelers, a deal was struck.

What started as a "low-key" deal with a few trucks coming to the car show, turned into a verbal agreement between Mr. Crane and dad.

"Dick's last words to me before he died was, 'Let's do a truck show.'" Dad said. "Dick said I want to do a truck show, and I want you to do it with me."

While he grieved over the loss of his beloved wife, and suffering from lung cancer, Richard Crane passed away before he was able to see the truck show come to life in St. Ignace.

The St. Ignace Truck Show was the original name dad and Mr. Crane picked to bring working show trucks to town. After Mr. Crane's untimely passing in 1996, months before the first St. Ignace Truck Show, dad met with his family and renamed the show "The Richard Crane Memorial Truck Show."

Mr. Crane's son, Rick, shared a lot of great memories of his father, the show, and working with my father.

"What a thing they put together," Rick said. "After your dad followed my dad and chased him down, they did a lot of great things. It really started something, didn't it?"

Rick was In St. Ignace for the very first car show and was the one who brought up the Triple Black Eldorado in the first place. Rick's first memory of attending the first St. Ignace show was meeting a World War 1 veteran and how nice the show was. His biggest take-away? How the show started so small and grew into such a great event, gaining worldwide recognition.

"I tell you what, your dad gave that city not only that summer show, but a great fall with the truck show," Rick said. "And man, did it boom."

Rick told me when St. Ignace was in the prime years of the show, "The Upper Peninsula actually tipped there were so many cars in that small city."

When Dick Crane passed, Rick and his family wanted to ask dad for something to honor him during the show. "We thought he would put up a sign, or rename a street," Rick said with a laugh. "I called him and asked your dad for some kind of tribute."

They never imagined dad would name the entire show after his father. Rick said his family was blown away and forever grateful. "He called me back and said, how's that?" Rick said. "I was looking for something like Crane Avenue, but that is your dad. He is very good to his friends."

Now in its 25th year, the truck show brings with it a huge following and the most spectacular 18-wheelers imaginable. Lined up grill-to-bumper, taking up the entire main street, the truck show, like the car show before it, exploded onto the national stage.

The weekend of the 2001 Truck Show came five days after the tragedy of 9/11. "That turned out to be the best truck show of them all," Rick said after fearing the show would be canceled. "It was so impressive with all the trucks having American Flags and the patriotism being displayed."

Rick drove a big rig over the bridge for the first time and was blown away at how many people were in Mackinaw City waving flags and cheering.

The highlight of the Truck Show is the legendary "Parade of Lights." Dad wanted to really make an impact. The call went out to all on-road truckers to get on their CBs and "yack it up," dad said.

"I can see your dad getting the town shut down," Rick said. "But shutting down the Mackinac Bridge? I still cannot imagine him getting that approved. There were so many agencies involved in that rally. Just, wow."

Reflecting, Rick told me his father would be so proud. "Your dad turned this into one of the best truck shows in the nation," he said. "Nobody else can use the Mighty Mac, shut down a town, and have the entire town part of the show like your dad did."

Rick never expected the truck show to grow from the original nine rigs the first year and was astonished to see the rigs take up the entire town the way the car show did.

"One year, we had more than 200 go across the Bridge," Rick said. "When the first truck did the route, crossed the bridge, went through Mackinaw City, and came back to St. Ignace, the last truck had not left St. Ignace yet. You couldn't believe such a thing unless you were there."

Rick told me that my father was a man who commanded respect for the work he did, how he did it, and how many partnerships he formed to make everything work.

"I am sure a lot of the town hates him during show time, but, wow, what a man, what an amazing person," Rick said. "Like my father, Ed was an old school man. His word was his bond. He got things done because of the trust he formed with his city."

And much like Richard Crane, when Ed Reavie enters a room "The Boss is in the room. No need to introduce himself. They both had this amazing presence to them."

Now retired, Rick still helps out with the family business but spends his time taking care of that triple-black 1976 Eldorado, so he can have it back in St. Ignace to lead the parade once again.

Going to the Louisville Truck Show, dad promoted the first Richard Crane Memorial Truck Show to be held the second weekend after Labor Day.

Mr. Crane told dad how much he loved seeing the bridge When in town and dad wanted to do something about that as well. He called the Mackinac Bridge Authority with the command, "Light that sucker up" they did. Dad's next great idea was to showcase those amazing 18-wheelers on the Mackinac Bridge. "The Parade of Lights" turned into a visual spectacular to rival anything, anywhere.

More than 200 trucks lined the streets. People walked up-and-down Main Street to the smell of diesel and the sound of Jake Brakes. Like a street carnival of the past, The Richard Crane Memorial Truck Show changed the genre much like the Car Show did.

The one common denominator is my father.

He created the St. Ignace Car show, changed the way shows worked across the country and brought in the biggest stars in entertainment and the car industry. It was like bottling a lightning strike. To do it twice was almost unheard of, but he did it. It's not the time, the place, or the circumstance. It's the man. Period.

Such was the national fame of the show that dad got a call from someone telling him he was "An Ice Road Trucker" and he wanted to come to St. Ignace.

Falling on his sword, dad told the man, Alex Debogorski, he never saw the show and told him to tell him about it.

After he did, dad called David Goldthorpe and secured a room for Alex. David comped the room as he was a huge Ice Road Trucker fan and knew who Alex was. That led to a five-year run in St. Ignace with Alex being one of the most popular celebrities to come to town. Banking on that celebrity, dad set out to find C.W. McCall, he of the legendary song "Convoy". Problem was, nobody knew if C.W. was still alive, let alone able to come to the Truck Show. Never one to listen to people's opinion, dad set out to find if C.W. was still alive. The number he called was answered by a man named William Fries Jr. who just happened to have the stage name of C.W. McCall. When dad asked him what he was doing, C.W. answered, "I am a political activist and pissed off at just about everybody."

Dad asked C.W. to come to the show but was told C.W. was in ill-health and could not come. What he did do was pure dad, he had him call the local radio station and do voice spots for the truck show.

"It was an experience," dad said of talking with C.W. "He was a radical bugger but man alive, that song was a huge hit and was still the trucker anthem and I was so grateful he cut those spots for us."

Dad didn't settle for catching lightning in a bottle twice but went into another direction to get more people to St. Ignace. He got a phone call from Bob Bomgrass, of Owasso Tractor Sales. Bob told dad he was following his shows and he pitched him an idea.

"Why can't we do a show with farm tractors?" dad was asked. "I have about 1,000 tractors that would love to drive up and go over the bridge and have a show."

He'd been told so often that he couldn't do a successful car show or truck show in such a remote place that he loved the idea and immediately took on his third genre changing event. Or was it the fourth?

Bob called the head of the Mackinac Bridge Authority and was told to contact dad about a tractor convoy over the Mackinac Bridge.

Its very first year, 1,300 farm tractors swarmed into St. Ignace to huge crowds and support.

"I had no idea that there were that many farm tractors in the country, let alone in St. Ignace," dad told me with his signature laugh. The St. Ignace Tractor Show was the week before the big rig show. For it's first year, dad was to lead the tractors over the bridge. Unfortunately, the gales of September hit and dad, on a farm tractor, was pelted with rain and high winds the entire trip. There is a famous photo of dad fruitlessly holding onto a battered, inside-out, and torn umbrella as he braved the fall storm.

When I saw it in the paper I called and told him the umbrella was actually using him for protection at that point and asked why he still held onto it.

"Because I knew it would make a good photo," he said with a laugh. "I had nowhere to go. I was on the goddamn bridge and when that thing (the bridge) started wiggling, I started counting how long I had left to live." Forever the showman. Once back in St. Ignace, he needed help from two football players to pry him off the "buddy seat" and set him down on dry land.

"I had no idea how to get off that tractor," dad said. "With my frail legs, I needed those boys to get me safely on the street.

The thought of 1,300 tractors in town was mind blowing. I will repeat; it's not the time or the place or the circumstance. It's the man.

With 225 big rigs, 1,300 tractors, C.W. McCall doing radio spots, and one of the most popular reality show actors in history, dad was again hailed as a revolutionary show promoter.

Chapter 22: Talking Trucks with Alex Debogorski

Guest of Honor, Richard Crane Memorial Truck Show, Ice Road Trucker

Descended from Polish survivors of the Holocaust, Alex is a fixture in driving competitions like "King of the Klondike" and LumberJack competitions, including strongman events.

Alex is a lover of competition and arguing politics, and he told me a great story of when his town upset him so much that he ran for mayor.

"I used car doors and car hoods for my political signs," Alex told me. "If you run for office, don't use perforated cardboard or plastic signs."

When people kill trees for political signs, you see, it brings a tear to his eyes. When asked why he used car doors and hoods he explained, "It is a renewable resource. That's why."

The car doors were placed at night because, "We were too embarrassed to do it in the daytime," Alex said. "We drove around in a car full of junk and hung them off fences, up on medians, and on street corners." He recounted a few times falling and sliding into ditches. "I was laughing so hard, I kept asking myself what we were doing, eh?"

The car door said, "Roll down the window; it is going to get hot. Debogorski for Mayor." The downside of using hoods for political signs? "People kept stealing them to use as toboggans to go sledding. I mean, geez."

I needed closure on how the election of 1992 came out and Alex said his 550 votes cost the other men in the race to not like him as he blew their chance. The person Alex beat never ran again.

"They kept wondering who was writing my speeches for me," Alex said. "Here I was wandering around town covered in grease with the crotch ripped out of my pants. They didn't figure I could write."

Get that image out of your head. You're welcome.

The town was accustomed to Alex's shenanigans, including the 500 pigs that escaped his farm and wandered into town. We talked about pigs, rabbits, and chickens for a while. I felt like I was in a bar having a Labatts with Alex as he spoke. What a great guy.

His star turns on the History Channel came about by accident. The original production was into reality shows and someone had the idea to do a reality show about the men who drove supplies on the most dangerous terrain in one of the most inhospitable regions on earth.

The production team went to Yellowknife and the company for whom Alex worked agreed to do the show and then the team went out in search of characters to follow in their trucks.

"It turned out whenever they interviewed someone, either that person or someone in the restaurant told them to track the Legorski fellow down."

And the rest is history.

"I had already obtained character status at that time," Alex said laughing. "I thought it was all a big joke, so I told them about the government breeding Jackfish (Northern Pike) with piranhas and they escaped into the river and started to eat all the aluminum boats."

He was still not taking the show seriously when a female director interviewed him. He told her she had "nice hips and should be good for at least a dozen kids."

The next year, she had a baby and named it Alex. "Draw your own conclusions to that one." To Alex, there was nothing at all interesting about his work and he wondered why on earth anyone would want to watch someone drive a truck through snow and ice.

"I think they picked me to help promote the show with all of my foolishness."

Fast forward several years, Alex found himself booked to come to St. Ignace. The fame of Ice Road Truckers took Alex to all the big truck shows in the States.

Going show-to-show, Alex says he loved coming to St. Ignace, except for one time.

"I got so sick I thought I killed the entire town," he said with a laugh. "I figured once I left town, the entire town would have died off. I could only stand for a few minutes. I was so weak."

He has traveled the world and loves being with the people, "Hugging, tickling them, and telling them dumb jokes. I want them to feel good about coming out to meet me."

The last time Alex was in St. Ignace he said he was shown a photo of him with a couple's 12-year-old son who is now a Marine.

"The great thing about St. Ignace is when these people came to see me, and now, their family is growing up and doing things all over the world," he said. "I got a chance to impact that family and their children."

Alex told me that the greatest part of the St. Ignace Truck show was working with the townspeople and my father. "The entire setting, the parade of lights, going over the bridge, it was fantastic. Your dad is a man's man. I enjoyed every minute of my time there."

He missed the 25th show because of the Pandemic and is glad to have another chance to come back. Preparing for "The Winter Road" trip, Alex wants to make it back to St. Ignace.

Before ending our interview, Alex asked me how a bear likes its carrots. Playing the straight man, I asked how the bear liked his carrots?

"RAAAAAWWWW!" he answered.

Not missing a beat, I asked Alex what did one snowman say to the other snowman? When he returned the favor, I told him, "Smells like carrots."

This is my life now. Sharing stories and jokes with an Ice Road Trucker. I am blessed.

PART SEVEN

The Roaring 90s!

Chapter 23: Cruising into the 90's

"It was out of this world and so very much alive. We had attended many classic car shows over the years including Concours d'Elegance shows across the country. Ed Reavie set the highest standard ever for car shows."
Alex Tremulis, *Designer of the 1948 Tucker Sedan.*

The 1989 show brought Wally Parks, founder of the National Hot Rod Association, and again mixed a brilliant alchemy of genres to form an elegant buffet of world automotive attractions, personalities, and outright fun.

Adding in the NHRA fan base with Mr. Parks (also Founder and Editor of Hot Rod Magazine), dad hosted a huge concert with Lou Christie, belting out Lightning Strikes, Two-Faces Have I, and many others.

Like a Springsteen song list through the years, dad added new acts and stars and kept the past ones to make a "Who's Who" of entertainment and automotive worldwide in tiny St. Ignace.

Cruise Night was a thunderous, booming success as tens of thousands of people lined the streets and poured bleach and water on the roadway for the boldest of hot rodders to execute their burnouts.

A five-mile long, stationary assembly of Michigan State Police Blue Goose Patrol cars with the red bubble top lights activated, underscored the insanity of the event. No word if any challenged hot shot kids to drag race them. The show of force was necessary to slow down the monstrously muscled and horse powered to hell hot rods, street machines, and customs and stop them from burning rubber down the street.

It appears the mother ship had landed on West US2, awash in a ribbon of flashing red lights that stretched for miles in both directions.

In 1989, I returned showing the results of two workouts a day complimented by eating pizza every night and grazing nonstop on the buffet at Central Michigan University's cafeteria.

I had graduated high school at 155 pounds, but I returned this year one inch taller and a buff 200 pounds in a black satin jacket, I was assigned to Dick Biondi as he waded into the screaming crowds of fans, all of whom were in throes of a malted hops frenzy. Their boundaries floated down a river of whiskey, cheap wine, and warm bottled beer. Revelers bounced off of me as I turned a shoulder into them when they came at Dick and tried to grab, hug, or otherwise screw with him.

"Careful, that big fella must be his bodyguard," one drunk who bounced off me said to the other drunk approaching. Mr. Biondi was a very slight man and my father told me to keep him safe, so I did.

I remember a shirtless, well-muscled, intoxicated young man hefted a boulder over his head, danced awkwardly with it, and sent people scurrying out of his way as he toppled to the ground with it in his hands. I told the intoxicated youth to call his mom and apologize to her for failing her as a man.

I'd lived in St. Ignace all my life and seeing this scene playout before me was a shock to my senses. Everything was surreal, like waking up in a different era, or being in a movie waiting for the director to scream CUT as the madness swirled around my head.

The people, the music, the roar of horsepower, the smell of nitrous, the awesome growl of the glass packs, Thrush Mufflers, Brute exhaust systems, and everything that went with it was a recipe for fun and disaster all at once.

In an "only in St. Ignace" moment, dad presented a tribute to the Tucker Automobile during the car show. Designer Alex Tremulis, Preston Tucker's daughter, and grandson appeared at the Guest of Honor lunch.

I remember them staying close together in a state of constant paranoia of being followed and watched by members of the Big Three car companies, even going so far as to point out several men in the crowd as spies there to keep tabs on them.

I didn't have the heart to tell them that just about everyone at the table was with the Big Three and many more were in the crowd.

They were another example of dad's insatiable desire to get each and everything he loved to come to town.

Adding the chief designer of "The Tin Goose" was just another layer of excellence on top of all the excellent people, cars, entertainers, and legends dad cajoled into coming to the show.

And, showing he prefers to be told "are you crazy?" to not trying, dad was successful in getting the red drapes used in the movie "Tucker a Man and his Automobile" to showcase the car.

How did he get them? Why, he asked George Lucas himself, that's how. How else do you think he would get them? Another example was Ernest Hemmings, the founder and publisher of Hemmings Motor News, a 500-page periodical, still in publication. As he told me about Mr. Hemmings, he said that his latest copy arrived in the mail the previous day.

Named a Hemmings Hobby Hero, dad followed up that recognition and brought the man himself to town as Guest of Honor. He also recounted his visit to see Mr. Hemmings in Bebington, Vermont.

Hanging in dad's office is a personally signed copy of Hemmings Motor News Volume 1, number 1 which Mr. Hemmings brought to town.

Back to yet another astonishing car show.

More than 60,000 persons and 3,250 show cars came to St. Ignace, blowing the minds of the country, as nobody had a clue how dad did what he did to bring this kind of horsepower to St. Ignace.

After our trip to the US Nationals, dad brought Linda Vaughn to St. Ignace in 1990. Thousands upon thousands of her fans lined for blocks to get an autograph.

As most legends did, once they came, they came back. Linda was a staple at St. Ignace for nearly 20 years, seemingly drawing bigger crowds every year.

Letter from a Legend – Alex Tremulis

Dear Ed,

I wanted to thank you for being persistent in inviting me to attend the 14th Annual Car Show. It was out of this world and so very much alive.

We had attended many classic car shows over the years including Concours D'elegance shows across the country. You have set the highest standard ever for car shows. Your residents and helpers were most gracious to us all. It was an event that shall remain in our memories forever.

I enjoyed meeting with Wally Parks who is responsible for all of those men in their fabulous flying machines. He was a great leader and a credit to our profession. He greatly deserved the honor of being your Guest of Honor at this show.

Your show reminded me of the oldies tune, "Those were the days" my friend and I thought they would never end. For me, this was an event of my dreams. God willing, and like Douglas MacArthur said, I shall return. But for now, be happy, be happy, don't worry. Thank you for your gracious hospitality,

Best wishes

Alex Tremulis

Writer's note: Mr. Temulis passed away 18 months after sending this letter. His design works spanned some of the greatest eras of the industry to include working in a design capacity for Cord,

Duesenberg, General Motors, Ford, and his most memorable, The Tucker Car Corporation.

Hired by Preston Tucker, Mr. Tremulis designed the 1948 Tucker Sedan seeing the "Tin Goose" from sketches to reality. While working for Ford, Mr. Tremulis was asked to design a car people would drive in the year 2000.

His design of the Ford X-2000 was brought to life in the form of a working prototype in 1999 and showed at Auto Shows around the world. Mr. Tremulis was contracted as a consultant for the 1988 Motion Picture, "Tucker: The Man and his Dream.

When I met Mr. Tremulis, he reminded me of Kress, my grandfather who is a big part of this book. Mr. Tremulis sported a Detroit Tiger Baseball cap with snow white hair underneath during the Guest of Honor luncheon and sat next to me. He was very sharp, cranky, and insightful and it was an honor speaking with such a legend.

PART EIGHT

A Family Tale Sadness, Sorrow, and Sacrifice

Chapter 24: Dad, Mom, and Me

"And the cats in the cradle and the silver spoon
Little boy blue and the man in the moon
"When you coming home, dad?" "I don't know
when"
But we'll get together then
You know we'll have a good time then"
-Harry Chapin

The most personal entry into this book gives a window into the relationship between dad and me. Simply put, we didn't have one. In fact, we didn't like each other. At all.

Inside the Reavie home, all was not well. In 1978, an event with my mother changed all our lives.

I struggled with telling this part of the story, but I felt that, for the rest of the story to make sense, this one needed to be heard. While the show was magical, things behind the scenes were not. From 1978 until 1991, it was a nightmare for dad and, after 1991, for my sister and me.

It is distressing for me to write this. I anguished over it. Got sick over it. Wrote, and re-wrote. It's May 6th, Jack is doing his second edit, and I felt I needed to say more. I reached out to him, discussed it, and he supported it.

This part of the book steps away from the show and talks about the Reavie family. Just us. It is deeply personal, painful, and supported by the family. It may shock you senseless, but that is a consequence of reality, and writing from the heart.

Mary Ellen Reavie, Danielle and my mom, died March 9, 2021, after a five year battle with blood cancer. She waged a beautiful fight but, in the end, she had nothing left. At the end, her cancer was in everything to include her brain.

Writing this brought out so many bottled up emotions. For the first time in my life, I looked in the mirror and saw a broken man staring back. It was painful. I knew for the first time, I needed help.

I sent a message to my primary care provider at Mayo, a magnificent man who had, for years, implored me to get help. He saw me when I began to unravel in the Child Crimes Unit, as having a clear mental break and PTSD by a thousand cuts. There are only so many beaten, sexually assaulted, and burned kids your mind can take before you become the monster you chase and your soul blackens, your mind bends.

One child, a six-year-old boy, was so brutally beaten that he was not expected to live. His injuries were grotesque and included lacerated internal organs, hair torn out by the roots, injury to his genitals so severe it was hard to imagine. His arm and leg were broken, as were several ribs. His teeth were broken out.

I looked at him as he lay moaning in his hospital bed and the look on his twisted up and contorted face still haunts my dreams. In his eyes was so much pain. Unimaginable pain. His look screamed "please help me and make this stop."

That began my descent down the rabbit hole. The next month I was on call and took a case involving an 18-month-old who died from the horrific actions inflicted upon her. It took me nearly a year to unravel the bullshit and get someone charged with her murder.

I was fractured before this, and now I was broken. I held that little girl's hand as a machine kept her alive. I told her I would find the person who did this to her.

Within months of chasing the man that hurt the little boy, it was my boss, Nic Jimenez who pulled me aside to tell me I had changed. First, I pursued this animal for months. It took MONTHS of therapy before that beautiful child was able to say that man's name and how he hurt him.

For the first time in my career, I had gone with our Fugitive Apprehension Team, gave them my handcuffs, and stood by as they rammed in the door and put my cuffs on him.

I had previously taken my Superhero Team to Phoenix Children's Hospital to visit this horrifically abused little boy. Captain America and Superman were unable to get him to look at them. Only my Black Widow Cosplayer, a beautiful soul named Jamie, was able to gain his trust. Jamie held his hand and talked sweetly to him for nearly 30 minutes, and he responded.

Both of those cases on top of the other turned out my lights. Gone was the happy, joking, life of the party Sean replaced by a dark, angry man prone to outbursts, nightmares, and behavior that ultimately led to me being suspended. PTSD by a thousand cuts with the first being inflicted during my own childhood starting in 1978.

So, that is the mental state I was in while writing this. It was not easy. Vulnerability is something Reavie men never show. Until now. My reasons are cathartic and hopefully, are taken for what I intend. Jack told me some people were not going to like this. He said it is my story to tell and also later told me this was the purest written part of this book and it hit him hard.

After 1978, I did my best to love my mother. This is not a bad son moment. This is reality. The reality that dad, my sister, and I lived and kept from everyone until I wrote this.

My wife sat in astonishment as I read this to her. Her eyes were glassy, a look of sorrow that suddenly explained a great deal of my self-loathing, depression, anxiety, fear of failure, and internal health problems and why I am the way I am.

She had empathy for my mother now. She saw firsthand the last 12 years of my mom's life and was in complete disbelief at her antics and behaviors. She seldom wanted to visit her, as she didn't want to hear her husband and sister-in-law being endlessly trashed, belittled, and cut to the bone with a blend of aggressive, passive aggressive behavior that chilled her to the bone.

To ensure that this part of the book didn't take my father by surprise, on Christmas Day 2021, during a 90-minute phone call, I read this to him.

I heard him gasp, and then break down crying. I knew what I had written was not only accurate, but still a raw, open nerve for us both. It was the first time we ever talked about it. Ever. We both bottled it up inside and let it eat us alive.

He agreed this needed to be told. The raw, real, story of not only the shit show of our family dynamic, but the very reason dad and I never had a relationship for the first 22 years of my life.

As I read to him, he sniffed and fought back tears. He remembered how awful it all was. How it impacted my sister, me, and him.

What happened to my mom in 1978 changed all of us and we all made drastic decisions on how to survive the nightmare of what became our family home.

Dad and I both resonated with the Harry Chapin song "Cats in the Cradle." I am sure the finality of that song was in his mind as I got older and further away.

I knew he was resigned to the fact that I had no interest in his car shows or cars in general. He tried with me; he really did. He had no example of how a healthy father and son acted, so he did his best. I see that now. Then? Not one bit. I stopped caring. The callousness of my heart was like leather.

His entire worldview of what a strong relationship was came from his father, Kress. Any therapist would look at that and try hard to not be shocked. Dad was treated as a tenant, an annoyance and, for a long time, a failure not worthy of love.

My mom, Mary Ellen, was the stand-in for dad until I was about ten. She was a great mom. She was tall, pretty, fun, outgoing, and had a great sense of humor. I remember she was in bowling leagues and dressed up for Halloween with her lady friends. They were all ladybugs one year and I think the Munsters the next. Big hair and green faces. It was cool to see that.

She doted on her only son and always told me that Kress had openly wept when I was born as he hugged and thanked her for giving him a Reavie grandson.

Elaine was embarrassed that dad worked in a grocery store, and horrified that he married my mother, who was of Native American descent. When we moved from Spring Street to Hillcrest Boulevard, she mentioned loudly that the latter address was more befitting a banker.

Mom and Dad were told constantly that they were terrible parents. Elaine gave mom books on proper parenting and openly despised her Catholic faith and her heritage.

Elaine famously told my sister that she needed to go back across to the other side of the tracks when Danielle visited our family on the reservation.

I am certain that dad married my mother (who was a tall, stunning, brunette with a million-watt smile and high cheekbones) simply to piss off Elaine. It worked.

My favorite photo of mom hung on the wall of her family's home. It was of her and her sister (my auntie Pat). One had on a pink dress and the other, blue. They were still in high school. They both had brilliant, perfect smiles on their young faces. Auntie Pat, Patricia Ann, mom's closest friend and sister, died in 1978.

My grandfather, Francis William Martin, one of the most beautiful souls to walk the earth, died within three months of a cancer diagnosis. He had a tumor the size of a golf ball that grew out of his head. He died December 8, 1980, and my mother, still reeling from the loss of her sister, was never the same again.

I was a nerdy little dork with few friends, and my imaginary friend who later became the logo for my Foundation. I was mostly a loner in school, but with three really good friends, Clyde, Jeff, and Trey. Glen Woodward Law III (hence Trey) was my best friend. His home and his mom, dad, brothers, and sisters were my lifeboat.

The Law family showed me what a loving family unit was all about. All of them. Trey, Chris, and Brett were the brothers I wished I had. Gina was older and Garth and Margo were born when I was a teenager but, when I see them, it makes me happy.

I see Chris every year at the car show and we share a deep hug as his six beautiful children wait their turn to say hello to me. If you parked near the show and gave money to "The Lady in the Shirt" you met Mrs. Law and her family.

I don't know how messed up I would be without that family. The late Glen Jr. and Joan, thank you for allowing me to practically live at your house. I loved Mr. Law like a second father, and I seek Mrs. Law out when I am home to let her know how much her family means to me. I can't say it enough.

The last time I saw Mr. Law was after the car show, in June of 2009. I stopped over to say hi and he asked if I wanted to go for a ride. I think he knew. He was not well. His heart was seriously damaged.

We drove around for hours. We shared stories about growing up, about when I worked for him at the drugstore. The family had several businesses, and he employed his children in all of them. "The Show" clothing store was the only theater in town owned by Mr. and Mrs. Law.

We drank Root Beer and drove. I still remember his favorite song was "Captain of the Heart" and he installed it in the jukebox in his home, which had a yard big enough for a baseball diamond and a tennis court.

Any child who wanted to play baseball, just needed to show up at 6 p.m. nightly. There was even a dugout. He pitched and it didn't matter if 30 kids came; they all played, and each had to bat before the inning was over.

We tried to hit a ball over the 20-foot-high chain link fence into the tennis court. Robert Paquin did once. He was a neighbor growing up, and physically gifted. It was cool. There was an arcade in the basement and Trey always had every gaming system. I loved that house. I loved that family. I was there every day.

Before I left, he hugged me and told me he loved me like I was his own son. The feeling was mutual. We both cried. He knew. I think I did, too. He died in early 2010 and left a legacy like few have in our town.

I texted Trey (who goes by Glen since he went to The University of Michigan) and told him about this chapter. I told him his family saved my life. I called dad and he agreed. He told me he often took Danielle to the Law house when things became unsafe for her at our home. Danielle told me the Law family helped mold the person I am today, and I agree with that.

It wasn't always that way. Mom and Dad did fun things too, like dad recording his voice at 78 RPM on his reel-to-reel player to sound like Santa's elves talking to us as Santa placed presents around our tree.

He then recorded his voice at 33 RPM to talk like Santa. "Hello Danielle and Sean" the speakers blared in a slow, older sounding voice. We were the luckiest kids in the world to have Santa take time out from his busy night to leave us a message.

My parents, clearly having a crystal ball, got me both a police costume and a Superman costume that Christmas, the last in our old home on Spring Street.

I remember the mother of my early life being fun, happy, goofy, and loving her baby boy. I still smile when I remember dad and her going out and mom coming home HAMMERED.

She kept yelling in that giggly, drunken banter, "I want to go home and see my kids." My laughing father replied, "You are home, you knucklehead, be quiet." My sister and I were both laughing. I think Danielle was ten and I was eight.

I remember her in the backyard helping me with my swing on a tee ball device dad had built for their little boy. An event dad still claims as one of his finest moments. She clapped and praised me when I hit the ball.

During my very first t-ball game, I rounded second and the throw from the outfielder plugged me right in the back. I ran over third, into the stands, and jumped into my mother's arms. I was a momma's boy, after all.

I remember riding down the hill to where the old Wyer's home and the McCann Elementary School was. It was steep and I had the great idea to copy my sister by going down with no hands on my snappy red, white, and blue banana bike.

That didn't go well, and my parents had the horror of watching me go head-over-ass, cartwheeling down the hill.

I was torn up bad. Asphalt is not kind to children in tank tops and shorts. Mom reached me first, picked up my bleeding body as I screamed, and carried me up the path behind the Holly family home, cut through the yard, and then across the street to our house.

She never put me down, comforted me, and then took tweezers and pulled the rocks and tar out of my wounds, cleaned me up with peroxide, followed by the dreaded Iodine. She was kind, compassionate, and comforting. That is still in my head like a movie. I've been cursed with that type of memory. I can play it back in my head.

My childhood was no different from any of my friends until a snowy Saturday morning in 1978 when my mother had a break from reality.

I got up early (usually at 6am) to watch Saturday morning cartoons. Dad got up shortly thereafter and I don't know where he was in the house.

I sat on the living room floor, watching the line-up of cartoons, and my day was set until at least noon when the "Shazam/Isis Hour" came on and ended when my sugar buzz was at its peak. I was ten.

I heard the bedroom door open, but she didn't come out, only moaned. This terrible, ghastly moan. I remember holding a spoon of cereal, frozen there. "MOM??" No response. I felt a horrible energy take me over, weigh me down, and left my bowl of King Vitamin and Super Friends cartoon to walk around the corner and look down the hall.

I remember how she staggered out of her bedroom that Saturday morning. She held the door jamb with one hand, her head in the other. I asked her what was wrong. The hallway was dark, illuminated only by a small night light on the wall. She was in her nightgown (which I never saw her in, always a bathrobe) and the light behind her cast an eerie, otherworldly glow around her.

She stood there, hand in face, slumped in the door jam. I took hold of her and called for my dad. I asked her what was wrong.

She motioned with her hand, index finger extended and twirling, and said, "spin, spin". By the time dad got to her, she was collapsing, which was the most horrible thing a child could see. She went down in sections as her body gave up one limb at a time.

I was small and couldn't hold onto her and neither could dad, so she fell, dead weight, into both our arms. Dad helped her into bed, and she mumbled incoherently.

I handed her a Batman coloring book (shaped like Batman's head) and a pen and asked her to write what was wrong. I put the pen in her hand, but it fell out. She couldn't open her eyes but her head went back and forth as she moaned and mumbled.

Dad called for an ambulance as something was clearly, horribly wrong. I still remember her being carted out of the house on a stretcher and loaded into an Ambulance.

It was cold and I saw her breath billow out as she gasped and moaned, eyes closed, mumbling, talking to someone that wasn't there. She had to be strapped down by her wrists as she was flailing about, trying to touch or hit something that no one could see.

I stood in the driveway, in below-freezing cold, and watched as the ambulance disappeared behind the huge snowbank that ran down the entire cul-de-sac to the service road.

I remember dad running inside to get his keys. I am pretty sure one of the neighbors came to the house to stay with me. Maybe the Greve family. Lana and Danielle were friends. That I don't remember clearly.

She was institutionalized for weeks and never the same. We were not allowed to see her. I spoke to her, but she sounded like someone else. Her voice was short, clipped, and curt, filled with anger.

Dad said that she ranted and screamed while strapped down in a bed. She was on suicide watch. It was so horrible. So goddamn horrible, he said. He sighed heavily into the phone as we talked, clearly impacted by this memory. His wife and our mother rode away in an ambulance and, two weeks later, something else came home. I had never met that person. My dad's life, my sister's life, and my life were never the same. Add the deaths of her sister and father in short order, we lost our mom, too.

Medical knowledge of that time was not well versed in mental health crises, let alone what to do about it.

It was not mom's fault that she was mentally ill, that she was over medicated, under medicated, paranoid, angry, sad, often psychotic and frightening.

It took me 40 years to know it wasn't my fault that she did the things she did, said what she said, hurt me the way she did.

From that day in 1978 until March 9, 2021, my mother lived in a perpetual state of drugged-out melancholy or drug-fueled delusions and anger. She became addicted to the large amounts of drugs prescribed to calm her, to energize her, to make her feel better. To help her sleep. Valium, Feryinal with Codeine, Norco, Tramadol etc.

She popped Valium like popcorn and was never in control of herself. She heard things that simply were not there, a constant argument in her head and it was usually me. And she raged against me, hit me with whatever she could get her hands on, swatted me in the face, chased me down the hall, and pulled me by my hair. She grabbed wooden spoons, Sears catalogs, anything. I didn't know what to cover and was hit everywhere.

She saw the world one way, and it was different from everybody else. Often, paranoia set in when "all those people" talked about her behind her back. She hurled accusations at my father day and night, accusing him of all sorts of wrongdoings that simply could not have happened.

She knew when his workday ended, and if he wasn't home in the time allotted for the short drive, she raged at him in a chilling verbal assault.

Some days, she was my biggest fan. Others, she terrified me. Each time, I wanted her to reach out to me as any son would with his mother. I remembered being carried up the hill. I remember her playing catch and reading to me.

Those times were gone, and I never realized they wouldn't come back. I always hoped they would because hope is stronger than fear. I hoped until the end.

When I begged her to help me make the little league team by playing catch, she told me it didn't matter and I wasn't good enough, anyway. I remember breaking down at the table after she said that. I ran down the hall crying as she mocked me. "That's right, run away and cry."

The memory of her belting me in the face in front of my two close friends for the sin of making a mess by mixing two different Kool Aids together is still with me. After she hit me, she threw a towel at me and demanded I get on the floor to clean it up.

I closed my eyes, felt my cheek blaze and tingle, so I didn't have to see my friend's reactions. I wouldn't look at them. They asked me if I was okay. I wasn't. They never came back. And I was never okay again.

I hid in my closet and read Spiderman comic books. I stayed after school for track, basketball, golf, or football. I didn't want to go home. In the safety of my closet, I heard her screaming at something or someone as she threw things, screaming at me, telling me to shut up. I remember her waking me up in the middle of the night, screaming at me to shut up. I was sleeping. My sister stood up for me screaming back that I had said nothing and to leave me alone.

Most days, I sat in my closet and shook, pretending to be Spiderman, swinging off to save myself. I even drew buttons on the closet wall. One was to lock it, the other to make me invisible. I placed my foot against the door so she couldn't open it.

This memory, blasting into my head in 2015, is what led to something great. As a Crimes Against Children Detective, I got the idea for my Foundation while interviewing a terrified 9-year-old boy.

He sat, arms wrapped around his knees, head buried, and would not talk to me. I was stuck. Interviewing child victims involved open-ended questions and nothing direct. He was too afraid to look at me let alone talk to me.

The origin of my Foundation came from my desperation to reach him which formed my next question to him; "Who's your favorite superhero?"

He instantly changed. Head popped up, eyes wide. He jumped out of the chair, screamed "IRON MAN!" and proceeded to run around the room making sound effects with his hands, pulsing energy out of his imaginary gauntlet just like Iron Man.

After he sat down, I told him my favorite was Spiderman (whom he also loved), and we talked about the new Avengers and Antman movie, and now, he trusted me and told me what happened to him. An arrest was made.

On the way out, I desperately wanted to give him an Iron Man t-shirt or action figure. I ran to my sergeant's office. Sergeant Tim Shay heard what I wanted to do, (a community donation drive for superhero action figures and t-shirts), and told me it was a really good idea. Thanks for the validation, sarge.

"Put on the Cape A Foundation for Hope," was born that day. Less than a month later, I held a simple event to get donations of superhero-related shirts and action figures to give to children who came to our center.

Eight years later, tens of thousands of abused children seeking help in eight greater Phoenix Child Advocacy Centers, benefit from that moment. Hundreds of thousands of dollars have been donated for their care.

For the first time, after a lot of therapy, I will tell the part I left out of that story. There was something else that happened before I asked the child that question. Something I never told anyone. Not my dad, sister, nor wife. Not even my board of directors or superhero team. I held it inside of me. Terrified to tell people.

I was running out of time to get him to open up to me. I closed my eyes to think. Suddenly, I saw myself in the closet, mother raging at me, my foot against the rattling door as she pounded on it. Scared and crying, I opened my Spiderman comic book to feel safe. In my mind I zipped a webline and swung away. So far away.

In a flash of pain, my eyes opened, and I saw my younger self myself sitting in front of me. I had to fight back my emotions. I wanted to see if superheroes could help him the way they helped me; so, I asked him.

Just writing this made me shake and caused tears to well up. It was added on April 20th, as Jack was finishing his second edit. I didn't want to reveal it but knew I had to. Somebody needed to hear it.

I think people understand me better knowing this. Sergeant Shay, remember whenever you called me into your office? Remember how worried I was? Scared I did something wrong? It got to the point you would preface your needing to speak with me with, "You aren't in trouble." Remember? For the last 40 years, I was in trouble. Lt. Jimenez, I think you saw that, too.

It explains so much about how white-hot my passion is for my foundation and how violently I defended it. It is MINE because it is ME. I am so defensive when challenged about decisions I make. Constructive criticism is only such if I agree with it.

That will make a great book one day. The healing has begun but I have so far to go. It's Mother's Day, 2022, and I text my sister telling her how hard a time I'm having with this. Memories are flooding back.

She said she was having similar issues. I text her, "Mom f**ked me up so bad" and then I broke down and wept for 30 minutes. She agreed mom focused her mental illness issues onto me.

My sister struggled daily and eased her pain in other ways which are hers and I will not dishonor her by making it public. She finally won her internal war later in her life. I am so proud of her.

I never gave up trying to get validation from my mom, whom I loved no matter what. I wanted the pre-1978 mom to come back.

Mom made life hard on all of us. She raged against dad and me when we came home from Cruise Night at 2 a.m. and accused us of being in a bar and drinking, being drunk, and carrying on with women. She called us selfish bastards, then slammed and locked her door and made dad sleep on the couch.

On one of the biggest nights of dad's life, the night he spent hanging out with Carroll Shelby and Zora, she was waiting for him and verbally murdered him in a fit of seething hatred and rage that I still hear.

She accused him of "F****g some cheap whore" all night and how she hated him for it. She punctuated her soul-scarring rant with this gem: "I am talking to a divorce attorney in the morning," then slammed and locked the door.

Dad and I cleaned up and went right downtown as cars were already lining up to park. It was crazy to even think the two worlds were of the same universe. An hour ago, he was toasting with Carroll and Zora, the King of the freaking world. Now, he was broken and reeling. But he kept going, and we pretended it never happened. I was the only one that morning who saw his heart hanging out of his chest.

We don't pretend anymore.

And as I write this, my heart is aching, dad's favorite song, "A Whiter Shade of Pale" has started playing, and caused me to stop and listen, tears welling up in my eyes.

"And although my eyes were open, they might as well just be closed."

We kept on and internalized our emotions which caused a myriad of physical ailments, many of which I still have. Internally, I am a mess, rarely not sick with stomach aches, bloody discharges, bile discharges, sour stomachs. I cannot eat many things without getting sick. Scottie? Marco? I think things make sense now.

It seemed the bigger the moment, the more her drugged, broken mind reacted. This, after some of the biggest names in the world praised dad for his vision, his work, and his achievements.

When Gordon Buehrig was waiting at the Flame restaurant for the first Guest of Honor Brunch, we all stood in the living room waiting for her to come out so we could go.

Dad's hero was in town. Gordon was the biggest automotive legend there was. And he was waiting for dad. When mom finally came out, she was in a sweatshirt and jeans and announced, "Nobody wants to see me anyway, you just go and have fun at your little party."

This occurred every year. She rarely attended events, and we never knew "which mom" would appear in the morning. Or if she would appear at all.

Friends rarely came over. I was alone. My father found his release and relief with the car show. My sister dealt with things on her terms, and I sank deep into anguish, still seeking my mother's approval.

I remember Nancy Marchand's portrayal of Livia Soprano on the incredible show "The Sopranos". I was watching it with a friend and he said, "Oh, come on, nobody's mother is that bad."

How could I tell him that was the best representation of the personal hell I lived my entire life? No matter how old I was.

When I came home to see her during Christmas, 2020, I got yelled at and made to feel like a fool when I stupidly used the "wrong shovel" to clear the snow off her porch.

That shovel was for dog poop, you see, not snow, and I should have known. I ruined it and she could not use it now. She belittled everything I did from making the coffee, to doubling her gas bill because I was there. Even though that bill wouldn't be there for another month, it was still my fault. She made me feel horrible about wanting to watch a football game and said I was still the same self-centered person she remembered when I was growing up.

When I left to visit dad and watch the game, the caregiver told me that as soon as I left, mom turned the game on and watched it by herself. When she was asked why, she said, "It's my favorite team and I am not sharing it with him."

She did tell me something heartfelt though. Knowing she had only a few months to live, she looked right at me and said, "I can't believe you didn't make me a grandmother. I'll never forgive you for that." Danielle said she told her the same.

It was a brutal stretch, including her raging and screaming when dad had to use her porta potty as he could not wait for her to get out of the shower. When I asked her if she thought it was better that dad piss himself and be embarrassed, she said, "Yes. Serves him right."

When I left to fly back home, she told me, "Your visit was nice; for the most part" and closed the door behind me. That was the last time I saw her alive. Nice memory.

There was a brief moment after her diagnosis, and when she stood strong and decided to fight her cancer, that the mom of old started to emerge.

Dad and she started to talk and had lunch together, the first time in 30 years. She was strangely happy. Calm. Sweet to me on the phone. When the cancer worsened, she was given pain meds, and the inky black tentacles of addiction slithered around her and drew her back into the darkness.

She took 10 Tramadol a day and once the drugs took hold, we lost her again. Mom's best friend, Judi Sved, helped Danielle as much as she could and witnessed some other level behavior from mom. All of it directed at Danielle because I was 2,000 miles away.

When mom was in hospice and close to death, my sister Facetimed me to say good-bye to her. It was the second time I lost my mother. The mom in 1978 that never came back, and the one life dealt us. It was very hard on Danielle and me.

During a therapy session, I was asked to take the "Adverse Childhood Experiences" test. This is the test to measure the depth of abuse suffered as a child. I scored so high that my therapist could not conceal the shocked look on her face. I was asked how I coped, considering I don't drink, smoke, or do drugs. That I had all the markers for teenaged suicide but, here I am. I couldn't answer her. Maybe it was to tell this story for the first time.

The toll on dad and me was a severe one. People saw us together at the show as father and son, not knowing that up until that moment, we neither spoke nor saw each other outside of holidays.

People thought I lived at home with him, or he just sprinkled water on me and I popped up. Truth was, I did not enjoy the shows. It was uncomfortable knowing that mom would be off the rails and I was expected to be a good son.

I became ill when the time to go home neared. Stomach on fire, anxiety through the roof. I tried to make her happy by bringing her a show sweatshirt, which was always the wrong color or size. "Would it kill you to remember what I like?"

With dad, talking was simpler. Our conversations were:

"Hi Dad."

"Hey Sean."

"What's up?"

"Same old."

"Okay, talk to you later."

We didn't hug. We didn't drive around together, and Car Show weekend was the most time we spent together. I made dad pay me to help him. I wanted nothing to do with his life or his show. I was all he had regarding the family wanting to help. I knew it, and I exploited it. It was my revenge for the times he wasn't there. I was young, selfish, short tempered, and uninterested.

In 1989, Wally Parks, founder of Hot Rod Magazine and the NHRA, came to St. Ignace. The show was another incredible success and dad met so many more of his heroes.

After the show, he was given two all-access passes to the U.S. Nationals for Labor Day Weekend. Mr. Parks rolled out the red carpet for him. All access to everything.

I thought nothing of it and went back to school for my last semester, scheduled to graduate in December of 1989. I had other things on my mind. Lots of parties and lots of women.

I had only 11 credits my last semester as I had transferred from a smaller school and lost several. I had mostly electives including a woman's study class that I took to meet a blue-eyed brunette. I went back a week early to party, see my roommates, drink, play basketball, and enjoy my last five months as a college student. At 6' 2" and 200 pounds with contacts, clear skin, and a nice haircut, things were much easier.

I returned from a quick trip to the SBX Bookstore and walked into my house at 1025 Franklin Street where my roommate Chris told me I had a call (no cell phones yet). It was dad. He'd called about ten minutes ago and said he would wait for me to come home, so Chris had set the phone on the counter.

I warily picked up the receiver and said hello. Dad sounded different. He sounded nervous and vulnerable. He never called me, nor I, him. I had no idea what he wanted, and I was puzzled.

After small talk, I tried hard to get off the phone so I could go play more basketball or meet with a new lady friend I heard was sweet on me, so I told dad it was nice talking with him.

"We will get together then dad, I'm sure we'll have a good time then."

He stopped me, he was hesitant, trying to control what struck me as emotion, and asked me to not hang up as he wanted to talk about something.

He reminded me of his upcoming trip to the U.S. Nationals, the all access passes, the tickets to the all-star events, meeting with racers, how much fun we could have, and then it came.

I shook my head and smirked when I heard him go through the same old story of mom going off the rails and refusing to go to the U.S. Nationals to "hang out and get drunk with your idiot friends" and locking herself into the bedroom.

He was preparing to leave the next morning to go to see his heroes at one of the premier events in all of motorsports, and he was alone. He'd been invited by a legend, the man who built the NHRA. He would meet the who's who of greatness.

He had two chairs in the NHRA's tower suite. Free parking. Free room. The key to some of his dreams was to matter to his heroes. His heroes were waiting for him.

Now I think back with all that waiting for him, standing alone in the living room wondering what the hell just happened. Broken again. Made to feel like a failure again and that he didn't matter. On top of all that, he was reduced to begging for someone to go with him.

That someone was me.

I still hear him asking me, a chill going down my spine. He spun it and sold it like he did to get Carroll Shelby and George Barris to St. Ignace. The difference is, I didn't want to spend that much time with my father. Not at another car event.

It was easy for him to swing by because the exit to my house is right off the highway. He'd stop, I'd jump in, and we'd burn rubber off to Indianapolis and have FUN, dammit. The entire weekend ON HIM.

I calculated the length of the drive. Staying in the same hotel room? Hell no. I did not want this. I had a life. I was finally out, away from my mom, I had friends and lots of women to meet. HELL, NO was I going to suffer another miserable weekend at one of his car things. I was an adult! Time to take a stand. Not continue to suffer because of my father.

I told him I was busy. I told him I had school. I had a job, and I needed to get things done before class started the next week. I was to graduate in four months. I was saying without saying, "Save your breath dad, listen to that song again. Your boy was just like you now."

Once I said my laundry list of excuses, the silence on the phone was deafening. I heard him sigh. His next question, bereft of any emotion or hyperbole froze me in my tracks.

"Sean," he said, pausing to make sure he had my attention. "What are you trying to tell me?"

"I've long since retired, my son's moved away
I called him up just the other day

I said, I'd like to see you if you don't mind
He said, I'd love to, dad, if I can find the time
You see, my new job's a hassle, and the kids have the
flu
But it's sure nice talking to you, dad
It's been sure nice talking to you
And as I hung up the phone, it occurred to me
He'd grown up just like me
My boy was just like me"
-Harry Chapin

This was it. The crossroad of my life and relationship with my father. I never heard so much pain or internal angst in one single question. It froze me. My mind raced. The answer to this question would change the course of my life.

Were the two of us destined in life to be a song lyric? A stereotype? To keep the Reavie legacy of a loveless relationship between father and son alive and well?

Or...

I swallowed, took a breath through the paralyzing silence, exhaled, sturdied myself and responded.

"What I am saying, dad, is this. What time do you think you are going to be here so I'm ready?"

And so, on August 29, 1989, a Tuesday, for the first time, I began a relationship with my father.

PART NINE

Healing and Hope

Chapter 25: Road Trip

"The best car show in the World?"
Australian Street Rodding magazine

Uncomfortable is the word describing our long trip to Indianapolis from Mt. Pleasant, Michigan.

Truly, we'd rarely spent more than a few hours together and that was always around other people. It was the usual banter about school, life, and mom. All the same answers. At this stage of my life, I loved Ponderosa Steak House for their awesome buffet and chicken wings. Dad and I had little in common anymore, but on this trip, we discovered we were practically the same person.

He saw the Ponderosa billboard first and suggested it. We both piled up on chicken wings and mashed potatoes. Halfway through, we realized we were competing to see who ate the most chicken wings. I ate 33. Youth. He and I were both the same regarding competition. It made me smile a little. Maybe he was, "just like me" but in a good way.

During the trip, we learned we both watched the People's Court religiously, had the exact same passcode for our voicemail, and preferred the Denny's Grand Slam for breakfast. Upon arriving, we went to the racetrack and walked into the main office. Dropping Wally Parks' name was a hoot to behold.

"Yes Mr. Reavie, we've been expecting you!"

While in the office, we got all-access passes for a private box in the tower suites, private parking, and pit passes. While dad was signing them out, a young kid with a bad haircut and thin mustache came into the office. Dad knew him but I did not. We talked with him for a while, he was a really nice young man and dad told me that he was a Top Fuel Dragster superstar in the making. Ironically, that nice young man called "the Kid" went on to win the US Nationals in the Top Fuel Dragster division as we watched from the Tower. Tragically, that same young man, Daryl Gwynn, was seriously injured in a 1990 crash in England and confined to a wheelchair the rest of his life. A few years later, we returned and met him again under very different circumstances.

On our way back to the hotel, we had a nice conversation about the event. I felt the energy in the air and maybe, just maybe, I was turning around on this automotive thing. Our ticket package included two tickets to the NHRA award show where dad and I saw and heard John Force speak for the first time. We got spiffy, secured our tickets, and walked onto the elevator.

On the way down, a man kept staring at dad's all-access pass and offered him $50. By the time we got to the bottom, the man bid $600. Dad respectively declined his offer each time with a laugh. He politely told the persistent man that Wally Parks meant more to him than $600 and before the man could counter, dad held up his hand and said, "Or any price."

We had one more floor to go and Kenny Bernstein stepped on the elevator. He smiled at us and dad shook his hand. I had a clue he was a big deal but didn't know him, either.

I did, however, know the next man on the elevator, Don "The Snake" Prudhomme. The Snake was one of the greatest to ever roar down the quarter-mile. He was a stud.

Dad and he spoke for a bit before Don joined his table and we went to ours. Ironically again, "The Snake" won the Funny Car class that year. Perhaps the new father son duo was a good luck charm?

The event was amazing, and we listened to John Force hold the entire room captive with his insane brand of spontaneous humor. Wally came to our table and greeted both of us. People craned their necks to see who we were.

We spent a long time afterward talking with drivers, dad was like a little kid, running around, grabbing souvenirs from tables (a long history, along with Curtis Fischbach), and collecting artifacts to store in boxes in rooms he built on to the house to hold said artifacts.

We stayed up late, got up early, ate at Denny's, talked about the previous night, and both had smiles on our faces as he used a "short cut" to get to Indianapolis Raceway Park.

We arrived, waved our badges at security, walked up to the NHRA suite, and went inside. The tower suite was something else altogether. There I met all three of John Force's daughters. They were babies. Now, they race alongside their father. I was only 22 years old. By the time this is published, I will be 55. Damn. What happened?

Racers and their families were in and out all weekend. I recall a buxom blonde woman entering the suite. I thought she was Dolly

Parton, but when I heard dad utter, "Oh, my God." I knew she was much more than that. We met Linda Vaughn, the First Lady of Motorsports, together. She fascinated me in a different way than my father who, for the first time in a long time, stood mute, staring as she worked the crowd with the elegance of a true professional. The Hurst Shifter Girl would become a huge part of our future lives when she came to St. Ignace and stood in as my wife's Matron of Honor when I was married during the 1993 show.

When Linda arrived in St. Ignace in June of 1990, she came up to me, extended her hand, pulled me in for a cheek kiss, and said, "Hi Sean, you are such a handsome young man."

She remembered my name. That is who she is. Bright, articulate, and strong. She is an incredible woman. I recall being stunned by Dave McCllelland as he strode up the quarter mile, his voice booming like it was touched by God just for this moment. The cars roared to life, the crowd went wild, and the event started.

Not caring about this in the past was no longer a problem. I was fascinated with the power and precision of the machines on pit row. Dad and I got to stand on the track, wearing protective headphones, as the Top Fuel dragsters took their turn.

They were beautiful behemoths and slid past us like Great White sharks in a lagoon, barely causing a ripple, leaving an exhaust trail of nitro-methane in the air.

Gliding through a water slick before "the box," when the drivers did their burn out, it was as if the tires instantly came alive. They rose up in a deafening roar that rattled my sternum, blew me backward, and left me gasping in impressed terror.

What da FERK!

I looked at dad and he knew his only son was hooked; finally. That event became legendary for one of the first 300 mph passes in Funny Car history.

We stayed late, got up early, hit the Denny's for the Grand Slam, and talked non-stop about the previous day's insane horsepower and excitement. We hobnobbed with legends, met movers and shakers in the automotive world, and never missed a second of action.

We split our time between the suite, the tower roof, and the pits. We watched every bit of the turbo charged, horsepower extravaganza we could, and soaked in the insane symphony of power, precision, and outright automotive savagery.

I had no idea.

The drive home was better than the drive down and we talked non-stop. We shared our experiences like two long lost friends, which we were, except we were not friends. We started our friendship that day. We stopped in to see the Kruse Auction and I learned to not make furtive movements with my hands and arms lest I find myself the owner of a fine American made automobile.

I can only imagine the high that dad was on during the last three hours after he dropped me off at school and we shared the most awkward hug outside of Cain and Abel.

I can picture the smile on his face. The pride in knowing he was not going to spend the rest of his life battling with an estranged son as he had with his own father. His heart was full. I can also picture his face and the opposite of that pride and joy when he pulled into his own driveway, to see everything he owned strewn across the front yard, his suits hanging from the porch railings, shoes in the grass, records scattered everywhere.

Mom naturally thought he'd spent the weekend with someone other than his son. This was our life. Now you know what Ed Reavie overcame to build his legendary show. The dark, black hole in which he lived alone with no apparent escape.

And me? I hope this soul baring forces people to look in the mirror and not let so many years of their life be lost by holding on to secrets like I did. Talk to someone. It means you are strong, not weak.

Mental health is a crisis in this country. The biggest battles are behind doors and walls, and in our hearts. I was terrified to reveal this. I did it so somebody else can get the absolution I never had, to find help. People can see behaviors in children and recognize the signs of abuse. Even as an adult, I still had them. Not YOU, I was told. You are so successful. You are Superman. Look at the awards. Look what you accomplished. Why are you depressed and sad all the time?

During one of my Foundation's events, a man in his 30's approached me and asked what I was doing. When I told him about our mission of healing and hope for abused kids, his trembling hands reached into his wallet and, with tears in his eyes, he handed me every bill within.

"I wish you were around when I was a kid because I had nobody to help me."

Brother, you have no idea. So, when you ask me "why" I do what I do, now you know why. Because there was nobody to help me, either. Be the change you want to see in the world. Start with yourself.

Letter from a Legend – Wally Parks

Dear Ed,

Words cannot express all the appreciation I feel for the wonderful times we had as your guest during your show in St. Ignace. Seeing that part of the country was the first time for us being part of your show, meeting all the nice people whose interest centers on cars, and most of all, getting to know the Reavie family made the week one of our best.

Topping it all off was the tribute you paid to me as your Guest of Honor during the luncheon. It was an occasion I will always treasure. I hope you can come down to the U.S. Nationals in Indianapolis over Labor Day weekend. Please let us know if that is feasible.

Wally Parks

Author's Note: Wally Parks is the Founder, President, and chairman of the National Hot Rod Association. Mr. Parks was at the forefront of establishing the sport of drag racing as a legitimate amateur and professional sport. Mr. Parks was Guest of Honor in 1989.

Mr. Parks provided the pathway to dad and me learning how to love each other. I often wonder if Mr. Parks had not offered those tickets to dad if any of this would be possible.

PART 10

Photo Album Ode to History

A young Edward Reavie hugging a relative's car.

*Ed, at 15, clearly looking forward to church
with Elaine, Kay, and Kress.*

Lesta, Kress, and the intimidating 6' 6" Edward A.

A young Edward K. and the family 1940 Chevy Pickup truck. Note the parking lights on the fender, the only year that design was in production.

The perpetual scowl of Kress Reavie.

Knowing his son is home customizing orange crates (middle child) instead of cleaning outhouses and white washing the rocks.

Edward A's solution to his family problem making him an entrepreneur ahead of his time.

Edward K's first car. His sensational 1953 Ford Carnival Red convertible (GingerSec techs looked up "Carnival Red" and colorized this photo for this book).

The official plaque given to all members of the "Rod Benders" who cruised the streets of St. Ignace relentlessly.

The 1940 Chevy Pick-up belonging to Kress that Ed and Bucky "customized" by removing the fenders and painting white walls onto the tires.

Ed's second car; A 1956 Ford Victoria. The Peacock Blue car was named "Little Star" and the tires were driven off by Ed's relentless cruising.

The only known color photo of the 1953 Ford. Ed owned 53 cars in his lifetime, and several are highlighted in this book.

The fabled 1965 GTO that beat Bucky, a motorcycle, and a State Trooper. My sister, Danielle, in her babyseat awaiting the next heat of Edward K's drag race.

The GTO, with Ed behind the wheel, was unbeaten in street racing and organized races.

The VW Type 3 Fastback. The car at the nexus of "The Sean Shank Redemption."

With Richard Teague on top of the 552' tall North tower of the Mackinac Bridge. The bridge climb was a favorite of many VIPs when they came to the show.

The legendary Zora Arkus-Duntov.

Carroll Shelby hands out awards during his guest of honor run. Mr. Shelby's visit tipped the auto show world on its ear making the media pay attention to the goings on in the small Northern Michigan town.

Automotive royalty. Richard Teague (VP-AMC), Zora Arkus-Duntov (Corvette), and Carroll Shelby (Mustang, Cobra) sit with Ed during the show in 1984.

Zora behind the wheel with his wife Ellie, who set a land speed record of 2 hours and 15 minutes from Detroit to St. Ignace, and Ed on the shore of Lake Huron.

George and Shirley Barris with Ed (with the Munster Coach).

During the luncheon, Ed always made sure his mother attended. Here, at 90 years of age, is Elaine with Linda Vaughn.

Press conference of legends to include Gordon Buerhig, George Barris, Dick Biondi, Ed, and author Pat Chappel (The Hot One).

George Barris and Gordon Buerhig outside during the luncheon.

Ed in all his glory riding in the Barris Batmobile with George and Shirley Barris (and Tracy Larivee).

Linda Vaughn saying words about the legendary Carroll Shelby during the luncheon.

Jack Walker, Chuck Miller, Ken "Posie" Fenical, Dave Bell, Pat Chappel (back) with Terry Cook, were all ears as Gene Bordinat II talked.

Mr. Bordinat passed away six weeks after the show. Ed with the King.

Linda Vaughn and Jack "Doc" Watson during his Guest of Honor brunch.

The backdrop for the auto show was not bad at all

Ed with NHRA Founder Wally Parks at Tom Monaghan's lodge. A fabulous Sunday event complete with the $6.5 million Bugatti Speedster Royale on display.

Mr. Parks received his Guest of Honor plaque Ed custom made for each guest often calling wives and assistants to get personal photos as he did with Mr. Parks.

Legendary VP of Design for General Motors Bill Mitchell and Ed.

Relaxing in his living room with Carroll Shelby, Ed was fast becoming a legend in the world he so admired. The Bud Long Neck was a theme for the weekend shenanigans with Mr. Shelby. Ed still has the bottle of beer, sealed in plastic, in his collection.

Don "Big Daddy" Garlits and Ed downtown St. Ignace.

"Big Daddy" Ed Roth and Ed catching up on old times. Mr. Garlits said he had never seen anything like St. Ignace. Mr. Roth called Ed an artist of auto show promotion.

The legendary St. Ignace Car Show grew two miles on the shoreline of Lake Huron.

This series of historic photos appeared in magazines from New York to California, Australia to Japan, and Sweden to Florida.

At its peak, 3,200 show cars and 100,000 people crammed into a town so small, it had no stoplights and only 2,200 residents.

Ed, Diane Barden, Carroll Shelby, Kathy, and Frank Livingston.

*Old School Cool. For long-time St. Ignace residents, the all-brick Pembles
Grocery Store will bring back lots of memories.*

102

Dave Bell with Chuck Miller during the Guest of Honor brunch. Roy Sjoberg opined the brunch was a way to talk about your heroes, turn around, and see them sitting behind you as was the case with Mr. Miller who met Dave Bell for the first time at the brunch in 1986.

Miss Nostalgia Productions Jennifer Brown and Linda Vaughn.

*In 1989, Dick Biondi missed his transport from the airport and simply
walked into the brunch. The author (goofball in suit) gave Mr. Biondi the
mic. Bottom right is Tucker designer Alex Tremulis with Mr. Biondi
addressing Mr. Wally Parks.*

Later that night, Ed and about 10,000 drunken revelers had the pleasure of listening to Mr. Biondi MC the insanely wild and fun Cruise Night.

Freddy Cannon, Danielle and Ed Reavie. The author's sister gave up so much of her life to care for her ailing father.

Linda Vaughn getting ready for the Down Memory Lane Parade.

Winning John Forces' Tool Box.

In his home with American Graffiti stars Candy Clark (Debbie) and King Pharaoh Bo Hopkins. Paul LeMat (John Milner) stood with Ed in the same room.

With Paul LeMat (Jon Milner) during the St. Ignace show

*Ed jumps the ropes to get a photo with Milner's Deuce Coupe, and Falfa's
bitchin' black 1955 Chevy. You may be detecting a theme here.*

These are Happy Days. Ed with "The Fonz" Henry Winkler.

Ed with "Potsie" Anson Williams, and "Ralph Malph" Don Most. To most who knew him, Ed was a modern day Fonzie.

The Down Memory Lane Parade is legendary.

The Happy Days gang enjoyed their Guest of Honor run walked the show area meeting fans.

The Richard Crane Memorial Truck Show lit up the town and the Mackinac Bridge during "The Parade of Lights" seeing more than 200 show trucks cross the Mighty Mac into Mackinaw City and back to St. Ignace.

Ice Road Trucker Alex Debogorski with Danielle Reavie.

On his first trip to California, Ed met with the legendary Tommy "The Greek" Hrones in his shop and watched him work. The two talked for hours and Tommy sent Ed a custom toilet seat for his collection.

Ed meets with Bob Wingate in California and fulfills the ultimate dream of hanging out with Carroll Shelby at his shop.

Standing in front of the Legendary shop of George Barris. Ed bought the first ever Motor Trend magazine in 1949 which featured a story on George Barris and made Ed a fan for life.

Johnny Tillitson, appearing one week after his daughter died, brought down the house with a song dedicated to her.

Ed sits with Beverly Lee of "The Shirelles" at the Guest of Honor Luncheon. The small-town Rebel was fast becoming legendary.

Ronny Dove came off the stage and into the crowd to sing to Mary Ellen Reavie with Ed breaking out a huge grin.

Backstage with Leslie Gore and Freddy Cannon before the show. Like a kid meeting Santa, Ed met all his heroes imaginable on his home turf.

Legendary artist Dave Bell gave St. Ignace national exposure through his work and Henry Highrise cartoons appearing in car magazines.

Ed commissioned Dave to design his Nostalgia Productions logo which is a creative blend of Ed's National Champion 1955 Chevy Belair and the Hirohata Mercury. (Dave Bell Collection).

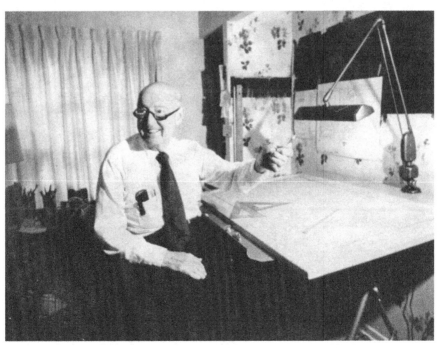

Becoming the show's first Guest of Honor, Mr. Gordon Buerhig opened the door for other legendary men to come to the show. (photo: Gordon Buerhig)

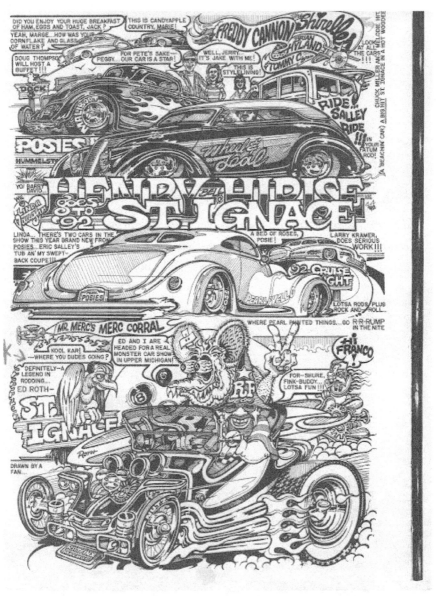

Another fantastic Dave Bell shoutout to St. Ignace during his run at the show (Dave Bell). A not-so-subtle shoutout, concerning my sister's smoking habit, kept Mr. Bell looking over his shoulder each year he came.

The parade brought in some serious metal.

The Truck show had awesome displays to include "Smokey and the Bandit" Trans Am and this beautiful 18-wheeler of "The SnowMan." Ed came close to landing Burt Reynolds for the show but Mr. Reynolds was in declining health.

The first winner of the Ridler Award, Al Bergler, did the "cacklefest" three times for the crowd.

Dave Jenkin's Bitchin' '57 Chevy Bel Air is one of the most radical rides ever.

The Down Memory Lane Parade showcased cars like the 1967 GTO.

The Down Memory Lane Parade also showcased this crank-started 1913 Cadillac.

Cars stretched for two miles with 100,000 people respectively walking by, under crystal blue skies and the lap of Lake Huron's gentle waves onto the shore and boardwalk located directly behind this row of cars. There was nothing like it anywhere.

St. Ignace had something for everyone. Admission was free, endless stores and restaurants awaited as did ferries to Mackinac Island.

Called "The Greatest Run Ever" St. Ignace was the Field of Dreams for car enthusiasts.

Ed Reavie at his desk

The legendary voice of the NHRA, Dave McClelland and his wife Louise.

Zora Arkus-Duntov in "Duntov's Mule" the X-87 (photo: The Ken Lingenfelter Collection)

Darryl Starbird joined the long list of Guests of Honor to brave climbing the Mackinac Bridge tower for an unprecedented view of The Straits.

John Schneider and the author with the General Lee during the Guest of Honor Luncheon.

Richard Crane passed away a few months prior to the first St. Ignace Truck show prompting Ed to rename the show after his longtime friend. (photo: Crane Family)

Staging for the Parade of Lights

Tom Shannon, Linda Vaughn, Bryan Hyland, and Freddie Cannon before the parade (photo: Jerry Patlow).

Linda and Top Hat John (with Victoria driving) wave to the crowd during the parade. Mackinac Island and Lake Huron in the background.

The 1991 S-10 Nostalgia Productions Truck.

The author FINALLY is allowed into the driver's seat of the iconic Turquoise and India Ivory 1955 Chevy Belair. Which, if you haven't noticed yet, is the color scheme of this book's cover.

When asked why he held a broken umbrella during a torrential rainstorm crossing the Mackinac Bridge, Ed answered, "Because I knew it would take a good picture."

Ed in his museum office reflecting on what he built.

*With 2021 Guest of Honor Tom Peters and 2012 Guest
of Honor Top Hat John Jenza.*

Friends for 30 years, Ed and Top Hat.

Ed's magnificent 1955 Chevy Belair Hardtop.

Guests of Honor Jack Walker (2017) and Chuck Miller (2010), Ed was two years removed from his final show as a promoter but still the show's icon and biggest fan.

"Just a shy, humble, country boy," was Ed's favorite thing to say. That humble country boy is firmly a legend in the world he cherished since he was a child.

"I did get the picture on my way out, so there's that," said Ed after getting tossed out of the museum for ducking under the ropes for this photo.

Father and son. Not a song lyric.

2021 St. Ignace Cup Winner Marv Wiegand's 1960 Rambler Wagon took home the hardware and $5,000.

Gary Alumbaugh's 1928 Ford Model A Pick-up took home the prestigious St. Ignace 6 award.

St. Ignace 6 winners Rob Van Camp's gorgeous 1967 GTO.

Paul Jurewicz's Dream Roadster.

St. Ignace 6 winners Kelly Welling's 1948 Hudson.

Mike Copeland's 1984 Dodge Rampage.

In 1955 the 15 year old Edward, while at Silver Sands Resort dreamed about the California car culture.

He's a Rebel*. In 2020, at 80 years old Ed returned to the resort and reflected on his own historic show that for the first time, had California car guys dreaming about St. Ignace; as legendary as any show in the country.*

*Murray Pfaff called the author and asked what car, if he could choose, would
Ed Reavie want to see at the June 25th book signing event. Thinking of the
Hirohata Merc and the Batmobile, Sean called his father and asked. Without
hesitation Ed said, "Burton UpJohn's 1904 Peerless." Going to work,
through a series of emails that were quickly answered, Sean located
the new owners of the car who were honored to bring this beautiful
work of art to St. Ignace in honor of Ed Reavie.
(Thank you Eric Minoff and Terri Coppens for making this happen.)*

Author's Note: *The fall of 2020. The first-time mom and dad got together to talk since November 29, 1991. This broke 30 years of silence between them and from a metaphor perspective, this is a very powerful photo. During the writing of this book, dad and I talked about the heartbreak of our lives with her, each hearing the hurt and struggle of the other for the first time. It was highly emotional, and cathartic and Danielle and my father agreed with me that our story needed to be told for some manner of absolution for us all.*

Chapter 26: The Last Supper

Thanksgiving of 1991, two short years later, I brought my fiance home to introduce her to the family. Dad and I had gone to the U.S. Nationals in 1990 and 1991 and continued to build our relationship.

I enjoyed the car show for the first time and worked with him as his son and not as an outsider who wanted to be anywhere else but next to him. It was nice. When I pulled into the driveway, a strangling feeling of doom hit me. The energy was evil, desolate, biting. I closed my eyes for a moment and hoped beyond hope the feeling was misplaced. I took my bride-to-be's hand and walked through the door.

We were met with an empty, dark kitchen and no cooking food. The smells of turkey, stuffing, and pumpkin pie were displaced by coldness.

Mom had our Thanksgiving dinner catered in, didn't lift a finger, and didn't speak to any one of us. My sister was miserable, angry and did not give two ferks about being there, and it showed. Dad was miserable and defeated as he scooped food from aluminum pans and looked down at his plate. I was horrified. I chose this occasion to introduce my future wife to the family. Mom sat there, lips pursed, eyes aflame with anger and spite.

"Would it kill you to pass the rolls, they aren't just for you," she hissed at me. She always took great care to belittle me in front of my friends and now, my fiance.

It was ghastly. We spent the dinner trying to not make eye contact. I did my best to clean up after but, since we were eating on paper plates, it wasn't hard.

Just like past holidays, it sucked. The Grandparents, each on the other side of the tracks, had nothing in common and constantly argued over politics. Kress, the consevative business owner and president of the school board. Francis Martin, the oldest of 12, managed to make it past 5th grade and spent 50 years working at the filling station downtown.

One memorable highlight happened when I was young as eight angry, uncomfortable people ate in silence. Mom stood and leaned over the table to light a candle, and inexplicably let out a titanic fart, freezing everyone in place.

The uncomfortable silence was horrifying. Mom stood frozen, eyes wide open. With the candle wicks still fizzing, Grandpa Reavie, the Kress of legend, said nonchalantly, "Is there a charge for the entertainment?" Everyone laughed. The best childhood memory of the holidays was my grandfather reacting with humor to my mom farting at the thanksgiving table.

That is the best one. You may be wondering, "what is the worst one?" Getting grounded to my room on Christmas day ranks up there.

Back to the Last Supper.

I spent two hours of gut-wrenching agony in the house, embarrassed, hurt, and realizing I'd had my fill of this bullshit. I looked at my fiancé and sighed. I wanted nothing more than to leave and never come back. And that is exactly what I did. I told all of them I was leaving and if they wanted to speak to me, they knew where I lived. I told them I was not doing this anymore. Ever. I closed the door and left the dysfunctional dynamics behind us.

The next day, my parents filed for divorce.

We now refer to that Thanksgiving as "The Last Supper," as it was the last time my mother and father spoke or interacted until the fall of 2021; 30 years later.

My sister and I likewise did not have any kind of relationship and rarely spoke. She reached out to me in 2001 to tell me she'd met the man of her dreams and asked me to come to her ceremony. I did. I had lost my sister for 10 years, beginning at age 24, and I simply couldn't take it anymore. My father never had a relationship with her to begin with. He didn't come that day because mom was there. Now, at 34, I came to meet her husband and try again.

Danielle and I rebuilt our sibling bond over the years. It was hard. We both had the love of family metaphorically beaten out of us and seeing each other was just a reminder of the most painful years of our lives.

I am happy to say, Danielle is now my sister and has been since that day. I love her husband Steve dearly for truly he was the right, and only man, for someone who burns as hot emotionally as my sister. He was the lynchpin to bring us back together and for that, I am eternally grateful.

PART 11

Shifting Gears

Chapter 27: The First Lady

Roaring into the 90's was incredible.

The 1980's took the show to dizzying heights and was a life changer for dad.

Gordon Buehrig, Dick Teague, Zora Duntov, Bill Mitchell, Carroll Shelby, George Barris, Bob Laravee Sr., Gene Bordinat II, Don Garlits, and Wally Parks as the first 10 Guests of Honor.

A perfect 10 for 10 of legendary automotive horsepower headlining his incredible show.

How do you top that?

On June 30th, 1990, Linda Vaughn, the most famous woman in the history of motorsports, walked down the streets of St. Ignace in a hot pink jumpsuit with a checkered flag design down both sides.

Yes, that got the decade off to a good start.

Her presence commanded attention simply because of her larger-than-life personality. Simply put, she is the best at working a crowd of anyone I ever met.

"Thank you for shifting my gears all these years" she called to adoring male fans, said with a sincerity that dripped affection even though she said it thousands of times in her life.

Chip Miller, the founder of Carlisle Productions, was another of dad's heroes who'd built the automotive flea market circuit to incredible success. He complimented Chip on his success and told him how much he meant to the car culture, Chip sat dad down and drew a comparison for dad. He told dad to consider the geography surrounding Carlisle, Pennsylvania. To take a protractor and draw a circle to see the cities from which he drew his crowds and built his business.

Pittsburg, New York City, Philadelphia, Boston, and New Jersey had tens of millions of potential customers. Looking at dad, he told him to consider St. Ignace and draw the same circle. One had to travel hours to find a city of remotely comparable size to Iggy. And from that group, dad built a car show that became the envy of the country.

"You tell me who's the hero? It's not me buddy, it's you" Chip told my dad.

When Zora visited St. Ignace, the door opened for men like Jerry Palmer (Executive Director of Design for GM-North America) and Larry Shinoda ('63 Corvette, Boss 302 Mustang designer) to attend as honorary guests or full-fledged guests of honor.

Mr. Palmer came several times and made a point to introduce himself to me. Great mind, humble man and responsible for some fantastic designs. Talking to other legends during this process, many spoke highly of Mr. Palmer and said he significantly influenced them as designers.

The 90's saw Cruise Night explode to legendary status, spinning off dozens of similar events around the country and influencing the founders of the world-famous Woodward Dream Cruise.

The legends kept coming; Gene Winfield, Joe Bailon, Larry Watson, Ken "Posie" Finical "The Shifty Doctor" Jack "Doc" Watson, Skip Marchetti, Freddy "Boom Boom" Canon, Leslie Gore, The Crystals, Gary US Bonds, the most powerful and successful show promoter in the country, Bob Laravee Sr., coming straight from the pages of automotive history.

The VIP cruise on the Arnold Line Catamaran was a two-hour trip on Lake Huron that sailed under the mighty Mackinac Bridge as the sun set, around Mackinac Island, and gave guests another reason to talk up the country's greatest car show.

"The three days of the show gave people things they could never find at a show anywhere else in the country," dad said proudly. "I still cannot believe it."

The show was stuffed with legends, and show cars exceeded 3,000 for the first time with 100,000 spectators. They crammed into every nook and cranny in the small town.

Traffic backed up for miles because as you know, St. Ignace had no traffic lights. "All those people, they were all here. In this small town. How did I do all this?" Dad said befuddled at his own successful way in promoting his show.

New shows were added, including "On the Waterfront" a swap meet and car corral. As muscle cars, street machines, and hot rods pushed out all original, much older cars, dad created "Antiques on the Bay" to showcase those cars.

Magazines from Japan, South Africa, France, Denmark, Australia, Germany, Spain, and Sweden covered all the aspects of the show.

Seasoned automotive journalists gazed in astonishment as they stood on the elevated South end of the show and looked down. They beheld not only the gloriously sparkling backdrop of Lake Huron, but more than one mile of pristine show cars and tens of thousands of people of all ages.

Thousands of photographs of St. Ignace were splashed across covers of Hot Rod, Rod and Custom, Street Rodder, and just about every car culture publication.

Nearing its 20th Anniversary, St. Ignace started as a dream inside the head of my father who, truly, refused to let go of the best years of his life. Recreating his love of that era's music, cars, and feel, dad introduced our small town to the world. Ernest Hemmings, so blown away by what he saw, declared dad a National "Hobby Hero."

Franklin Hershey, the designer of the 1955, '56, and '57 Thunderbird, rode around with Dad in his 1955 Chevy simply unable to believe what he saw. To honor Mr. Hershey, dad had a tribute to the Thunderbird and hundreds filled the streets.

On display in Feature Car Row? The first Barris Custom in the state of Ohio; a bitchin 1951 Chevy Bel Air Royal painted in "Eggplant and Purple Orchid" two-tone, was nosed and decked with a Continental Kit. This amazing car, owned by a priest, and its clone, were side-by-side in Feature Car Row. Father Ernst became a Monsignor, and only then did he bring the car out of the garage and have it taken to St. Ignace.

"For years, he was called the 'Car Enthusiast from Ohio', as he didn't want his parishioners to know he had all those great cars," Dad said with a laugh. "Burns Barryman brought up the clone. It was the most gorgeous Chevy ever made."

A quick story to show you how my father works. While I am doing the final draft on this book, I wrote down a question about the car and called dad. I simply wanted to know what year and model it was.

That was it.

He told me the make and model, I told him I was buried (a week away from turning in the manuscript) and had to go.

Thirty minutes later, he called back informing me he found the 1952 Motor Trend issue in which the car was featured and had an eight page biography of Father Ernst with the news he was also a "Pharaoh" and as such, was in the rare club with Bo Hopkins and Dad.

While I appreciated the info, I told dad I simply could not put any more information into this book. "Really? but this is really good information. I have info on the Continental Kit and the Ohio License plate still on the car when it was in California.

And if you are wondering NO, "Rebel without a Clue Two" is not in the works. Yet. Geez.

Anyway,

Iconic cars like JR Ewing's Ford Retractable, The Monkee Mobile, The Batmobile, the Hirohata Mercury clone, and other world-famous rides, were on display.

Norm Grabowski, "The Father of the T-bucket" was a bushel of fun driving his custom beer cart up and down main street. "I am not sure if he got arrested or not, but he sure was a lot of fun," dad said with his signature laugh.

Stopped by police. Not arrested. So, I was told.

Such was dad's renown that he received letters from three state Governors, all the major networks, top shows Including Good Morning America, The Tonight Show with Johnny Carson, icons such as George Barris, Mickey Thompson, George Lucas, Jay Leno, and many others congratulating him on his success, wanting to know how he did it, thanking him for resurrecting the genre.

"Not bad for a kid nobody wanted on their team," dad said with a sinister chuckle. "I love every minute of it." The thing about my father, and me, is we hold grudges. Is it healthy? Not at all. Does it make us feel better when we succeed despite other people? Maybe.

After all the years of living vicariously through the California car culture, reading about, and meeting, the California car culture heroes, the self-proclaimed "Rebel without a Clue" had yet to cross the state line of the Golden State. Yet to see for himself the wondrous history and culture that the state was known for across the world. He decided it was time.

Chapter 28: California Dreaming

When the best-of-the-best of the California car culture came to St. Ignace, they took home stories of seeing things at one show in a small northern Michigan town that was not seen anywhere in the country.

Condensed within that small town was the biggest collection of automotive history imaginable. Hearing of this mythical place across another majestic bridge, others came. Dad experienced "build it and they will come" before the movie Field of Dreams worked the same principle on the screen.

Yet, shocking as this may be, Ed Reavie, the ultimate California dreamer, had yet to visit California. He remedied that twice; in 1991 and 1997.

It was my conversation with Judy Gross that inspired this entire section. When I spoke to her about using her book "St. Ignace Car Culture" as a reference, she told me to ask dad about a famous pinstriper he met in California who knew it was him even though the two had not met.

So, I did and dad talked for nearly an hour about his first trip to the Golden State. We were both shocked that it never came up in our three months of interviews but were glad we finally discussed it.

As I spoke to him about a trip he took to California, he could not remember the year he went, but then something magical happened. As we spoke, he said, "Oh, wait, here is the ticket, it says August, 19 1991," he said with pride. "And people always give me grief for saving things."

Don't tell my sister.

Dad visited Frank and Kathy Livingston, planned a trip to George Barris's shop, The Grand National Roadster Show in Oakland, and also, a side trip.

He was fascinated by Dean Jefferies, loved his work since he was a teenager, building America's Most Beautiful Roadster. "We were patching our cars with bondo and dodging potholes, and Dean and Larry Watson were getting their cars on the cover of Hot Rod Magazines and cruising in Southern California.

It was a trip of a lifetime for him as he toured Joe Bailon's shop and watched him spray paint his signature creation, Candy Apple Red Paint, on a new build.

"We thought we were car guys," Dad said. "Um, no. They were around the same age and light years ahead of us in everything."

Driving with Frank and Kathy, Frank shouted out, "Hey, that is George Barris's shop, let's go see him."

The group walked in and George was on his hands and knees in a filing cabinet. This was 12 years after Mr. Barris came to St. Ignace mind you.

Dad called out to him with a hearty hello. Not turning to see who called out to him, Mr. Barris said, "Hey Ed, don't go away, I am in the middle of something."

George Barris recognized my father by his voice.

How does that happen?

As he showed dad around his shop, dad saw the Batmobile, projects for movies, and cars being readied for the Oakland Roadster Show.

"There were people everywhere in there. This was like a dream," dad said. "Mulholland Drive, Hollywood Boulevard, all that automotive history, there was no end to it."

The trip was also dad's first cross-country flight. The Rebel with no clue, the bag boy, the wild child, was 57 years old to finally realize his dream. He was in California and his heroes knew him by his voice.

But that paled in comparison to what happened next.

Dad told Frank that he'd seen Dean Jeffries shop, but Frank told dad that Dean was a recluse, did not like people and thought it was not a good idea to visit him.

And we all know how that went.

The shop was surrounded by wrought iron fences and guarded by fierce, barking Rottweilers. Dad walked around the side of the building, saw his hero, Dean Jeffries, a man whom he never met, coming out of the side of the shop as he heard the commotion being caused by Ed Reavie trespassing on his property.

Stopping in his tracks, Mr. Jefferies looked over and said, "Ed? Is that you?"

Dad was shocked that one of his heroes, a man who never put eyes on my father, recognized him. I hope it was this moment dad realized HE had risen to the level of legend and esteem in which he held his heroes.

How does this happen? To whom does it happen? Men like my father who never stop believing in their vision and dream.

Dad was invited into the shop, saw the Monkee Mobile, and was told flatly by Mr. Jefferies that it was he who created the Monkee Mobile, not Mr. Barris. It was a point of contention that drove the two apart and caused dad to walk a cautious line.

"It was like a priest meeting the Pope," dad said. "To be with the man who first uttered the word "bitchin" regarding the car scene was something I will never forget."

Dad and Dean conversed like old friends and spent three hours in Dean's shop. This mystified Frank Livingston who told dad, "Dean never spent three hours with a human being in his life."

Kathy told me, "Dean was not good with people and a bit cantankerous, but your father had the perfect personality and showed the respect to the culture that immediately put Dean at ease and then, there we were, talking with him in his shop."

From that point on, Dean Jefferies and the Livingstons became very good friends. "Your father's show was so good," Kathy said. "Everyone out here wanted to go there to see it."

Traveling the California car scene was a dream come true for dad, as he met all his heroes and was introduced to their heroes with the magical California energy everywhere.

"They knew everybody, and everybody knew them," dad said. "And now, they all knew me. Wow." Even at 82 years of age, my father still doesn't realize he is a peer to his heroes as he became a hero to so many.

Taking a side trip to see the man who started it all was a shock to the system. Meeting Tommy "The Greek" who started in the 1940's, was stuff of legend.

Dad walked into the warehouse and he saw Tommy who shouted, "Who the hell are you?"

"I am with Frank Livingston," dad said.

"You are not with the city, are you? I hate those bastards!"

"Sir, my name is Ed Reavie and I think we are going to be great friends."

He spent half the day with Tommy the Greek, talked about the early cruising scene after World War II, the first shows, and his pinstriping business that turned legend. Tommy told dad about how all the icons and legends, Barris, Jefferies, Bailon, Watson, came together and started the "California Cool" car scene.

When dad got home, a package from Tommy the Greek was on the porch. It contained a hand painted toilet seat.

"I still have the box it was mailed in," dad said. "I am looking at it right now. It's a keeper."

As I knew dad had many toilet seats, I asked him how such a thing, painted toilet seats, became collector items.

"The legend is, Joe Bailon was in his shop, hit a can of paint with his elbow, spilled it onto the closed toilet seat next to the work bench," dad said. "He stepped back and looked at the weird pattern the paint made, and said, 'well how about that?'"

The hallway leading to dad's office has six custom toilet seats on his wall from Ed Roth, Paul Hatton, Joe Bailon, The Alexander Brothers, and Tommy the Greek. All autographed. In his hallway. In St. Ignace.

You can't believe such a thing could be true. I dare you to even try. But it is. This is my father. Why only six toilet seats though? "That's all I have room for," dad said. Can't argue with that bit of logic.

He returned to California in 2003 for Wally Parks' 90th birthday celebration. "It just happened to coincide with the Winter Nationals," dad said. "How about that?"

The party was hosted in the NHRA Museum, and dad thought he was in a living, breathing, Hot Rod Magazine. "Everyone was there. All the legends, the drivers, the writers, the builders, and me."

The next day, dad had a thought. "I wonder where Bob Wingate's shop is?"

Dad called him. Bob was stunned and asked where he was. When he told him, Mr. Wingate told dad, "Turn around, look at that motorhome to your left, I am the one waving to you."

Right place, right time. Right man.

"How did I get here?" dad said of all this. "Do I belong? I was here and yes, for the first time, I think I belong. It just stunned me."

Dad ran into Bruce Meyers and was invited to his home to see his collection in Beverly Hills, two doors down from Jay Leno. This stunned Frank Livingston, a man who lived the life full time in California, as Bruce Meyer approached dad first and introduced himself.

Frank told dad, "I've lived here all my life and never met him and here you are talking with him like you are old friends. How do you do that?"

Kathy and I spoke for nearly an hour and she said dad was the perfect blend of person to make what he did so successful. He had a gift in the way he talked with people.

"He was so quick witted, so spontaneously funny, and made people feel like they've known him all their lives," Kathy said. "He treated all of us like family and his love for the culture was out there for everyone to see."

Later, during the VIP Brunch at the Grand National Roadster Show in Oakland, a who's who worldwide of automotive in attendance, it was Ed Reavie, promotor of the St. Ignace Car Show, introduced from the stage by the president and promoter of the greatest show in the country

"Your dad treated everyone like rock stars," Kathy said. "And when he came to California, they returned the favor."

He got the same honor from Bob Larivee Sr. during Autorama and said he is so proud to have that much respect from the two biggest show promoters in the country, and the two premier shows in the country.

The trip to California was "Bigger than life for me," dad said with pride. "I've read about all those men, all those places, my entire life and to be out there, in the middle of it, with them, changed my attitude in so many ways and reaffirmed my love of the car culture."

The biggest take away from it still gives dad chills.

"They all welcomed me like family, treated me like royalty. I will take this to my grave," he said. "Memories like this are the greatest part of my life. The best shows in the country, from California to Detroit, to Daryl Starbird in Oklahoma, knew me and gave me the greatest gift ever; they acknowledged me, and I finally felt a part of the car culture that shaped my life."

Chapter 29: Shifting Gears with Miss Linda Vaughn

1999 Guest of Honor, The First Lady of Motorsports, Motorsports Hall of Fame 2019

Linda Vaughn was a game changer.

With her unmatched charisma, grace, and sophistication, Linda took St. Ignace by storm from 1990-2010.

Mammoth crowds gathered for her autograph sessions, cries of "LINDA" filled the air wherever she went. She always stopped to take a photo and thanked the large crowd gathered for "shifting my gears all these years."

When I told dad that, after nearly six months of trying to get in touch with her, the interview happened, he showed a great deal of emotion. Linda is an icon in the motorsports world and carried that iconic image with her for two decades in St. Ignace.

He tried for years to get Linda to his show, but she was always booked. It took a phone call from a fellow icon to get her to come.

"Carroll Shelby called me and yelled 'God Dammit Linda you need to come to this show, it's your kind of show!" Linda said with her trademark laugh and Georgia drawl. "So that is what got me to start coming, Shelby got me good. This time I came. I fell madly in love with all of you in St. Ignace."

She remembered our first meeting at Indianapolis Raceway Park in 1989, and told me, "St. Ignace was wonderful, and it got better each and every time. Part of my summer was to come up and see you all."

Getting Linda to St. Ignace included getting her bags of Mackinac Island Fudge. "My favorite was getting the peanut brittle," she reminded me. "I brought back $100 of fudge and peanut brittle every year."

Once in St. Ignace, such was the draw that she came back 19 times in a row. "The passion of everybody, it was family, there was something different every year and I met more new people. It was incredible."

Working for the good people of Chevrolet who, Linda said, "Were double passionate about St. Ignace" was another great joy of being at the show.

Getting whitefish at The Galley Restaurant, right next to the large GM display, became a tradition. The entire team enjoyed a large dinner of whitefish together every year.

Craig Shantz and his team made things so much more enjoyable than any show Linda attended. "St. Ignace had a back home type atmosphere," she told me. "It was genuine. The love, the passion, the fun, everyone smiled. I never had a bad time in all my years. I was passionately in love with y'alls show."

I told Linda how many of her friends were coming to the show to see dad, and she immediately said she wanted to come to see him and her friends.

Being the only female Guest of Honor of the 45-year history of the show was incredibly important to Linda. "It was an honor Sean; it was an honor from your dad and I thank you so much for that."

Dad's endless passion still impacts Linda. "He was a true believer which is why I love him so much because he was honest, upfront, and a real fan of what he does. He loves what he is doing. I still love what I do, even after all these years. If people still want me, I will still go."

Incorporating the City of St. Ignace into his show and not the other way around was something about which Linda marveled. "He understood the town. He knew the culture, and he made this all happen through his passion."

Reminiscing about the show, I told Linda the 8-year-old boy at his father's side for the first show is now 55, she quickly added with a laugh, "Yeah, let's not talk about age."

The down-to-earth nature of my father is what made it work, Linda said. His passion equaled the passion of his heroes and allowed him to become one of those heroes himself.

"He certainly is," Linda said. "He is the creator. He did it all through pure passion and love and it showed. I changed everything around with my schedule to come back to St. Ignace every year."

It was Linda who reminded me she was the matron of honor at my first wedding. Although she had done this once before, she told me, "It was nothing like yours," referring to being on a boat under the Mackinac Bridge at Sunset being serenaded to "In the Still of the Night."

Linda and I spoke at length about the men and women who formed the genre and how sad we were to have lost so many over the years. Talking about our dogs, Linda said she has a dog named "Curly Joe Cocker" and after all these years of travel, was finally able to have one. Telling her about my French Bulldogs, Ralphie and Satan's Tater Tot, made her laugh.

"This will be a bestseller," Linda said of this book. "The stories you are telling need to be heard. Word of mouth from just us will help with that."

Not a month went by that dad didn't ask if I had talked to Linda yet, and this book could not be complete without an interview with the only female Guest of Honor in the history of the show. Mission accomplished, dad.

And, Nostalgia Productions LLC, made sure she came to town.

Chapter 30: Talking Car Culture with Mr. Jerry Palmer

Executive Director of Design for GM North American Operations. Corvette Hall of Fame. Chief of Design, Corvette (4th Generation)

Legendary Corvette designer Jerry Palmer was a fixture in St. Ignace for years. His work on the Camaro and Corvette lines led to incredible designs of those iconic automobiles.

Unknown to me, "Mr. Palmer" as I called him each time, I met him and during this interview, until he corrected me and told me to call him, "JP", had his early roots in the Upper Peninsula of Michigan.

A bar on West US2 called, "Millers" (eventually Little Hog Island Party Store) was owned by Mr. Palmer's Godfather, Jim. Baptized by a priest befriended in a bar, Mr. Palmer and his siblings were baptized in Naubinway. "I would go to church on Sunday, but I did not want to go to Catechism," he said as we both shared a laugh as I also had an issue with the same. Don't even get me started on my father's aversion to the church.

Mr. Palmer recalled Christmas morning in 1951, when he got a Lionel train set and built onto it, visualizing how to add to it while in church to pass the time. I mentioned the car brochures that kept my father occupied and we shared a laugh.

"Small world, your father knew Jim Miller," Mr. Palmer said.

Like all great automotive men who came to St. Ignace, Mr. Palmer (sorry JP) heard about this incredible show through another icon in the industry.

In this case, it was Bill Mitchell himself who brought photographic evidence of what an incredible show it was, photos that piqued the interest of all who saw them.

"I was overwhelmed at the quality and the number of the cars," Mr. Palmer said. "I met so many great people up there, especially the 'Yoopers' who were all characters and wonderful people."

St. Ignace holds great memories for Mr. Palmer. When he went back after the show, he encouraged and leveraged his team to go to the show themselves to see parts of automotive history.

"There was no bigger advocate for St. Ignace than Jerry Palmer," said Brian Baker, 2016 Guest of Honor and Vice President of the Automotive Hall of Fame. "He talked about it all the time and he was the reason I started coming."

The GM/Chevy contingent became the biggest presence at the show and occupied a huge spot right in the middle of the show grounds. "Everyone within 50 miles had a Chevy jacket on and we brought a huge contingent."

I shared a great story (told later in this book) about Jon Moss and my dad concerning Dodge and their display and told Mr. Palmer about my Challenger and the changes I made on it. After he asked me how many horses, I told him 425 to which he replied, "Good!"

"If I guy parks his car and doesn't turn around and look at his car, he is not a car guy," Mr. Palmer said with a laugh.

I shared stories about the show and my father, when Mr. Palmer said very matter-of-factly, "Your father was a wonderful man who knew his cars, he knew what car had what horsepower rating, and the difference in the engines between a '55 and '56 Chevy. He knew his business."

His 1932 Hi Top and the modifications he made, are a point of pride for him. Mr. Palmer told me it is good to always have something to look forward to and mentioned his ride is up to 450 horsepower. Car guys are great.

"St. Ignace is always fun," Mr. Palmer said. "I have so many great memories. It was something you looked forward to all year. It was the first major event of the summer."

During the winter months, when all the toys got put away and it was cold, gray, and dreary, Mr. Palmer said someone always called and asked if he was going to go to St. Ignace again. "YEAH! Let's go!" was his reply.

The excitement over what cars to bring both personally and professionally, that haven't been seen yet, was what got a lot of people over the wintertime blues.

"It snowballed from there," Mr. Palmer said. "I called my friends asking what they were taking up. Coming to St. Ignace, you always saw something new and different and that is what made them special."

A fond memory of the concept car going in reverse during the parade was already shared in this book, but the two of us got a good laugh from the first telling; all but the fuel pump leaking all over the ground near people trying to light their smokes.

"That would have made headlines," Mr. Palmer deadpanned, telling me that his passenger ran toward them, screaming to not light them. Turns out, the high-tech wiring system completely malfunctioned sending every possible signal through to the engine, wreaking havoc.

They took the car back to the proving grounds, and Mr. Palmer told me the car carrier loaded it into the transport when, out of the blue, the second deck of the car carrier collapsed and slammed to the ground with the car on it. It was destroyed.

The concept car was rebuilt using salvaged materials and turned into a prototype. It is still somewhere in the General Motors Archives and being shown.

"It would be so cool to bring all the show cars (from GM) that have appeared in St. Ignace, back to the show. Rolling off a list of cars, including the Mako Shark, Mr. Palmer said the right people need to make that happen. Right people, I hope you are reading this. Let's make this happen for the 50th St. Ignace show.

Mr. Palmer brought so many performance cars to St. Ignace, and said it was to stimulate people to purchase a Chevy.

As I ended my interview with Mr. Palmer, I thanked him for making such a profound impact on me as a young man. Every year that he came to the show, whenever he saw me, he approached me, extended his hand, and introduced himself. Here was Jerry

Palmer, legend. Corvette King in the tradition of Bill Mitchell, Harley Earle, and Zora, coming up to a 20-something kid and thinking enough of me to shake my hand and tell me who he was.

It taught me a valuable lesson that no matter your standing in life, making someone feel important is a part of being accomplished. Inclusion is everything. Empowerment is everything.

I explained to Mr. Palmer about my charity work and recognition received and let him know that I do the same thing to people I meet, most of whom respond to me, "Yes, I know, we came to hear you speak."

As I explained this to him, Mr. Palmer exclaimed, "That's fantastic!" Even though he did not remember doing this, I told him about how those moments amazed me and made me feel part of the auto world.

"The great thing about the show is you got to talk to people, tell them stories, let them hear how these things happened, how they came to be," he said. "This is a great American experience. I am pro America. I love cars, I love the people. The times in St. Ignace were great."

He recalled having lunch in a downtown St. Ignace restaurant with legendary race driver Phil Hill and was amazed to hear stories about his era of cars.

"The guys sitting in the audience were the big guys making it all happen," Mr. Palmer said. "It was quite a deal. Your dad had the recipe, he never screwed around with success."

Laughing again, Mr. Palmer said, "He put you through college with the t-shirt deal, right?"

Laughing right back, I told him, "Yes, indeed he really did."

"A good time was had by all, it really was," Mr. Palmer said.

And again, thank you J.P for spending so much time speaking with me and bringing back so many great memories.

Chapter 31: Unprecedented

"St. Ignace is where the action is."
Freddy Cannon, *Holds record for most appearances on American Bandstand and four appearances in St. Ignace. Also, the author's best man during his wedding in 1993.*

Charles "Chuck" Jordan, one of the most successful and influential designers of the 20th century, headlined the 17th Annual St. Ignace show.

While at M.I.T, Mr. Jordan won the Fisher Body Craftsman's Guild Model Car Competition, earning a scholarship.

Harley Earle's personal assistant, Howard O' Leary, invited the young Charles Jordan to come to work for General Motors after graduation.

And what a career he had.

Jordan rose quickly through the ranks, and Harley Earle himself named him Chief Designer of GM's Special Projects Studio. From 1957-1967, Mr. Jordan was Chief of Design for Cadillac.

In 1987, he was named Vice President of Design for General Motors. During his reign, Mr. Jordan was responsible for a great deal of iconic cars for which General Motors is known. A fine example of how high in regard St. Ignace was held by the top designers in the world.

Linda Vaughn came again, brought legions of new fans, satisfied old ones, and once again, brought the past alive in the here and now.

The cast of Honorary Guests was astonishing: Jerry Palmer, Bob Kaiser, Pat Chappel, Kay Buerigh, Doc Watson, Thom Petterson, Bill Couch Jr., Chuck Miller, Frank Livingston, Harold "Baggie" Bagsadarion, The Crystals, Bryan Hyland, Freddie Boom Boom Canon, Doug Thompson, The Shirelles, Mr. Merc Sterling Ashby, legendary artist Dave Bell, Crane's Detroit Business Founder Keith Crane, and legendary Thunderbird guitarist Jimmy Vaughn.

Add Cruise Night, the Down Memory Lane Parade, and the show itself. This was one show. Not a series. Not through the years. Not in the decade of the 90s'.

One show.

All those legends, all those cars in one place. like nowhere else in the world.

Later in my life (52) I was seriously injured on duty, I could not move around much. I ordered a guitar and decided to teach myself to play. I learned that I was able to "hear" notes and once I learned the key in which a song was written, I played along on the corresponding scales.

One of the first songs I learned to play was "Voodoo Child," along with "Sunshine of Your Love," "Layla," tons of blues songs, and some of my own.

I graduated from a beginner acoustic guitar, purchased for $150 on Facebook Marketplace, to a Fender Telecaster (butterscotch blonde like my idol Bruce Springsteen). I often shared with dad the songs I was playing. He told me he was friends with a guy who was a good guitarist and whose brother was a guitarist of some renown but dad, in the twilight of his mind, could not remember his name. He finally told me his friend's name was Jimmy Vaughn. I stopped in my tracks and said, "Are you talking about Stevie Ray Vaughn?"

"THAT'S HIM!" Dad announced proudly. "Do you want Jimmy's phone number?"

Such is the life being son to the original Mr. Reavie.

The beginning of the 90's saw dad embrace another part of the culture, and he started raffling off unique show cars.

His first car was a Bugatti Type '59 replica. He sold a ton of tickets and, as is his want in life, created another income stream to secure his lot.

Adding a fleet of vehicles with "Nostalgia Productions" on the side, Ed Ryan, dad's biggest helper when it came to driving the car around the show circuit, and later in charge of the Vendors, was an invaluable partner.

A professional model car contest was outsourced to give it the attention it deserved. I had moved away and started my life, living first in Hillsdale and later, Lansing, Michigan. Each one was four plus-hours away. I had little interest in the model car show as it took me away from being with dad and getting him point A to point B.

Dad's biggest skill was seamlessly meshing so many different passions in the same genre into one show. Fans of one segment soon became fans of all. Young and old, rich and poor, they all came to the show and left the better for it. As promotor and face of the show, dad saw a lot of cool things. One, in particular, is at the top of the list.

"We were driving together in the parade and I pointed for you to look at who was sitting on the bench," dad said with a laugh.

Only in St. Ignace could you see Chuck Jordan and Keith Crane sitting side-by-side on a bench, eating ice cream, and watching the parade of all American metal cruising under sunny skies, cool temps, and the vibrant hum of the good old days.

"That's America right there," Dad said. "Two men of their caliber, friends, just sitting there having an ice cream cone and looking at cars. It's the best, just the best."

The "California Kid," the 1934 Ford, owned by Pete Chaporis, was on all our clothing that year. It was the best-selling year in history and Bob Scudder, dad's partner on the clothing side, (and owner of Sign and Design in Pellston) had to run back to Pellston as they quickly ran out of items.

The t-shirt business outgrew our local supplier, Marv Winkelman, and dad was contacted by local radio personality Jim Scallin about a top-notch shirt designer who handled big orders and was perfect for the growing show. It was Bob.

I still have my shirt and jacket from that year and that car was hot. Jimmy Vaughn drove his candy apple gold paint Buick Riviera from Austin, Texas and waved to the crowd during the parade.

In early June of 1992, dad created a new show called "On the Waterfront," with Larry Shinoda as Guest of Honor. Please see the **table of contents** for the history of On The Waterfront, Antiques on the Bay, and Richard Crane Memorial Truck Show.

Bob Scudder was indeed the perfect blend of cool and creative, and a pleasure to work with during the heyday of Cruise Night.

So many shirts were sold that dad paid my entire college tuition. I recall walking into his office as if I were in the movie Casino, with all the cash he had on the table. At any moment I expected Robert Deniro to enter the room with a hammer and give dad two options.

With three successful, incredibly popular shows, dad kept what worked and scrubbed what didn't. In the early years, he had a picnic for everyone Saturday night after the show. That was before the parade and cruise night.

As the show grew, there was no way to accommodate that many people. With The Down Memory Lane Parade, organized to perfection by Merv Wyse, and the now-beyond-imagination Cruise Night, he didn't have time for no stinking picnic. There was action afoot and St. Ignace, as Freddy Cannon crooned from the stage, was where the action was.

Chapter 32: Mastermind

The creative mind of Ed Reavie developed multiple events to add to his world-famous car show; each could stand alone as a singular event and be successful. Added to his list of produced events, and it becomes inconceivable that one man could organize all this, as it was his HOBBY and not full time job.

The part of his show that overshadowed all else started when he was 16 as our bleach blonde rebel first "legally" took to the road to cruise with his fellow Rod Benders. His vision was cleared after seeing American Graffiti in 1973. After a few so-so years, Bob Goldthorpe and dad were the perfect mix to make it explode into the greatest show on asphalt.

Truly an event you had to see to believe.

I present to you the history of the most notorious automotive event in the State of Michigan, and possibly, the entire country.

Cruise Night

The Juke Joint was Jumpin'

Before the Cruise Night even happened, Dad lived it with Bucky and his friends who took their bitchin cars to Chiefs Drive-in on the North end of town near the St. Ignace Airport.

With their glass packs, hot cars, peroxide-aided blonde hair, leather jackets, and ducktail hairdos, the cruising was epic. Soundtracked by Buddy Holly, Elvis, The Beatles, The Rolling Stones, Bill Haley and His Comets, Motown, Chuck Berry, The Beach Boys, and all the great Rock and Roll of that era.

"Cruising exploded worldwide, as did our music," dad said. "We had Chuck Berry singing about riding along in our automobile with no particular place to go." "Just Cruisin" with Smokey Robinson, The Beach Boys had Fun, Fun, Fun, Jan and Dean cruised to Surf City."

"The cars were right in the middle of it," dad said. "It didn't matter what kind of car you had, what mattered was the radio and the music." The soundtrack of dad's life played from his multitude of automobiles as he listened to the top jocks of that era. For dad, "his" cruise was a validation of an attempt to recreate the best years of his life from 1956-1970.

"Each brought thousands of cars and thousands of people," dad said. "And it will never, ever end. As long as someone cranks up their tunes, shows off their car, and drives up and down the street, cruising will be alive."

One of the best moments of my adult life was when I purchased a limited edition 2014 Dodge Challenger RedLine. Through the years, I put on new side mirrors, a new spoiler, changed out the exhaust system, put in a cold air intake, and even changed out the gas cap. The car is a monster with 400-plus horses and a zero-to-60 timer built into the dash. When I was a detective and called out in the middle of night, this option was used on the empty roads from my home to the parking garage where my city vehicle was housed. Allegedly.

It has a Hurst Grip shifter and there is no greater thrill for me than to take it out to the Sonoran Desert Trail, turn up my tunes (usually Born to Run), activate the "sport" option, hit the gas, feel my body slam against the seat, and leave rubber behind me.

When speaking to legendary Corvette man Jerry Palmer about my car, he simply said with excitement "That's great!" He didn't mention the Mopar element, he was just thrilled I had a bitchin car and I was cruising. A true car man. The car is eight years old and has 52,000 miles. I will drive it until I can't.

Like the father, so the son.

I also get off topic pretty easily or as those who know me say, "wow, you randomly changed topics on me there." So, back to the story.

Cruising was a huge part of dad's life. He followed the legendary Joe Bailon and "Miss Elegance" and George Barris with his cars. Those men were three time zones and an entire world away.

One of the byproducts of our two-month conversation was dad digging into his files and finding things he'd forgotten long ago.

The first ever Street Rod to appear in St. Ignace (in 1976) was owned by Bob King. As we just talked about cruising, dad tried to find Bob King, an old banker friend, and was successful, talking with him about his 1923 T-Bucket with a 327 Chevy V8.

Bob Blair purchased the car from Ray in 1976 and ultimately, the car was sold to Jimmy Vaughn, a long time cruising friend of dads.

I still remember on a Sunday morning, I was in the 8th grade, dad got a call from Bruce Dodson telling him that Jimmy and his young son, Todd, tragically died in a car crash in that car.

Todd and I played basketball and little league together and I still recall the two of us being in the final of the Knights of Columbus Free Throw Championship. We tied and had to go to a shoot off. Todd went first and made two out of five. I made three in a row to win. Todd was to be in my high school class the next year. It was a tragic day in our town and for his wife Robin and daughter Sonda. "Jimmy was a car guy," dad said. "I could easily see him as my number two as the show grew."

Cruising was such a huge part of dad's life that he often struggled with being a new parent and running a household. When I was six years old, dad and his old friends saw a movie that changed their lives. Up there on the big screen were their formative years. The music, the cruising, the non-stop fun that came from a time most thought dead. There were two schools of thought in the early 1970s; Rock and Roll was dead as was America's love affair with the automobile.

Gas guzzling boats flooded the streets given little imagination for style. The airwaves were flooded with the sugary pop of The Carpenters, Neil Sedaka, Barry Manilow, and Abba.

The Beatles broke up, The Rolling Stones were passe, and the gas shortage stemmed cruising as dad knew it. However, that night in 1973, dad saw "American Graffiti" on the big screen and it changed his life, again.

"Even those that didn't like it (the movie) liked it," dad said. "It was infectious. George Lucas was a genius. Everything he did was right."

Knowing he had to do something with the momentum of American Graffiti still being everywhere, dad contacted Lou and Dorothy King, owners of The Chief Drive-in, and proposed an "American Graffiti Night."

Carhops on roller skates served a handful of cars that showed up in 1976. Dad gave a cassette with American Graffiti style music to play but the manager did not play it.

Word spread over the next few years and dad constantly tweaked the event from about 10 cars in 1976, to international acclaim as the greatest show on earth in the late 1980's and early 1990's.

"It became a monstrous event," dad said. "We tried to emulate Mel's Drive-in and didn't do too bad for a backwater town, did we?"

Starting small and eventually earning the nickname, "Woodstock North" the St. Ignace show attracted more than car show people, it attracted fans of fun, chaos, shenanigans, and criminal tom foolery.

The family event eventually became a circus and turned the sleepy lakeside town into a tire screeching, boozing, dangerous cloud of blue smoke that threatened not only the show's success, but also the safety of those who made it what it was.

Speaking about his once fun, rock and roll cruise night, dad told me "It got way out of hand. It turned into a monster."

In the late 1980's to the mid-90's, West US2 looked like an August morning in 1969 in a Bethel, New York alfalfa field. People were strewn everywhere in makeshift campsites erected without permit or permission. The stench of decadence surrounded the highway shoulders and on ramps, both North and South. Those who came were not car people and had no dog in the hunt. They quickly turned the town into the danger zone as hopped-up drivers burned rubber in souped-up cars and fishtailed to screams and yells downtown. A throng of equally inebriated patrons spurred on the behavior by pouring bleach on the road. Rubber burned, fuel injectors sprayed, screams erupted, and dad's blood pressure rose as he stood in the living room in a state of total befuddlement.

The first time I remember him showing his emotions about what could go wrong was when the two of us stood in the living room of our hilltop home, overlooking downtown. It was well past midnight. All the windows were open and if "holy shit" had a sound, it was that sound which filled the house. The entire house was filled with roars both from man and machine, as though being invaded by the crew from Mad Max. Such was the chaos, that there was a string of several years when dad and I did not go to bed, as we listened for crashes, sirens and the inevitable phone calls and fallout.

Men, women, and children crapped and pissed where they were, took drugs, and played rock and roll and rap music on their crappy stereo systems. Large amounts of them, in the throes of a malted hops frenzy, gave zero fucks about consequence as they thought laws did not apply to their bloody good time.

Nobody anywhere saw anything like it before. The security for all of this fell on the tiny St. Ignace Police Force with less than 10 officers, overwhelmed with the equivalent of a year's work in one weekend.

Tim Matelski started his law enforcement career during the first show in 1976, as a college student studying criminal justice. He watched over the cars in the Chalet North Motel. When he graduated and became sworn as an officer, Tim served the city of St. Ignace for more than 30 years, the last 23 as Chief of Police.

While in the academy, Tim recalled being called back to St. Ignace by the Chief of Police to handle the overflowing cars and crowd. One of his first orders was to approach the crew of the IceBreaker and railroad car ferry "Chief Wawatam" whose engineer decided, some say intentionally, to clean out their stacks during the show, coating the cars and patrons with ash.

Told by the Chief to go to the Wawatam and tell them to stop it. Just when Tim walked into the boat, they stopped. He turned around and went back, to praise from his boss. "I never talked to anyone," he said laughing. "They just stopped."

On top of the ash-spewing ship, this particular year it snowed for the first and only time in the history of the car show. That afternoon, it got so hot that Tim remembered his boots sticking to the pavement. Welcome to the Upper Peninsula.

Tim never missed a show weekend, worked every Cruise Night and watched it go from fun, hanging out with your friends and driving your cars, to a logistical nightmare of cars stretched for miles up and down West US2 leaving mayhem in their wake.

In 1986, Tim was promoted to Chief and was tossed right into the mayhem of Cruise Night. "I remember driving up West US2 and people on the sides of the highway were throwing beer bottles at the car," Tim said. His partner, Bill Borland, screamed, "These people are crazy."

The jail got so full, Tim said, "Those the least drunk, got released." In the mornings, the line of people waiting to get into the court to pay their tickets for public intoxication, racing, public indecency, and speeding, stretched around the building and into the street.

Such was the chaos, it was only a matter of time before something terrible happened resulting in drastic steps to stop it before that happened. The year after a crew of drunken hooligans broke out windows in downtown businesses, that drastic step was taken.

Enter "Zero Tolerance."

Even in the promotion of this book, 30 plus years later, people still piss and moan and bitch about "the show being ruined" by this policy. St. Ignace people, car people, businesses. Seemingly, the only way people can enjoy themselves is in a constant malted hops frenzy, crapping on sidewalks, and hurling insults and beer bottles at the police and innocent teenagers in marching bands. Now that is an impactful policy.

"We had a problem," Tim said. "We had women claiming they were raped, windows were being broken out downtown and it was enough. Enough was enough. We had to stop this."

While many think it was the Michigan State Police who enacted the zero tolerance, Tim said the idea was his and he had to fight for it to be implemented. "I was told by my city officials and the State Police, it would never work and we could never stop people from camping on the sides of roads, let alone people doing burnouts on the street."

Tim researched into camping and campsites and quickly realized that by cutting the grass on the highway, the City was unknowingly creating a campsite for anyone who wished to plop down a tent and campfire.

"I went to the Health Department, telling them that to be considered a campsite, we needed running water and portable toilets," Tim said. "If they cut the grass, they are inviting people to come up there."

Bringing the head of the Health Department to the State Highway Department, Tim said she told them what was needed to maintain public health requirements. With the dollar signs and manpower needed to do such things, the Highway Department quickly decided they were not going to provide those things and as such, the grass was left to grow.

Tim got two cases of yellow, "Police Line Do Not Cross" tape and strung it on extra posts around the area. "If we had to camp out here ourselves, all night, to make sure nobody camped there, that is what we were going to do."

Mary St. Antoine, the health department representative who helped pitch the idea to the Highway Department, gets all the credit from Tim for helping stop that madness from occurring.

I can only imagine the shocked look on people's faces when they arrived to stake claim to their little piece of shangri la where rules don't apply to their good time, only to see six feet of course, sticky grass and weeds for as far as the eye could see.

The reaction was immediate and complaints from both townspeople and would-be campers became well known.

"I became known as that no-good SOB who wanted to kill the car show," Tim said. "Fire Matelski and save the car show became the rallying cry for area business men."

Tim got grief from the highest reaches of city government from "going too far," stood his ground and shot back, "Show me the sign out here that says come to St. Ignace and act stupid."

The former "Glen's Market" across the street from the highway campers also reacted with anger and outrage over the decision as it meant a huge loss of revenue from alcohol sales. In the years to follow, the families who left the show because of the rowdiness out of fear their cars would get damaged, came back and made the show a family event again.

Zero Tolerance did not just apply to public displays of depravity, it also meant what people did in their cars. Officer Fred Paquin got a lot of credit from Tim as he worked the overnight shift and drove the policy home hard with the officers in his span of control.

Time recalled a bar brawl that Fred tried to break up, got bit on the leg in the process as he rolled around on the floor with the out of control drunk. Tim said Fred took out his mace and somehow, the stream of insanely caustic pepper spray ended up filling the man's mouth.

"That took the fight out of him," Tim said with a laugh. I had to agree as would most recruits in the academy who are required to eat a face-full of it to pass that exercise.

As an Instructor at the Arizona Law Enforcement Academy for five years, I once told a class of recruits who asked me about the upcoming "pepper spray day" while I was teaching them, it is akin to having someone soak your head in kerosene, then lighting a match and putting it out with fire ants.

Tim remembers going to the court hearing for the mouthful of mace man and the man was having a hard time not smacking his lips during the hearing. The judge, wondering why this man with the red face and watery eyes (the effects can last for days) was doing such an annoying thing, got this answer from the man; "I think someone shit in my mouth."

The answer sent me into a coughing fit from laughing so hard.

Street racing was another issue with people throwing water and bleach on the streets for the cars to do a burnout. This brought about high-risk safety issues.

The Big Boy scene during the Cruise Nights was nearly unmanageable. "All we could do was patrol the area, get out and walk around, and try to talk to people the best we could."

Simply parking a patrol car in a lot or on the street and activating the lights seemed to calm people down a bit. "This was back when I was a patrolman and it was a lot of fun to mingle with the people," Tim said. "Then I became chief and I had to work. I was the one responsible for this mess."

The chaos over all those years only produced one death when a young man lost control of his Corvette in the wee morning hours in 1981 or 1982. He raced over the railroad tracks at a high rate of speed, lost the backend, overcorrected, and went head-on into a tree on the main dock, killing him instantly.

Tim was the first officer on scene with Fred and remembered that awful night. "The 'Vette hit the tree so hard that the frame wrapped around the tree and sprung back. Every bone in that young man's body was broken."

Tim still remembers the driver's name and said the young man who died was picked up at Bootsie's Drive-in on the North side of town near hotel row, and the two took off for a ride through town. On the way back North, the accident happened.

"That was a hell of a way to lose your husband," Tim said recalling the emotional outburst from his wife when she was told.

With all the law enforcement agencies in the area, I asked Tim if it turned into a jurisdictional nightmare.

"Any of the bad stuff was left up to us," Tim said. "Michigan State Police assisted us but we took care of the things that happened within the city limits."

The car show took on a "twilight zone" feel where laws don't apply to those attending. When the police started cracking down, Tim told me my father was thankful for the hard work they did to bring the show back to a level of normal. Tim said that, through the years, there were many near misses that could have brought terrible press to the town and my father. One in particular was at the end of the parade where the Biblical rain hit.

The streets were soaked with water and one group had just left their lawn chairs where they'd watched the cars from the side of the road. A Corvette came along, punched the throttle, lost it, and fishtailed right into the chairs moments after they'd left. The amount of luck through the years was something for which Tim couldn't account. Hundreds of thousands of people in a town built for 2,000, and only one fatality.

I asked Tim his favorite part of the show, and he didn't hesitate, stating, "When it was done." Working 14-hour shifts, coming in at 5am, Tim recalled one year that the unseasonably high temperatures caused him to collapse from heat exhaustion.

He was taken to the hospital but refused to take any time off during the show. He came in at 5am the next day without missing a beat. "It was just Car Show, you did what you had to do. Everyone pitched in to make it work."

Tim recalled meeting Zora Arkus-Duntov as one of his great moments. He also really enjoyed meeting the Happy Days gang, Anson Williams, Donny Most, and Cindy Williams. Weddings took place, people came from all over.

"You never know what the show was going to bring," Tim said. "It was an amazing experience every year. Never in your mind could you think something like this could happen here, something this big and impactful."

Tim's one regret was never being able to attend the Guest of Honor Brunch to see all the superstars of the car world. "I had to work, but that is okay. We all did our part."

He retired from the force January 1, 2000, became head of the St. Ignace Marina, and turned that it into a real money maker. As for the events my father started, Tim is firm in his resolve about what they meant. "Your dad saved this city," Tim said. "It was the start of the summer. People come here every year to see this show. Your dad did a lot of work and people don't realize how much. It was all year for him."

Through the years, roles were defined, and things got easier. Officer Mark Wilk oversaw removing the people from downtown, George's Auto Body hooked up any stray cars, Pete Heckman (city manager) made sure the streets were closed, and when the sun came up, people were ready to go.

The Michigan State Police took over security on US2 and, during the thunder and lightning of the 80's, had four miles of blue gooses, bubble lights spinning, parked down the middle of US2 to stem the insanity.

A lifelong friend, Kyle McPhee (yes, Bucky's son) recently retired from the Michigan State Police. Unbeknownst to me, Kyle worked in an undercover capacity during the show for many years and was up to his elbows in hellions, street racers, and tom foolery on a scale hitherto unknown.

Kyle and I immediately started sharing memories of our fathers and he laid this gem on me. "My dad was strutting around like a rooster because he was beating everybody on the street," he said. "And then your dad gets the GTO. That was the end of that."

Kyle and I grew up together, played basketball together, both became police officers, and both had crazy, car loving fathers who happened to be best friends growing up. We had a lot to talk about.

Happily retired, Kyle has four businesses now, teaches at ten colleges for Law Enforcement, and is an expert witness regarding VIN verification and does forensic examinations on burned out vehicles.

Kyle attended Ferris State University and never took a single law enforcement class. Attending the Automotive School, Kyle wanted to be involved in the industry. Sadly, the automotive industry was hurting, and jobs were scarce. He sat in his living room and pondered his future, when Bucky walked in and asked what he was doing. He told his father he wasn't sure, and Bucky offered up a line straight out of the Kress Reavie universe.

"Well, I'll tell you what you're not going to do, is sit on the couch and do nothing," Bucky told him. "You have two choices; go into the military or take the State civil service exam."

Bucky signed Kyle up for the Michigan State Police test and didn't tell him about it. Successful, "The rest is history, I passed the goddamn thing by pure luck."

He embarked on his law enforcement career in 1989 and I told him that, during my time at the St. Ignace News, I was the one that put his graduation photo into the paper.

Kyle started his career in the highest paced, violent, crime soaked Post in the State of Michigan, and stayed for four years. When he graduated the academy and got that assignment, his Post supervisor gripped his hand and didn't say "welcome" he said, "Hang the f**k on."

"I was running on the jagged edge of disaster for four years there," Kyle said, making a statement I am going to co-opt for a later book.

Much like my training and first three years in the precinct containing the legendary (for all the wrong things) Van Buren Avenue corridor, Kyle and his partner, Trooper Bryon Egelski, badge #383, got a baptism by fire.

Both decided to transfer to a different assignment and Kyle went from the frying pan to the deep fat fryer by getting assigned to undercover narcotics.

Kyle was trained in covert surveillance and fugitive apprehension, got sent back to the Lansing Post in 1997, and was promoted to Detective Sergeant in the auto theft bureau. His superiors saw his degree in Automotive Technology and decided his skills would best be used there.

In 1994, I met Bryon when Kyle came out of the crowd to introduce him to me. He looked like God decided to make a Trooper and made Bryon. Nice looking kid, strong, smart, and motivated. Sadly, two weeks later, July 11, 1994, Trooper Bryon Egelski #383, was killed in the line of duty. I remember how it crushed Kyle and, to this day, he honors him on the anniversary of his death. When I experienced the loss of one of my partners, Kyle was one of the first to reach out to me. Our brotherhood is strong.

Years later, in a goosebump moment, he went to get his sergeant's badge from the quartermaster and he was told to go to the file cabinet and get his Detective Sergeant badge from the ones in supply. He pulled on the sticking door, gave a mighty tug and sent the badges everywhere. One badge flew out and landed on the floor face down.

Picking up the badge, Kyle saw the number and froze; it was #383. "I kept that badge until I retired."

In an amazing twist, Kyle's son, Dylan, now wears badge #1455 for the Michigan State Police; the same as his father when he was a Trooper, yet to be promoted.

I fondly remember Kyle getting me on the Michigan State Police driving track to take the powerful Dodge Charger around the circuit. After only a few laps, I was told my time was only a few seconds off of what recruits needed to qualify. That was fun.

With his background in undercover work, Kyle was tasked undercover for the car show. I saw him many times, always looking as if he just came home for vacation; which was the point.

"We went to a lot of swap meets and car shows looking for that one percent looming about in the background looking to run a fraud on people."

Kyle found numerous forgeries at shows, even stolen vehicles. "We waited until the show ended before confronting the vendors," Kyle said. "We never wanted to make a scene that could hurt the city or your dad."

The St. Ignace show proved to have very little in the way of fraudsters and charlatans, Kyle said. Even so, he focused on educating law enforcement.

Kyle met with the Troopers assigned to the show from Posts around the state and gave lessons on how to properly identify vintage cars, where the VIN numbers were, how to find them in the system, and to help speed along any traffic stops.

"I was a resource for them if they got anything suspicious on the stop," Kyle said. "They would call me and I would meet with them at their stop, and help them properly identify the vehicles."

The show grew to the point where Kyle got involved in intellectual property theft, that being knock offs of Michael Kors, Prada, and others. "Those companies do not screw around when it comes to people stealing their brand," Kyle said. "They would fly into the show and come right down to their booth and drop lawsuits on them. It was no joke."

One of Kyle's greatest memories is going to Cruise Night. "There were so many people, we were afraid someone was going to do a burnout and go flying into the crowd and kill someone," Kyle said.

Going UC into the crowd, Kyle tried to find the instigator of the burnouts, flag them, and have uniformed Troops slowly walk in and approach, "and that person would disappear from the show."

He spent time at the Big Boy during Cruise Night, was shocked and could not accurately describe the scene out there. Much like everyone who attended that festival and celebration of the American automobile and the alcohol intake capabilities of her inhabitants.

"Seeing the utter wildness on US2 one year, I think in the early 90's, there were so many Troopers that they were lined up down the center lane all the way to Miller's Camp (several miles away) trying to slow things down," Kyle said. "The Troops and other officers on foot looked like an army. I wish there was an overhead photo of it because, wow, it was impressive."

I remember this vividly. Looking West, to see nothing but a long red ribbon of rotating bubble lights, piercing the darkness as far as the eye could see. I looked at dad and we both just laughed.

"I can't believe I am seeing this," dad said, proud that he was.

Kyle remembers people sitting right on the side of the road, in lawn chairs, stretching for miles, and for hours, did just one thing. "They kept pouring bleach on the road!" Kyle said. "You just couldn't believe it. Girls were taking their shirts off, people were out of control. It's something that if it was a TV show would have hit pretty big if they were there."

When I told Kyle this chapter was named, "Woodstock North," he laughed and wholeheartedly agreed. A long-time car guy, Kyle showed his Lemans Blue 1971 Chevelle at the show and currently has a historic Mustang he keeps in great shape.

Now retired, Kyle said he is going to spend time going to Barrett-Jackson and the Mecum Auctions. Toward the end of the conversation, he recalled the book "Herding Goats" by Al Drake and laughed because dad made sure Bucky got into the book (as did Kyle) in recounting the rivalry, and dad's destruction of Bucky with his GTO.

And, my father's son made sure Bucky and Kyle are included in this one too; and Kyle's son.

Cruise Night turned into a decades-long event, and once Chief Tim retired, the mantle passed to Mark Wilk to take his turn as the top lawman in the city and work on taming the beast.

I'd told Mark what I wanted to cover and he said flatly, "What do you mean? Nothing happened during Cruise Night, it was a piece of cake," and then we both broke out laughing, having lived it for so many years.

Mark graduated High School with my sister Danielle in 1983 and is a life-long public servant to St. Ignace.

While in college, he earned his ambulance attendant license and began his career as a paramedic after graduating from Michigan Tech University with an Associate Degree in 1985.

A full-fledged paramedic since 1991, Mark graduated from the police academy in 1987 and was a dual police officer and paramedic.

Promoted to Chief of Police in 2010, Mark dealt with Cruise Night shenanigans in 1987 until the end of what was the first stage of Cruise Night on US2.

"It was Mardi Gras," Mark answered to my question of his impression of his Cruise Night experience. He filled me in on being an auxiliary patrol man in 1983 doing parking enforcement and "the walking information booth" which he really enjoyed.

"You have to have the ability to talk to people," he said. "You have to be friendly to people, you have to like talking to people." The best part of his job was talking to those from out of town and getting to know about them, he told me (and I agreed).

The first few years of Cruise Night, Mark directed traffic on West US2 and soon started asking the hordes of people sunbathing on the side of the road when they were going to the car show.

When they responded, "What car show?" Mark knew the paradigm had shifted from the hard-core car crowd to the hard-core party crowd just in town to raise hell and scorch the earth.

When Tim Matelski was chief, Mark talked about one yahoo who was livid with them during traffic control, not believing they would stop him to allow other cars out of the side streets.

The man sat revving his engine and screaming the entire time until he was allowed to go. He left a rubber trail and cloud of smoke behind him. Mark wanted to do something about it and Tim told him to hold off a bit. Suddenly, the car's drive shaft exploded, with bits and pieces of the car strewn all over the road. It was now a burned-out hulk of metal and rubber. With a smile, Tim looked at Mark and said, "Justice is served."

Even though St. Ignace Police was the host agency, Michigan State Police and their manpower took over the show planning and security. Briefings were often held without sending an invitation to St. Ignace Police and, at times, it stressed Tim and Mark to the max.

MSP had a plan to park police cruisers sideways across the road at midnight and announce to people that cruising was over. When Mark told them they cannot do that, an MSP lieutenant told Mark that she did not answer to him. The decision created a firestorm between agencies.

Things got bad when people began parking and camping on the cloverleaf surrounding the highway on ramps,

"The story was that the police ruined the car show," Mark said. "That is not the case. We want people to come to have a great time. But to have a great time doesn't mean you have to flash your breasts, drink, and create problems for everyone."

The family event of the 1970's and early 1980's was replaced with a level of debauchery that drove the family's high-end car guys elsewhere.

"We wanted parents to explain to their kids what the cars were all about," Mark said. "Not what those things were on that lady's chest. It got completely out of hand."

Happy for Tim's "zero tolerance" policy, Mark said it saved the event. If you squealed your tires, you were arrested. If you had alcohol, you were arrested. If you were disorderly, you were arrested.

For a jail built to hold 28 people, Mark said they booked 130 people a night. "The rules don't change because it's a car show," Mark answered to people being shocked they were arrested.

"But it's car show," was a constant refrain of those partaking in the malfeasance, oddly thinking the laws ceased once over the Bridge and into the friendly confines of St. Ignace.

The policy began to work quickly as people had to empty their pockets and have their weekends ruined because they were being knuckleheads. They soon went elsewhere to party and, slowly, the families and car clubs came back.

Still, the shenanigans were epic. In years past, there was a time officers could walk along among the crowds and engage them.

"Then the tables turned," Mark said. "And you did not dare go anywhere alone because you might not come back uninjured."

Mark recalled an incident with several couples when a bundled-up female came up to Mark and said, "Officer, I have to show you my breasts."

Back peddling as the woman tugged on her sweatshirt, Mark told her, "Ma'am, I am sure they are impressive, but if you do this, I will arrest you. You are going to jail."

Still the woman persisted and hiked up her shirt to reveal two pear shaped cardboard cutouts taped to her t-shirt covering her breasts. "That's the type of thing you enjoyed," Mark said laughing. "You can have fun, you can have conversations, it was great."

One call involved a large body-building male who shattered the window of his girlfriend's car. When telling the male that he needed to be arrested, he was less than convinced. With the very large Bruce Bigger with him, Mark told Bruce it would take at least five officers to get him into custody. "The man had muscles on his muscles and was well over six foot," Mark said.

Using all their verbal judo skills on the hulking male, he finally allowed the officers to take him into custody. When Mark asked Bruce what they could have done if he resisted, Bruce told Mark he was set to deliver the infamous "grab and twist" to a certain part of the male's anatomy to gain compliance.

As an officer of the law with several high-risk arrests that go south and get dangerous, I can neither confirm nor deny such a move exists. All I can tell you is it works.

Later, on that Sunday, Mark got a call from longtime Mackinac County Sheriff Larry Leveille. He asked him who arrested the Hulk and brought him to his jail. When asked why, Sheriff Larry told Mark, "Had we not kept him calm, I was worried he would break my jail."

Mark retired as Chief and 35years as a police officer, took a part-time job as a Deputy for the Mackinac County Sheriff's Office and still enjoys working patrol in his home city.

I saw Mark in 2019 dressed in brown for the first time after decades of the blues. It was great to see him. While he spent his career in a small town and I spent mine in the 5th largest city in the country, we are part of the same brotherhood.

"Your dad has impacted so many people's lives," Mark said. "St. Ignace is so well known because of your dad."

In the past, St. Ignace was associated with Mackinac Island. Now, no matter where you go, people immediately say to Mark, "When I tell them where I am from, they say Car Show."

Recalling a training interview, he attended in Lansing early in his career, the administration board asked Mark a series of questions regarding the position. It was the last question, posed by the Commander, that made Mark laugh.

Instead of asking a question relevant to the procedure, the man, knowing Mark was from St. Ignace, asked Mark, "Classic or Hot Rod?"

"St. Ignace got put on the map by your dad," Mark said. "Sadly, a lot of shows rode on your dad's coattails and copied what he was doing, even holding shows on the same weekend."

Sharing one last story, Mark recalled when the Mustang owned by Bob Seger, a legendary rock and roll star hailing from the State of Michigan, was at the show.

One spectator refused to believe the car belonged to Mr. Seger, going so far as to even scoff at the ownership papers they presented. Such was the scene she created, police had to be called. Showing the woman the ownership papers once more, she still gave no quarter.

Hands on hips, the woman proudly declared, "That doesn't say Bob Seger, it says ROBERT!"

Such is the life of a public servant.

"Mark Wilk was a real cool-headed guy," dad said. "I never had a concern when I knew he was there." Once the Cruise moved to the Big Boy, all bets were off, and things happened you could not believe unless you were there.

When I reminded dad about the woman who thought feeding a bear was a good idea, losing her finger in the process, he had a good laugh and wondered if the lady still thought it was a good idea.

Working with Big Boy owner Bob Goldthorpe, dad saw the event triple in size and then grow to impossible levels.

Dr. Ernie Fever, a local DJ, spun the records in the back of the restaurant in the first few years. The parking lot was full of dancing men and women (but no bears) wearing the clothing of the era.

For the most part, things were under control. Dad reached out to the management of legendary Chicago DJ Dick Biondi, and lived yet another dream. "I listened to Dick every night of my life," dad said. "There were many DJs out there, but Dick was a personality. There is a difference.

Dick Biondi became an icon throughout the Midwest on the blow torch of WLS radio and their 150,000 watts. His staccato, hyperbolic approach resonated with the times. He brought a palpable excitement to the airwaves, spun all the hits, talked a mile-a-minute, and made dad and his friends feel as if they knew him.

"When I first talked with him, I asked him if he remembered the first song he played after arriving at WLS from Buffalo. "He told me Alley-Oop by the Hollywood Argyles."

Dick Biondi's legend and hyperbole was immense. One such legend was that, upon hearing "That'll Be the Day" by Buddy Holly and the Crickets, he loved it so much that he played it nonstop and barricaded himself in studio to keep management out.

Depending on what you read about Dick, the scene is recreated (using another DJ) in the Buddy Holly Story using Hollywood Hyperbole of course, but it added to the legend.

Dick was the first DJ to play a Beatles record (She Loves You), his fame grew across the country, and he truly was the first DJ to gain that kind of celebrity.

He covered 26 states and Canada every night and was the Superman of the DJ world. Dad jumped through years of hoops to get Dick to St. Ignace and still remembers when Dick came into the Guest of Honor luncheon at the old Flame restaurant and stood in the doorway, late because he missed the shuttle from the airport.

"As soon as I saw him standing there, I knew I immediately hit the big time," dad said proudly. "Dick Biondi was in St. Ignace. There was a gasp from the crowd, and everyone wanted to meet him."

Now that the legendary jock was in St. Ignace, he came back time and again to be the MC at the Cruise Nights, often wading into the teeming, obnoxious, and intoxicated crowd.

Dick was a man slight of build and he asked me to go with him as I was not. Donned in my satin jacket, people wrongfully assumed I was his bodyguard but, in a way, I was. Disappearing into a frothing sea of party goers, they tried to pick him up more than once.

With Dick Biondi spinning the hits on a stage made especially for him, dad took a shot at landing the man who was the voice behind the music in American Graffiti; Wolfman Jack.

He dialed many "possible" phone numbers received from his sources in the entertainment industry, until one day, "Mrs. Wolfman" answered the phone.

He pitched his car show, name dropped Dick Biondi, and was on a roll until Mrs. Wolfman interrupted tersely by stating: "Who the hell is this and how did you get this number?"

Dad didn't make the impression he had hoped, but he got on the radar. By the end of the conversation, Mrs. Wolfman had all of dad's information, and remarkably, sent him a contract.

Once the sticker shock subsided, (legend has it $25,000 was the appearance fee) dad let go of that dream. Talking with those who had the clout to sign him, dad learned Wolfman was a hit and miss regarding performance.

Like most people, the first time a face went with the voice, was during Wolfman's appearance on American Graffiti when "Bob Smith" was seen eating popsicles when Curt came to the station to make his dedication to the blonde in the Thunderbird.

Regarding Dick Biondi, dad said it was a dream come true. "It was a highlight of my life," he said proudly. "Chicago had a lot of great jocks, but nobody like Dick Biondi."

Dad talked fondly of Dick's time in St. Ignace. He would drive Dick around just talking about cars and music. "You can't buy those memories," dad said. "Cruise Night brought so much to the table, not only for the city, but for me."

I reached out to Mr. Biondi's representative to schedule an interview, but sadly, was unable to connect with him. This happened a lot with trying to secure interviews as many of dad's heroes are enfeebled by age and illness.

As Cruise Night grew, so too did the demand for merchandise. It was 1985 and the Cruise had grown to the bursting point. Ever the capitalist, dad asked around for not only a clothing vendor, but a company that did in-house design work.

Enter Sign and Design out of Pellston, Michigan and owner Bob Scudder.

"Ed was a car guy," Bob said. "Look at what he created. It was unique in the sense it was so remote and yet, so many people wanted to go there. Ed created this…thing. And it was so cool."

He brought a staff of 20 people to handle the influx of people, but neither dad nor Bob knew what to expect. Bob was stunned when, ten minutes after opening his booth the first night, he sold out and had to send his crew back to Pellston, about a 45-minute round trip.

"We sold out like that," Bob said. "We were near the front door of the Big Boy and we opened, and it was gone." For 23 years, Bob provided show goers with high quality shirts, sweatshirts, hats, and jackets, all with a new, original design.

At the height of the show, Bob estimated 10,000 pieces were sold, which blew his mind. "Those were the good old days, it was new and unrestricted; which became an issue."

In contrast to law enforcement's thoughts, between the township and the city police, Bob felt it became heavy-handed with the public, regarding the "Zero Tolerance". "I don't think it was a good choice, and I get there has to be a balance," Bob said. "You have 100,000 people in town and have to control that. The question is how."

Bob did not want to criticize the decision, but felt the city brought a lot of harm on itself by raising hotel and restaurant prices so high that it drove people to other locations, taking millions of dollars in revenue with them. "I know this was one of the things that really pissed your father off, he never knew what to do about it."

Bob began coming to Cruise Night just as it was catching fire, and spent 23 years as the only official, sanctioned clothier dad allowed to use his brand and his trademarks.

"It was a party man," Bob said laughing. "US2 was simply wild. It was a party. Car guys are car guys. They want to cruise, and the party grew around them."

The Big Boy was the epicenter, the nexus, the fulcrum of, "Some crazy shit," Bob said. The crowds swelled, people descended on his tent to the point Bob had to bring equipment on sight to print on demand.

"I brought up everything I had. I took every shirt, every sweatshirt, all my equipment. I printed everything we had, and then I opened for sales," Bob recalled. "And they cleaned me out in ten minutes."

The fun of the times was not lost on Bob. For example, "Get liquored up and poke a bear," Bob said of the woman who did exactly that, losing a finger.

Seeing a much different side of my dad than most, Bob said working with him was very casual. The relationship was discussions concerning which car to place on the shirts, colors, and how many.

"Your dad was very casual about it, I showed him, he said it was cool, I sent him a check at the end of the show. Simple."

When I told Bob, dad said making the t-shirts was a license to print money, he agreed. "It was well into the six digits," Bob said. "And, he told me he put you through college."

He did. Thanks, Bob.

Wishing he could do another design for dad, Bob said a personal commitment keeps him from coming each year. "You think about this, all the heavy hitters your dad brought to town, it's really incredible. This is a great project you are doing, the stories need to be told. It is so cool."

Dad's hands off, unassuming approach to their relationship was what made it work. "Don't get me wrong, he would check in to see how sales were going," Bob said. "I am sure it was to make sure he could pay for your next semester of school."

"St. Ignace Car Show? It was one of the best experiences of my life," Bob said. "It was such a great time. Things were a lot easier then." Excited for the future, Bob said it's time for the "silverbacks" to step aside and make room for this newer generation of exceptional builders.

"The Cruise was a thing of legend with so many great stories and I am glad I was there for it," Bob told me. I couldn't agree more.

PART 12

Solving a problem-Ed Reavie Style: Muscle Car Mania and Antiques on the Bay

Chapter 33: Solution Oriented Promoting

"Best Show on Earth."
Murray Plaff, *legendary designer and 2019 Guest of Honor.*

Starting Muscle Car Mania was another stroke of genius from dad. He enlisted Dwayne Starr, retired Michigan State Police Trooper and Funny Car driver. He created this event to solve a huge problem during the show.

Cruise Night had gotten wild and dangerous with people doing burnouts up and down Mainstreet, drag racing on US2, and flirting with tragedy every year. The City and law enforcement, including The Michigan State Police, St. Ignace Police Department Mackinac County Sheriff's Office, and Tribal Police, were all over dad to end cruise night, to institute a zero-tolerance policy, and to arrest everyone who did this dangerous death spin.

Instead of telling people they couldn't do it and ending the program completely, dad charged the eager drivers to do it. He put them in a self-contained, controlled area, and let them burn out and drag race in front of a paying crowd.

Thus, Muscle Car Mania was born. "Simple. Capitalism at its finest," dad laughed.

One thing I've learned from my father is that everyone has problems, and nobody cares to have cheese with your whine party. Minus a solution, life's setbacks are not exclusive. Solutions to those problems are what separates you from the majority.

Muscle Car Mania was a solution to a HUGE problem.

One of dad's funniest moments during Muscle Car Mania was a night at the Cheboygan Fair Grounds during the burnouts. A young man had borrowed his father's Corvette without permission and entered the contest.

He gave into the crowd as they shouted and screamed for him to literally flame out. So he hammered the tires until they smoked, flamed, and then exploded, grinding on the rims, sending sparks and flames out the back. This sent the Corvette into a chain of events where it first blew up the engine and sent parts through the hood. It inevitably engulfed the car in flames and completely destroyed it.

"Come to think of it, we never saw that kid again after that. Makes you wonder," Dad bemused.

Dad wanted to bring that show to St. Ignace, so he partnered with the local casino which constructed bleachers and paved a mini drag strip. Legendary NHRA and former show Guest of Honor Dave McClellen was the voice from trackside and people flocked to it, paid for the privilege, and everyone had a ball.

As the driver of a Jet Fueled Funny Car, Dwayne had reach in that community and soon, with like-minded daredevils coming to town to compete, it was another incredible success. Such was its success that dad called Wally Parks, who historically loathed Jet Cars as beneath the Top Fuel dragsters, funny cars, and street machines he made famous, and told him about it.

Through some stroke of fate, Wally invited dad and Dwayne to the U.S. Nationals for an exhibition run during the 2001 U.S. Nationals Friday night opening ceremonies. Dad looked around and was surrounded by NHRA superstars as they stood with him to watch.

He still got goosebumps as he told me this story. He was on the track, helped light the jet, and felt his glorious head of hair blow back as Dwayne catapulted off the line in front of a capacity crowd at Indianapolis Raceway Park. On the microphone? Mr. Dave McClelland himself.

That Wally Parks himself asked a personal favor like that from dad, showed how revered he was to his heroes. In fact, Dwayne got "pissed" because Mr. McClelland talked up Dad and his show the entire time he was in the dragster, waiting for his accolades which never came.

"Hey man, you have to pay your dues," Dad said with a laugh.

Chapter 34: Antiques on the Bay

Another major problem: the cars and people who came the first few years of the show, the old school, antique car owners, were disappearing as the show took on a much different look heading into the 90's.

The first St. Ignace Show, then known as the Straits Area ANTIQUE Auto Show, grew massively with an influx of modified street rods, muscle cars, and hot rods but it caused the old brass era cars to fall by the wayside.

"If you saw one Model A, you saw them all," dad said. "People lost interest fast because they all looked the same and they looked for the chopped 1932 Coupe."

The antique car owners approached dad with their concerns of being pushed out of the show. The realty was, however, that the new generation of car show spectators favored the chopped, slammed, flamed, nosed, decked, and fantastic muscle cars over the colorless, older models.

The show started being called "The St. Ignace Hot Rod Show" and went through its hyper-growth mode. It brought in ever more daring custom builds and sensational show cars. So, dad decided to once again make whipped cream out of sour milk.

The very first Antiques on the Bay started in 1997, one year after the Truck Show. The caveat was simple. The cars had to be antiques (25 years or older) and have no modifications. Kress would applaud.

As the Tractor Show preceded the Truck Show, so did Antiques on the Bay precede the St. Ignace Car Show. The Musser Family (owner of the Grand Hotel) donated a free weekend stay to the best of show winners. There were parades, bridge rallies, and again, an entirely different crowd.

The show was laid back and casual with no huge engines smoking nor tires burning. Cars that came from Meadowbrook and from barn stalls filled the streets.

Antiques on the Bay provided another income stream to the town for 26 years and gave people a place to show their antique cars.

"We went right back where we started from," dad said. "It was a beautiful show." With the demise of Antiques on the Bay, dad lamented the city was once again putting on one show for the masses.

One show, while profitable and impactful, put dad in a box and, like the public relations genius he was, he simply created a show to cover all aspects of the motor world from big rigs to tractor trailers, to Model Ts to hot rods.

"I hope one day, they bring it back," dad said. "It was terrible when it went away," dad said. "I don't want to dwell on it but it pissed me off."

The simple fact is that a committee of people, with money behind them, could not pull off a series of successful shows that one man made look easy.

With yet another successful show, dad attributed it to how he thinks about the shows he started. "I invite orphans," dad said. "Like the plain Jane's who never get a date, so I decided to fix that."

He invited station wagons and four-doors, dad marveled, "They came out of the woodwork," he laughed. "My god they were everywhere. What a great idea, if I do say so myself."

He highlighted the collectors that were not in the mainstream of car show participants, successfully worked niches, filled them, and drew huge crowds.

"Fall in St. Ignace is a beautiful thing, leaves are turning and so are the sun tans," dad said. "Two weeks after Labor Day, I created a swap meet of antique snowmobiles, toys, peddle cars, and a few 18-wheelers to fill in holes."

Labeling it a final call for showing any type of item with wheels, the "On The Waterfront Show and Swap Meet" again showed dad's forward thinking and his eye for things people wanted to see. One of those things was a helicopter ride, and people really loved it, and to this day, dad never figured out the opposition to it.

"Oh my God, the bitching over that helicopter got me in a lot of trouble," dad said. "One day of the year, something people came to town to do and paid for the privilege, and the powers-that-be hated it."

With his signature show series growing rapidly, dad produced Antiques on the Bay, The St. Ignace Car Show, The Antique Tractor Show, On the Waterfront, and the Richard Crane Memorial Truck Show, never taking a break to relax because, to him, this is what helped him relax.

Keep in mind, he still had his full-time job at the First National Bank. His ability to compartmentalize, organize, and execute, was beyond comprehension.

Years earlier, Tom Monaghan, the former CEO of Domino's Pizza, called my father the most organized man he ever met. Still, dad felt something was missing, some segments of the hobby were overlooked. Thinking back to his childhood, dad fondly recalled "The Howdy Doody Show" as a staple of television.

"I set out to find Buffalo Bob Smith," dad said of the legendary man who spoke through Howdy Doody. Dad found his agent, called Bob Smith and the two had a wonderful conversation. Bob agreed to come to the first ever "St. Ignace Toy and Hobby Show."

"He was in my house. He was here," dad said. "We set up a peanut gallery and had a great time." The St. Ignace Waterfront Fall Meet included the Toy Show, to rave reviews.

Legendary Honey Radio DJ Boogie Bryan told me he was so struck at seeing Buffalo Bob in St. Ignace that he was unable to approach and talk to him. "I was an adult and felt like a child again," Boogie told me. "I still kick myself for not saying hello to him."

"We did a lot of cool things here," dad said proudly. "Anything with wheels, we brought here. We did a little bit of everything."

There were also 30 to 40 custom-made pedal cars on display, with their own music and themes, just another element of variety not matched with any series of shows in the country.

The Howdy Doody Era? Check. Pedal Cars? Check. Every era of car ever conceived? Oh, yeah. The history contained in one man and in one small city such as St. Ignace is unique and impossible to comprehend.

PART 13

Bride Over Troubled Water

Chapter 35: In the Still of the Night

Stunned that my girlfriend didn't bail after "The Last Supper" we decided to marry in 1993 in Grand Ledge, Michigan. A funny thing happened on the way to the chapel; the owners bailed, stole everyone's money, padlocked the door, and left us high and dry.

I sought dad's counsel, and it was two seconds before he blurted, "Why not do it during the car show? Hell, all these folks watched you grow up! It will be perfect."

Well, that was easy.

It was June 24, 1993. I was in my tuxedo awaiting the arrival of my wife-to-be on the top deck of the Arnold Line Catamaran. Mom's house party, long ago outgrown, now happened on the three-deck, high-speed Catamaran boats that skimmed between Mackinac Island and St. Ignace.

My fiancé had been driven to the dock by Jack Walker in the 1941 Ford Roadster "String of Pearls" and stayed below decks as I awaited her on the top.

We stopped at Mackinac Island to pick up Mackinac Island Mayor Margaret Doud, whom I came to know working at the Mackinac Island Town Crier. She came topside and we headed to the Bridge.

The Catamaran idled underneath the majestic Mackinac Bridge and created a surreal backdrop as the sun sank into Lake Michigan, cast in a reddish, orangish glow, with wispy clouds glowing a rainbow of cotton candy colors.

Mayor Doud performed the ceremony, with Freddy Cannon in his place as best man and Linda Vaughn as Matron of Honor. My father told me it was a one-in-a-million chance and a story for the ages. Guess what? I am telling the story.

The boat free floated under the Bridge and a large freighter warned the captain they were about to "Flatten you like a pancake" if we did not move.

Sinking into the Straits of Mackinac in a flaming, twisted ball of molten metal and screams of terror was not on the itinerary, so our Captain told us to take a seat and we motored on to our destination.

"That was an amazing thing for me," Freddy Cannon told me. "Thank you so much for such a great memory. I was the best man during a wedding on a boat, floating underneath that amazing bridge at sunset. It really doesn't get any better than that."

"It was beautiful," Linda Vaughn said. "On the top deck of that boat under the Bridge, there was nothing like it. It was amazing to be part of that."

During Saturday's concert, Freddy dedicated a song to us, a moment he remembered when I got in contact with him again. "It was a beautiful moment in my life," Freddy told me. It was during that show that he performed a song he wrote for his wife Jeanette.

When I contacted him, I was sad to learn Jeanette was suffering with dementia and Freddy was at her side, tending to the love of his life. We didn't have a lot of time to talk but I told him how much he meant to my father and me.

"I have nothing but fond memories of coming to St. Ignace," Freddy said. "I loved your father and I loved that show. It was four of the greatest years of my life. Tell your dad I love him and thank him for everything he did for me."

You just did Freddy. God bless you and your beautiful family.

Chapter 36: Talking Cars with Mr. Jack Walker

"St. Ignace is my favorite show. Ed is the smartest man in the world. Look at what he created"
Jack Walker, *legendary custom car builder, builder of the Hirohata Clone, String of Pearls, Eclipse, and the 2017 Guest of Honor.*

Jack Walker first came to St. Ignace in 1986 and brought with him one of the most legendary clone cars ever built; The Hirohata Mercury.

"I was really impressed with the show and the high dollar cars that were in St. Ignace," Mr. Walker said. "I had never seen so many Reliable Truck transports in my life."

He first showed the car at Bob Larivee Sr.'s Autorama said once he returned home, he got a phone call from a man telling him he wanted him to bring the car to this place called, "St. Ignace."

Mr. Walker was just getting started in the circuit, said he didn't know anybody in the industry, and wanted to get out to promote the car. When dad called to make the arrangements for him to take the car to St. Ignace, Mr. Walker jumped at the chance.

One problem.

"I had no idea where St. Ignace, Michigan, was," he told me. "No. Idea." Mr. Walker contacted a friend to go to dinner and told him that dad had called and invited him to show the Mercury in St. Ignace, and he asked the friend if he wanted to come with him.

"So, we get the map out and my friend asks me where in the world St. Ignace was," Mr. Walker said with a laugh. "I told him I had no idea but it had to be close to Detroit because that is where your dad saw the car."

Mr. Walker looked at the map for a long while, finally located St. Ignace, and exclaimed, "Jiminy Christmas, look where I have us going. Do you see where we must go! A man is no better than his word and I told your dad I was going to go, so I went."

The trip to St. Ignace was a thousand-mile journey, but, true to his word, he made the long haul to show his car. With the Mercury on a ramp trailer, Mr. Walker pulled into the K Royal Motel and looked around.

"I had no idea where I was at but knew I was somewhere that was going to be big," he told me, after seeing hundreds of cars and thousands of people cruising up and down the streets well in advance of the show.

Then it rained and trapped Mr. Walker in his hotel room for an entire day. "I thought I would never go back but then the sun came out and I did the show and the 'never going back,' turned into going for 13 consecutive years."

The most amazing thing to him was seeing the entire town of St. Ignace being the show. "When I got there, the only person I knew was the guy who went with me, I didn't even know who your dad was because I had never seen him before," he said with a chuckle. "By the time we left the first function, we knew a lot of people. It was really overwhelming to meet so many people in one place and to be so friendly to you."

During the show, Mr. Walker strolled to the top of the hill and looked north at nothing but cars and people. It stretched for nearly a mile. "As far as you could see," he said. "It took me a long time to walk to that point because of all the people."

Mr. Walker thought of how odd it may have been to people who didn't know anything about the show (and they exist) and wondered what it felt like to park your car on the dock and go to the island, only to come back a few days later and see nothing but people and show cars and you can't drive anywhere.

That happened. More than once. Including a future Chief of Police. "They must have thought they were in a different world," he said laughing.

The entire experience amazed him, and such was Cruise Night that year, Mr. Walker had only this to say: "Unreal." Add to it, being downtown at 3am, in the dark, with the registration line already forming, and cars being parked for the show that didn't start for another six hours.

"With more than 100,000 people here, where did they all park?" Mr. Walker said with the rhetorical question.

A former Missouri drag racer, Mr. Walker went to a car show in Kansas City and saw a Corvette with gull-winged doors that was in a great state of disrepair. He found the owner and offered his dragster as a trade. The man accepted but told Mr. Walker the deal needed to include the trailer.

One thousand dollars later, Mr. Walker took the car to Tulsa, Oklahoma, had it fixed and repainted pearl white. Once it was fixed and painted, the interior was replaced, and the engine rebuilt.

In its ISCA first show, the car known as "The Condor" took first place. Mr. Walker showed the car around the circuit for seven years and won multiple Best Custom awards. He was hooked.

He purchased a truck called "The Eclipse" and enlisted Doug Thompson (the original customizer and Hall of Fame North inductee) to help him redo it. They turned it into an insanely cool custom.

It was during the customization of "The Eclipse" that Mr. Walker happened to come across his next project. One day he was on the way to his shop when a 1950 Mercury passed him on the street.

"You know what? I knew I needed to get one of those."

He told Mr. Thompson that their next project was to be a 1950 or 1951 Chop Top Mercury. Mr. Walker found a 1951 Mercury and went to work on it. When Mr. Thompson came to look at it, the friends decided, "We wanted to clone the Hirohata Car."

The Hirohata Mercury was George Barris's most famous custom, considered lost and part of legend. The project had been attempted once and the customizers failed to get the roof right.

When Mr. Walker decided to take the chance, he told Mr. Thompson they needed to clone the Mercury to perfection. "And that is what we did." They kept each other in line to ensure they stayed exactly to task, and even pressed the identical license plate Mr. Hirohata had on the original car.

The car took the industry by storm and was in great demand. Mr. Walker took it everywhere. The outdoor shows started to fade the green paint white and, while he was in St. Ignace, Mr. Walker met Chuck Walker (future Guest of Honor and Ridler Award winner) and hired him to paint it back to the original.

After the paint was completed, Championship Auto Shows Inc. (owned by Bob Larivee Jr.) called and asked to lease the car for two seasons to take it across the country. "If anyone told me that all this would happen with it, I would have called them crazy. It went legendary overnight. It was incredible."

Over his many years in St. Ignace, meeting Chuck Miller and Dave Bell was a highlight. With his otherworldly artwork and "Henry Highrise" cartoons, Dave Bell gave St. Ignace national exposure, and drew entire cartoons based on the show that appeared in Street Rodder Magazine.

I design logos for my own charitable foundation shows and I use Dave Bell's influence on how to put words into the designs as he did. Another legend in St. Ignace.

I told Mr. Walker that, if dad could own only one car, it would be the Hirohata Mercury. One of Mr. Walker's creations, The String of Pearls, was my wedding car. Catching up with him after so many years was one of the great byproducts of writing this book.

Mr. Walker shared a story of when he let dad drive the Hirohata Clone. He said he watched dad drive through town, waving to everyone, with hundreds of show cars and thousands of people lining the street.

"I told your father that the merchants in St. Ignace needed to be kissing his butt for the money he brought into the town. It was all him who did it. Who would've ever heard of that town without that show? Without your dad?"

Another perfect rhetorical question.

"Your dad was the smartest person in the world," Mr. Walker said. "I told him, you knew who all these people were, and you knew you would never meet them so you put on a show, invited them, and they came. Look what he created. This is my favorite car show."

Chapter 37: Doubling Down on Legendary

"If you want to have your faith in the car hobby rekindled, come on up to St. Ignace."
Keith Crain, *publisher Crain's Detroit Business and 2000 Guest of Honor.*

The 1993 show was, again, spectacular.

Steve McQueen's Indian Motorcycle Display from the Imperial Palace in Las Vegas was on display.

Tom Gale, head of Chrysler's Styling Department, drove a Plymouth Prowler from Chrysler World Headquarters in Auburn Hills to highlight a MOPAR Muscle Show.

Miss Nostalgia Productions Jennifer Brown debuted in her stunning red, white, and blue bikini and learned from the master show woman, Linda Vaughn, how to work the crowd.

At a show in Flint, Michigan, dad watched as a stunning young woman, clearly the crowd favorite, lost the bikini contest to the show organizer's daughter. The crowd booed the winner and dad applauded Jennifer as she was clearly the people's choice.

Dad approached her with a business card, told her she had a great future and wanted to hire her to work his show. He told her where he was in the event, and if interested, come talk to him. She did and was a highlight at the show for many years, and on trips around the state to promote his shows.

A red 1957 Chevy was raffled off. Jack Walker brought several of his beauties. Big rigs and show trucks from Dick Crane's American Truck Driving School convoyed into St. Ignace, adding another element.

Dad was a showman and brought in anything he thought would give a family exposure into every nostalgic niche.

Don't like show cars? Great, how about a concert with Gary US Bonds? Hate sitting in a chair near your car? Great, here is a fantastic gallery of art, clothing, shops, restaurants, and cafes occupying the entirety of St. Ignace's main street. Kids bored? Send them to the swap meet, toy show, and model car contest.

Need a break? Stand near the marina and take in Lake Huron's sparkling waters, take a boat trip to Mackinac Island, and just breathe in the smells of wall-to-wall fun.

Dad made people literally create ways to be bored. The show's energy was unprecedented. There were legendary racers Art Arfons with his iconic Green Monster Jet Car, record setting racer Phil Hill and two-time Indy 500 Champion Gordon Johncock for IndyCar fans.

Trophy-winning show cars from Pebble Beach, Oakland Roadster Show, Autorama, Concours D' Elegance shows nationwide, or your old buddies under-renovation Shelby Cobra all lined the streets of St. Ignace.

Everyone with passion for all things car culture came and broke single-day bridge crossing records, as nearly 50,000 cars came to St. Ignace just from the south, to say nothing of those who came east through Wisconsin.

"They just kept coming," dad said. "There was no end to them. From electric to Rat Rods. It was incredible."

There was a James Dean lookalike contest, auto auction, an automotive art gallery, a Hemi Under Glass Barracuda, classic Mercs in the Mercury Corral, The George and Sam Barris collection and awards.

This was all available to the crowds. A Japanese Auto Journalist came on his own dime and created the first bi-lingual automotive magazine to feature St. Ignace.

The show's growth was evident by the 78-page printed program that listed all the guests and cars. The 20th Anniversary Show, headlined by two-time Indy 500 Champion Gordon Johncock, and Roger Gustin, with the Lava Jet Car, and automotive business publisher Keith Crain.

I learned a valuable lesson from Keith Crain in all the years he came to show, he was professional and all business. Recalling a conversation he had with long-time mayor Bruce Dodson over bridge fair, Mr. Crain smiled and told the mayor, "Never argue with a man who buys ink by the barrel."

Years later, I was in Cleveland going through the Rock and Roll Hall of Fame. Near the Otis Redding plane exhibit, I saw Mr. Crain and a group of businessmen looking through the other side. I did not approach him, as I was not on the same relationship level with my father. I would wait for him to pass and smile.

As I was reading about the plane, I heard, "Well imagine meeting you here." I turned to see this bear of a man with his hand extended. He shook my hand and introduced me to his friends as he gushed about my father's show. He slapped me on the back and told them I was a chip off my dad's block before saying goodbye and walking off.

Sometimes the reason people are successful is because they treat everyone the same and by doing so, make you feel important. I never forgot that. I have piles of commendations from civilians because of the way I treat them. Learn from the best. Do what they do.

Thank you for the lesson, Mr. Crain.

Letter from a Legend – Keith Crain

Dear Ed,

It was a great 15 minutes of fame. You are a great host, not to mention the entire city of St. Ignace. I feel like Neil Armstrong, I've walked on the moon and now there is nothing else to do.
It was a great few days and I cannot tell you how much I enjoyed the event and the three days and I want to thank you for making it so enjoyable. I look forward to attending many events of yours

in the future and it is my wish for us to grow old together in our Hot Rods.

Thanks for the great time and I will see you all soon.

Keith Crain-Chairman
Crain Communications and 2000 Guest of Honor

Chapter 38: Talking Cars with Mr. Tom Gale

Head of Design, Chrysler Corporation and 2001 Guest of Honor

Bringing Tom Gale to St. Ignace was a major event for dad. Years prior, Mr. Gale had worked to get sponsors and amazing displays for the show, including the Viper display. The show was well known by the time Mr. Gale came to St. Ignace and he was already a resident of Northern Michigan when "St. Ignace" burst onto the scene in the late 1980's, early 1990's, he had a great idea about what lay ahead.

"Your dad really built something beautiful up there," Mr. Gale said. "The show matched my expectations when I finally saw it."

Cruise Night was a favorite. "Back in the day, Keith Crain, Chuck Jordan, and I just sat on the curb watching all the cars go by. It was awesome because we just networked with each other with no particular agenda or place we needed to be," Mr. Gale said. "It was just fun. Get an ice cream cone and sit there. It was one of the most enjoyable things and times we had."

St. Ignace was a meeting place for a lot of legends and Mr. Gale said it was wonderful to support my dad and honor what he was trying to do.

"St. Ignace doesn't get the credit it deserves for already being an iconic place," Mr. Gale said. "You have the Bridge, the Island, the Straits of Mackinac, and the incredible views." The surrounding area was perfectly utilized by my father, Mr. Gale said.

"It was an eye opener for a lot of people," Mr. Gale said. "Not only from Detroit, but from California. That was a pretty neat thing and the area is amazing. It was a well-kept secret."

The show was rich in legendary people and iconic cars. Meeting men like Gene Winfield and the other headliners. "The show to me was all about cruising, I enjoyed that so much."

One of my father's favorite stories concerned the launch of the PT Cruiser and that vehicle's mass appeal. There was a waiting list for the car and dad, never prone to hyperbole, loves telling the story of Tom Gale, the PT Cruiser designer, walking his work order to the front of the line to ensure he got his reasonably fast.

"I think we did try to get him a car by advancing the order for him," Mr. Gale said. "I had forgotten about that, but, yeah, we did that."

The success of the PT Cruiser was a lightning in the bottle moment with more than 1.3 million units sold, but it soon fell out of favor with the media, which rankles Mr. Gale to this day.

"It was different. For the time, it was perfectly acceptable. It brought the acceptance of five door cars to this country," Mr. Gale said. "It was remarkable. The journalists fancy themselves experts but have no clue as to what goes into the design of a car."

Mr. Gale's finest memory is when Lee Iacocca saved the company which allowed their designs to really flourish. They had more than 50 concept cars and Mr. Gale said many of them came to St. Ignace.

"To be in such dire straits in the 1980's to roaring back in the 1990's, was a proud achievement for a company to do as well as it did. Lots of people put their heart and soul into bringing the company back."

The comeback included the Viper, The Prowler, The Dodge Magnum, and other fantastic cars and designs, all of which came to the show. The show itself saw many different genres of car culture in the same place. There were antique license plate vendors, vendors selling wrenches, other tools, and memorabilia all to attract, "The gear head to the show," Mr. Gale told me.

My father's legacy is secure, Mr. Gale said. "It puts him right up there with the California show, the Oakland Roadster Show, Autorama, and behind them all was a person who was an enthusiast, that's the common denominator."

Having a single-minded purpose is essential to success in anything, Mr. Gale said. "Some people have no idea as to what is cool and what is not," he told me. "People have to have an understanding that this is in the heart and soul of the people driving it."

What dad accomplished, "was amazing. It's a great story. It was a remarkable time to be there," Mr. Gale said.

Chapter 39: Rat Fink in da House

"Ed Reavie is an artist when it comes to auto show promotion."
Ed "Big Daddy" Roth, *from his book "Confessions of a Rat Fink," and 1996 Guest of Honor.*

The colorful and interesting characters, straight out of car magazines, who walked through our home never ceased to amaze me. The biggest and wildest one of them all was none other than Ed "Big Daddy" Roth; legendary designer, artist, and human.

Late for his own Guest of Honor Brunch, Big Daddy strolled through the doors in ratty jeans, top hat, and a stained, blue sports coat. He opened the coat to show one of his t-shirts with the legendary Rat Fink design, to deafening applause. He later showed up at dad's house, covered in chicken wing bones that fell out of the car and onto the driveway, and asked if he and his son could crash at dad's place.

"They were interesting people, that is for sure," Dad said. "That was quite a day and they brought several more days with them."

Dad called David Swope, owner of the Golden Anchor Hotel to see if Big Daddy could crash at the hotel, as my then-wife and I had the only other bedroom. His son went with him and ended up sleeping under their trailer on Dock #2 in St. Ignace (show headquarters). Allegedly upset with the loudspeakers playing music late at night, his son unplugged the sound system, the PA, and just about every vendor's power source.

Twenty years into his show, dad looked back and marveled at all the people who, up to 1980, he'd only seen in magazines, but now sat with him like old friends in his home and talked about cars, the culture, and their heroes.

As a kid, dad was not popular, not into sports, was always picked last for games, and finally said, "the heck with it," and buried himself in car magazines, cars, music, and cruising.

"Through reading all the car magazines, I developed my own heroes. Other kids had sports heroes, I had car guys. Those kids never met their heroes, but those magazines planted a seed, and I was able to meet so many of mine."

I asked dad to look back at 1976 and fast forward 20 years and if he ever imagined all those legends in his town, walked up his driveway, had a beer, and talked about cars.

"No. You couldn't. So many things had to happen to do that. I got a lot of lucky bounces, but a lot of hard work made that happen."

He recounted the struggle of building the show in a small town that was geographically unfavorable to such an event and having to fight the city every year. I remember his frustration in dealing with the city council and all the hoops through which he was forced to jump, and how much it hurt and disappointed him.

"They are all gone now," he said of those who caused the struggle. "And I am still here. The show is still here. You can't get to the mountaintop by stopping for roadblocks. You have to figure out a way around them."

He traveled coast-to-coast in search of cars, talent, and legends which he had yet persuaded to come. He always had odd jobs painting houses, selling cars, detailing cars, just to support his hobby and the show.

"I step back and look into my room (his insanely cool museum of automotive history), blink my eyes and say, this all happened here, and I did it."

He designed his own blueprint and created his own version of what a show could be that other shows followed. Original ideas.

Think about it; the St. Ignace Car Show, if it were the only event he did, would still be a show of legend. Add to that everything else; The Down Memory Lane Parade (thanks Merv), Cruise Night, Muscle Car Mania, On the Waterfront, Antiques on the Bay, The Richard Crane Memorial Truck Show, the concerts, the tractor show, the toy show, the Thursday boat trip through the Straits of Mackinac, etc. It was almost dreamlike to see all of those events seamlessly put together the way he did.

When he started, few car shows were held in Northern Michigan, especially in the Upper Peninsula. I remember a show in Escanaba but not as well as poor Bob Blair. Ask him about that trip.

Now every city in Michigan hosts shows and events, imitating what he did.

The world-famous Woodward Dream Cruise had its nexus in St. Ignace. The future organizers came and watched in wide-eyed wonderment as thousands of cars, every make, model, and style, endlessly cruised the streets as tens of thousands of spectators cheered them on, poured bleach on the road, and howled in delight when the drivers gave them exactly what they wanted.

PART 14

Being Ed Reavie

Chapter 40: Luckiest Man on Earth

My father is a lot of things, among which is being one of the luckiest people on earth. Luck, of course, comes with hard work. I am not talking about that luck.

False teeth get flushed down the drain? It just happens to come to rest on a ledge in a sewer and is easily retrieved by the small hands of a six-year-old.

Foreign car built on the metric system and said car breaks down in a small town in the hills of Kentucky? The garage owner just happens to have the exact fuse you need in a pile of dust in his garage.

That kind of luck.

As a living witness to my father's shenanigans, I felt this was an ideal place to document a few of his stories. Within the Phoenix Police Department, my father is known as, "The Original Mr. Reavie" as my antics are well documented by supervisors.

"You did what?" and "Why can't you do things like a normal person?" were frequently asked of me. I replied to those questions with, "This is nothing, you should meet the Original Mr. Reavie," or famously, "What answer do you need to hear?" I will leave

Sergeant Jessing's befuddled, exasperated response for a non-family book.

When dad visited and met some of those supervisors, I was told later, "Wow, there really are two of you."

Anyway, here are a few of his best.

Chapter 41: The Sean Shank Redemption

Enter one of my favorite "dad" stories ever. One of such ridiculousness, outrageous parental malfeasance, and downright foolishness, that one could not believe it unless there were multiple witnesses. Which there were. And they are still alive and spoke on the record with me. Okay, it's just me, as my sister was so traumatized that she refuses to talk about it. Dad will gladly talk about it. Which is part of the problem.

It was the summer of 1973 and we lived in our house on Spring Street. The City was using dynamite to displace earth to install a new sewer line. Our house had a detachable garage where dad kept his brand new, red VW Fastback with the Hurst Shifter, wooden competition steering wheel and Brute Exhaust System.

He was worried that leaving the car in the garage might result in it being damaged if the shaking ground dislodged something from the rafters, so he moved it into the driveway (The house was between the car and the work zone.) As he walked toward the house, he heard a loud boom, and a "ZING" and then a soul-ripping metallic thud as a rock flew over his head and slammed into the VW's hood and created an orange-sized dent.

Dad immediately became sick from shock, as his car was worth more than life. He ran to the house and vomited multiple times into the restroom sink.

As he gasped for air, with water streaking down his face, he ran his tongue around his mouth and felt something odd. He looked into the mirror and noticed that something besides the contents of his stomach was gone; his "butterfly tooth."

The Butterfly Tooth is a false tooth device that attaches to what looks like a butterfly wing and is molded to fit perfectly onto the roof of the wearer's mouth. It is designed to replace a lost one and is held in by suction. Hey, this was 1973.

"So to recap, I threw up, lost my tooth down the drain, and I had a hole in my car," dad deadpanned. "It ruined what was, up until that time, a perfectly good day."

He saw the tooth in the clear drain pipe, so he filled the bathtub several times (years ahead of Bill Nye the Science Guy) and pulled the plug which created an onslaught of water and suction to pull the tooth all the way through the pipe.

Why did he want the tooth to go down the pipe instead of trying to pluck it out with maybe a clothes hanger? Don't ask. I soon found out.

Okay, I'll tell you.

The manhole cover and the raging brown sewer river was outside the house in the street. See where this is going? If you guessed straight down the drain, I will autograph your copy of this book. Find me in St. Ignace.

His horrible plan, that he could somehow not envision going wrong, was now in action. Often criticized for not including his children in any of his activities, Dad decided to make a family mission out of this.

He grabbed a crowbar out of the garage, went to the middle of the street, pried open the manhole cover, and stuck a flashlight and then his head inside the ghastly lower levels of bowel soup.

"I SEE IT!" he exclaimed as the light illuminated his little tooth and butterfly wing teetering precariously on the ledge of the sewer with gooey water streaming past it.

His next idea would have put him on the Child Protective Services most wanted list, had they been a thing in 1973. My father was a big man. He was 6' 3" and around 220 pounds. He was also in possession of two left feet and no thumbs when it came to things like this. So, he did the only logical thing he could do, and it was my fault for not thinking of it first (I was a pretty sharp 6-year-old who once cut all my mother's roses off her rose bush and made "rose mud stew") or for questioning him.

Looking at me and my pure white-blonde hair, sparkling blue eyes, horizontal striped shirt, Tuff Skins elastic waistband jeans, and a spanking pair of new Buster Browns on my size 4 feet, he did some quick math. He calculated that I would clearly fit into the hole and have an easier time descending the ladder, grabbing the tooth, and saving the day.

Plus, if something happened to me, he could make another one that looked just like me. What was the harm? This was a $10 tooth we were talking about here.

"Get down in the hole, I will stop traffic," he barked at me. My sister could not believe what she was seeing, but soon she became numb to these types of shenanigans and simply went along.

With sis holding the light and dad watching for traffic, little Sean went down the ladder and grabbed the tooth. It was an event about which my ancestors no doubt sang folk songs on the great reservation in the sky.

"I FOUND IT I FOUND IT" dad reported to me what I said. "You held it up in slow motion, like raising a victory flag! It was a proud dad moment for sure."

One of many, no doubt.

"And after descending the ladder into a river of foul-smelling awfulness, Little Sean came out the other side triumphant."

Did you read that in Morgan Freeman's voice? You're welcome.

He grabbed us both (I am assuming this is the one time my mom let him babysit his children without someone babysitting him), tossed us in the freshly dented car, and we roared off to see the town's dentist, old Doc Holley.

"You did WHAT?" Doc Holley barked.

He explained it all with a straight face, then handed the recovered device to Doc Holley. Well, he did leave out the part about sending his only son down into a tunnel of steaming excrement to retrieve it. He winked at me and put a finger to his lips.

Doc Holley examined it with his spiffy head lamp, ran it under water, shook it off, shoved it into dad's mouth, and clamped his jaw shut.

"Good to Go!"

Go ahead, ask my sister when you see her. Be warned, she will get triggered and lay down a stream of expletives that will wrap around your head and suffocate you.

As I said, I am in therapy.

Chapter 42: Elvis and Ed Reavie

The Clambake Car

"It was a thrill to me to have my butt in the same seat as Elvis," dad said of his experience being the only person other than Elvis to drive the historic Corvette Stingray XP-87 Racer. The legendary car was used in the Elvis movie, "Clambake."

Painted candy apple red for the movie because Elvis requested it, GM restored it back to its original configuration with a period-correct 283 V8.

The 1959 Corvette Racer has a unique history.

Designed by Peter Brock and Larry Shinoda (past show special guest.) Bill Mitchell purchased the chassis from a 1956 Arkus-Duntov tubular frame racer Corvette SS, and directed and funded the design in the secretive "Studio-X."

When the car was completed, Mr. Mitchell entered the "Stingray" in the 1960 SCCA competition and it was driven by "The Flying Dentist" Dr. Dick Thompson. Dr. Thompson won the C-modified class championship.

Originally silver, Elvis requested the car be painted a more exciting color and it was redone in candy apple red and a hood scoop was added. The XP-87 Stingray was the design inspiration for the "C2" generation of Corvettes (1963-1967) which took the

Stingray name. The '63 Split Window Stingray is the most iconic Corvette in History as it was the first, and only year, the split window was available.

Once the movie was completed and GM took the car back, it was restored back to its original silver color and condition and period correct 283-V8.

Today the car resides at the GM Heritage Center in Michigan. However, I believe it's currently on loan to the Petersen Automotive Museum in Los Angeles.

Dad was invited to the prestigious GM Heritage Center for a tour and walked on ground normally reserved for titans of the industry, which he now was.

The smalltown boy, the thorn in his parents' side, who took orange crates and customized them into cooler orange crates, was asked to come to the Heritage Center. Imagine indeed.

Bill Mitchell designed the XP-87 and only two non-General Motors personnel have ever driven it; Elvis Presley, and high school pushout, former grocery store clerk, and the 1973 Father of the Year, Ed Reavie, in 1990.

The XP-87 arrived in town 23 years after Mr. Mitchell came to St. Ignace. Dad gave General Motors a little collateral to drive it; his National Champion 1955 Chevy.

"They wanted to make sure I came back," he said with a laugh. "They surrounded the '55 Chevy until I came back. That told me it was the real deal."

Jerry Palmer, head of design for Corvette, famously told dad, "You logged more time in that car than I did."

Good company to be in; Elvis and Edward K. Reavie. "Not too many people can say that," dad said. "And I am the last one standing."

This is not to be confused with when dad jumped the velvet ropes in the Hank Williams Sr. museum containing Hank William Sr.'s 1952 Cadillac death car, opened the door, and pronged out in the backseat with his tongue hanging out while demanding I take his photo. In a museum that prohibits photos. Yeah, we were thrown out.

But I did take the photo.

Chapter 43: Ed Reavie and The Deputy Sheriff

"What we are dealing with here is a complete lack of respect for the law."

One of dad's favorite annual trips was the 600-mile round trip to Iola, Wisconsin. He took the 1955 Chevy and attended 25 consecutive shows, falling in love with the small Wisconsin town.

His passenger was Gary Olsen, my high school Geography teacher and driver's education teacher. Mr. Olsen was a big bear of a man who gave out a coveted "Autographed Check Plus" for students who went the extra mile in the drawing of maps.

Check plus was the check mark with the plus sign after it. The autographed check plus was just that, written out in perfect handwriting at the top of the map. I earned two fabled Check Pluses in my time in his class and it was a wonderful carrot he gave us all.

He was legendary in our town (Editor's note: He was my teacher, too and yes… a legend) and taught generations of students. I played basketball with his son Jon and another son Mark was a coach of mine. We lost Mr. Olsen and his daughter, Joy (Jon's twin), way too soon. Both losses crushed our little town.

On one of those trips to Iola, The Original Mr. Reavie ran afoul of Johnny Law in such a way, as a police officer, I cannot fathom. And I can fathom a lot. Stay tuned for a series of three books covering my life as a street cop in Central Phoenix for those.

"Central Wisconsin is like a Norman Rockwell painting with beautiful countryside, homes, and cheese curds," dad said, as he already started to laugh as he told me about his "slight" misstep regarding what a normal person would do at a traffic light that, clearly not being normal, he didn't.

"I dodged a huge bullet, maybe even a cannonball," he said, still laughing.

Iola was booked so dad stayed in a nice Waupaca hotel with other show goers, enjoying a picture-perfect day. Iola is a monstrous car show with more than 4,000 cars and 100,000 people who stream into the small country town.

The morning of the show, dad was excited to get going, get some breakfast and then see all his friends at the show.

"After I got ready, I jumped in the Chevy and headed out," dad said. "And soon, came error number one."

Dad came to the intersection and realized he rolled right through a red light. "Unfortunately," he said. "A County Deputy was on the other side stopped at his red light."

His rear-view mirror was instantly filled with blue and red strobe lights. "He caught me red handed," dad said.

Dad saw the County Mountie Hat as the officer approached, and the mirrored sunglasses, and a toothpick dangling out of his mouth, and noticed that the Deputy's belly extended over his duty belt. If "welcome to the chain gang" had a poster boy, he just wobbled up to dad's window.

Dad heard the jingle of keys and the static crackle of a radio because his window was already rolled down, and then the shadow of the deputy loomed over him.

"Don't they have traffic lights where you are from, son?" The Deputy asked.

"Um, actually sir, I don't."

"Are you telling me you don't have stop lights in your town?"

"Yes, sir, that is what I am telling you. That is why I didn't look for them and ran this one, sir."

Not laughing, the deputy bent down until dad saw his own terrified look in the mirrors of the Deputy's shades and asked for license and vehicle registration.

This party was just getting started.

He saw dad's room key and understood that he was a show-going visitor to his county, so maybe, just maybe, being disarmed by dad's obvious attempt at being coy, he told dad he looked legit and just needed to enter dad's information and would document his stop as, "educational."

Yes, that is a thing. I once famously did an educational stop on a rather fetching blonde who, crazy as it sounds, must have lost the top button of her blouse which was already strained to hold back the fleshy cargo within.

She used the, "I just forgot to register the car, certainly you understand how a single lady sometimes needs helpful reminders now and again."

I told her that I certainly did and, to help, I will write it down on official City of Phoenix stationery. With her head coquettishly cocked and flipping her hair over her head, she cooed a thank you.

When she saw a court date on the bottom of the ticket, i.e. stationery, for no registration, the look on her face was priceless. "Now you won't forget, see how helpful we can be?"

Again, sorry, attention span thing there.

Back to Smokey and the Rebel.

Dad watched the Deputy in his side mirror as he walked away to document the stop and was in full panic mode as he said to himself, "please don't turn around and look, please don't turn around and look."

He turned around and looked.

DAMMIT!

Returning to the car, the Deputy drummed his beefy fingers on the roof of dad's '55 Chevy.

"Mr. Reavie," he boomed. "Are you aware your registration expired in 1976? That was 27 years ago!"

Clearing his throat, dad answered immediately.

"No."

"You mean to tell me today is the first day you realized you've been driving this car for 27 years with no valid registration? That dog don't hunt, son."

Dad took a deep breath and told the now-flustered Deputy that he indeed knew it was out of date, but the plate was for show only, as he wanted to keep the California Cool of the original car. He also told the dumbfounded Deputy that he had the current Michigan plate under his seat.

"That's an odd place for a plate, don't you think?"

"Yes sir, it is. Would you like to see it?"

"I need to see it ON THE CAR!"

Laughing, dad said, "Lucky for me he was in a good mood or my ass would be hung out to dry."

Dad gave the Deputy the Historical plate and waited for him to come back so he could go get breakfast.

He missed breakfast.

The Deputy walked back to the car with a purpose and once again did the finger drum of doom on the roof.

"We have a problem."

Heart sinking, dad asked.

"I cannot find your car in Michigan. I cannot find your car in California. The Secretary of State in Michigan has no registration on file for this vehicle. Your car, technically, does not exist."

When dad asked if what he gave him was no good, the Deputy told him dad did not give him a registration, he gave him the title. There was no registration.

"Huh, how about that?" Dad responded.

"How about you get out of the car?"

Crowds formed as both dad and his car were well recognized in the show world and at the Iola show. Malfeasance was afoot in their small town!

"My stomach was rolling at this point, so I asked him if it was possible the records were purged after 25 years?"

Scratching his pink jowls, the Deputy said, "Here's the issue; you are driving a California car, claiming to be from Michigan, and I can't find you anywhere."

Now at loggerheads as the crowd snickered, with "Free Ed Reavie" signs already made, constructed, and being waved, something had to give.

"Do you have a screwdriver or socket set?" he asked dad. When told there was a screwdriver somewhere in the trunk, the deputy now laughed, "Mr. Reavie, the last thing I want to do is see who you have tied up in your trunk," then went to the police cruiser to retrieve his own.

Dad watched as the Deputy removed the California "DOE211" plate and placed the 27-year expired Michigan plate on it, then he asked, "So, what next?"

Looking dad up and down, had the large man known Kress Reavie, no doubt he would now understand.

"You don't understand," the Deputy said. "You can't come rolling into my town in a car like this. You run a light, I pull you over, and now I have a serious decision to make."

Dad swallowed hard. "I envisioned myself with my car being hooked up by a wrecker and taken to impound until I could prove it existed," he said. "And, as it was clear I could never do this, I would never get my car back. I was at his mercy."

Instead of writing dad a citation for displaying a fictitious plate, expired registration, no proof of financial responsibility, and disregarding a traffic control device, the Deputy had one question for dad.

"What are you going to do now?"

Dad said that, since breakfast was over, could the Deputy recommend a good place for lunch.

The deputy laughed so hard that he nearly lost his campaign hat, and dad knew he was in the clear.

"I really like you sir, tell you what," he said laughing. "I will escort you to a good rib place."

Driving behind the Deputy, dad let out a deep sigh and channeled his best Carroll Shelby after they were pulled over by the Michigan State Police. "Lovely town they have here."

The following year at Iola, Tom West let dad take his 1961 Impala convertible to put some miles on it. Dad always stayed at the same hotel and, when he walked out to get into the car, he saw a Sheriff Deputy truck cruising the parking lot looking at cars.

To dad's astonishment, it was the same Deputy no doubt, looking for a Turquoise and India Ivory 1955 Chevy Belair Hardtop Sedan with California plate DOE211 expired for 28 years.

Now that is luck.

As we talked about this, dad said he received an invitation for Iola 2022 in the mail, but sadly, "those days have passed but, the memories will always be there."

Chapter 44: Putting St. Ignace on the Map

"Ed Reavie put St. Ignace on the map." was often said to me while writing this book.

People say it metaphorically. Would it surprise anyone if I told you Ed Reavie LITERALLY put St. Ignace on the map? Any takers?

Yet another Ed Reavie story that, when I told it to those interviewed, amazed them.

How did dad literally put St. Ignace on the map? Thank you, I thought you would never ask.

One fine example of growing up in St. Ignace was that it was so small and inconsequential, the local news stations did not include it on the weather map.

This did not sit well with dad.

Not.

One.

Bit.

Does anyone not know where this is going?

Dad grabbed the phone book and called all the television stations in the area. At that time, I think we had five channels total. ABC, NBC, CBS, CTV, PBS, and all local news shows on those stations.

He called TV 9 & 10, and the other stations, and asked why St. Ignace was not on the local weather map. I mean, geographically, there was not a more beautiful backdrop of any city in the Upper Peninsula. Two Great Lakes and the Big Mac? Come on man!

To ignore the gateway to the true North (which is NOT anywhere North of Detroit, Trolls) was akin to leaving a car in stock condition.

To him, repetition is what gets people to believe in what you are doing. People have to see your face, hear your story, and be relentlessly bombarded with the literature.

You don't think he landed Carroll Shelby, George Barris, Zora Duntov, and Gordon Beurigh by asking only once? No, he was relentless, and caused Mr. Shelby to tell him he was "the most persistent son of a bitch I've ever dealt with."

The station manager of TV 9 & 10 soon found this out. He listened to this wild man pitch him as to why St. Ignace needed to be on the weather maps, and was told, "You just can't call and do this. There is a process, and this isn't it."

He asked what was needed to start this process, was told, and then dad shifted his relentless ways to the Mackinac Bridge Authority, to send the weather updates to the station every day.

That was the key ingredient. An official weather source, like an airport or the Mackinac Bridge Authority, needed to religiously send weather forecasts to all the stations so they could report conditions.

My father has a way about him. He can make you think his idea was your idea and, seeing it was your idea, wouldn't it make sense to do it? You already read the story of my sewer plunge, right? I am 55 and I still think that was my idea.

And guess what? Dad did just that. He called, daily, for weeks and reminded the Bridge Authority to send weather updates until repetition became a habit. When his calls were answered with, "Hi Ed, already sent them" his work was done.

Ed Reavie put St. Ignace on the map, literally and metaphorically.

The first day St. Ignace appeared on the local news weather map, we broke out in cheers.

My dad did that.

It was a great day indeed.

Chapter 45: Ed's Incredible 1951 Chevy!

The first car of dad's that I remember was a dark blue 1948 Chevrolet that I was told to get into and stop being difficult. My Saturday was spent in Traverse City, Boyne City, Gaylord, Petoskey, and all the other towns on the show circuit. Endless highways that all went to the same place, as far as I was concerned.

I can still remember the smell of that car. Musty. To me, it sucked. However, the 1948 Chevrolet Fleetline Aero two-door sedan sported rear Venetian blinds and wipers, a Fulton windshield, wide white walls, and blue dot taillights. Dad got the car repainted in original dark-blue and re-chromed brightwork. It was gorgeous.

California dreaming never left dad's mind. He vicariously lived the Cali Car Culture and wanted a piece all his own. Bringing that to town was one thing, having a part of it to call his own was an altogether different thing.

One day, he saw an advertisement for Bob Wingate Chevy in Los Angeles. He went through his flyers and was ready for something good. Something that screamed California cool.

He called Bob and chose a 1951 Chevy Convertible, black with red interior and all the options. The California Cool car to define my dad was on order and he could not be more excited to once again have a car of legend in his garage.

However, before dad could take delivery of his new dream car, Bob told him the car was appearing in the Rose Bowl Parade as part of Bob's display. The car would make the parade route, be placed on a transport, and delivered to dad the following week.

Right now, those who know my dad best are hearing about this car for the first time. Join the club. I never heard this story. You can call it fate or luck, either way, dad never laid eyes on that car nor did it ever park in his driveway or cruise the show. Its California Coolness was nerded up pretty good.

When Bob called him back Monday, he made sure dad was sitting down before he broke the news. The California cool car was in an accident during the parade and totaled. There was no car. Dream smashed. Dad apoplectic.

Now what?

Never a believer in coincidence, what happened next changed dad's life. After the shocking news of his dream car's demise, Bob told dad there was another car on the lot Bob thought he would like.

It was a 1955 Chevrolet Belair Hardtop Sedan and was in pristine condition. The India Ivory and Turquoise, rust-free car was loaded. Yes, Virginia, there is a Santa Claus and, at that moment in time, his name was Wingate.

After dickering back-and-forth and getting photos in the mail, it took months before dad purchased the car for $4,800 in 1975.

That car not only turned our small town on its head, but it also became a car of legend, appeared on dozens of magazine covers, and earned a National Championship in 1980. This magnificent car went on the show circuit for 15 years and won the Antique Automobile Club of America's, Junior, Senior, and Preservation Award. It appeared on 10 National magazine covers. The car that almost never was, changed my dad's life the way his car show changed the genre. It is the car I in which I cruise the same streets he did; dad in the passenger seat, smiling ear-to-ear.

He added several original options including a Wonder Bar Radio, fender skirts, blue dot tail lights, spinners, dual glass packs, and 35 other options.

It was years before he allowed me in the driver's seat of the '55. It was a running joke for decades and I was in my 40s before he gave me the keys.

My first drive introduced me to power brakes and, the first time I pressed them, nearly sent the two of us flying through the windshield. "FEATHER THEM" he said in exasperation. Because the car did not have seatbelts (and still doesn't), I heeded this advice.

Now, as he ages, I have the pleasure of feathering the brakes, dealing with the play in the steering wheel, and letting those glass packs roar. His health declined to the point he could no longer drive, but we still spent hours cruising, with me behind the wheel. As we drove through town, he acted as a narrator of history.

Each corner, each street, each building, he told me what was there and what was happening in 1958 when he was 18 and ruled the streets in his cars, hanging with his friends. I heard how much it all meant to him.

When he told me the '55 was a consolation prize over the '51 he craved, again, it was the first time I'd heard the story. Yes, another fact I learned about my dad.

His "consolation prize" gobbled up covers nationally, won every event it was entered, and did for dad what Fonzie did for a leather jacket. One can't help but compare the '51 to Wally Pip who called off playing a baseball game, to be replaced by Lou Gehrig.

But did you know there was another cherry 1955 in dad's garage? This is the story similar to the third child in the Happy Days home. One year Chuck was there dispensing advice to Richie while dribbling a basketball, and then he was gone.

Or maybe this car was cousin Oliver. The mini version of John Denver that they used to keep interest going in The Brady Bunch. Scrappy Doo? You get where I am going.

In a complete Ed Reavie moment, he picked up a 1955 Chevy Harvest Gold and India Ivory sedan with Neptune green interior, with only 18,000 miles on it. The car was the proverbial "little old lady who drove it to church every Sunday" car. Mrs. Foote, 92 years old, stored the car in her Cedarville garage.

Longtime friend and then-future Mayor of St. Ignace, Bruce Dodson, tipped dad off to the find. Dad contacted Mrs. Foote, explained his desire to purchase the car from her and pledged to give it a good home. Mrs. Foote wanted to hang onto the car, as it had sentimental value. He understood, was kind and considerate, and struck up a pen pal relationship with her, and never once asked in those letters to buy her car. Mrs. Foote lived four more years as dad kept open the lines of communication with calls and letters. Upon her passing, family members found the letters he'd sent, called him, and negotiated a deal for him to bring the car home. Dad loved everything about the car save for one glaring issue; "it had two too many doors," he lamented.

Another interesting thing; when Mrs. Foote bought the car, she did not want music in it and had a "radio delete" plate installed where the radio should have gone.

It appeared on several magazine covers and was a beautiful ride. Alas, dad could not get over the four-door sedan aspect and sold the car a few years later.

But it did last longer than Chuck and Cousin Oliver.

PART 15

Becoming Legendary

Chapter 46: Nearing a Quarter Century

"It's like a Hollywood Movie. Hot rods, customs, and lowriders. I've never seen this many cars, it was a Hollywood spectacle on a Saturday night."
*-**Terry Cook**, legendary automotive writer and multiple time attendee.*

Dave McClellan, a man with as golden a voice I ever heard, arrived with his wife as Guest of Honor in 1997 as part of dad's effort to expand his reach into the world of NHRA.

Legendary for his microphone skills and booming voice, Mr. McClellan was a humble man who enjoyed our little town, as he sat on a bench eating ice cream, watched the cars go by, signed autographs, and smiled ear-to-ear. He was so kind to me, and thanked dad and me for having him in our town.

I called Mr. McClellan for an interview and heard that golden voice on the answering machine. I left a detailed message and was happy to see the call come in from the same number an hour later. Sadly, it was Mr. McClellan's son, Michael. My heart broke as he told me about his father's battle with dementia and, at times, was unaware of even who his family was. We had a nice conversation and I told him how much his father meant to my own and what a nice, kind man he was. Michael told me a great story about his childhood with his father and I appreciated the time he took to call and tell me. Another one of America's legends I was thankful to meet.

One thing I always teased dad about was all the work he did to get men like Carroll Shelby, Zora Arkus-Duntov, and Bill Mitchell to St. Ignace so he could meet them while I did not lift a finger for such an honor, and yet met them at a much younger age than he did.

The Big Three were well represented in St. Ignace. They took out huge ads and brought some of their nicest historical cars and new rides to show off to the 100,000 spectators.

Dad then introduced a new award for cars owned, built, and presented by females. Hundreds of female-owned classic, custom, hot rod, and street machines lined the streets, vying for the award.

Reaching to the obscure, yet historical, dad booked Peggy Sue Gerron as a guest. The namesake of the classic Buddy Holly song, Peggy Sue, was also the first female to be a master plumber in the state of California.

Pinky Randal, world-renowned authority on Chevrolet, and a longtime friend of dad's, brought a huge display of classic Chevrolets.

He also went against the grain and named Boyd Coddington as his Guest of Honor. Mr. Coddington was a seven-time winner of America's Most Beautiful Roadster. Dad first met Boyd at his shop, introduced by Frank Livingston.

"I will never forget going into Boyd's shop and seeing Chip Foose sanding down a 1957 Chevy for a customer," dad said.

Boyd was a legendary hot rod builder, best known for his custom-fabricated alloy wheels machined from solid aluminum billet (an industry first). So iconic were his custom cars, that his style became known as "The Boyd look."

Boyd built "CadZZilla" for ZZ Top frontman Billy Gibbons. It electrified the custom car world and prompted Gray Baskerville to proclaim it, "the most incredible transformation he'd ever witnessed."

Boyd changed the face of street rodding, dad told me. Later, Boyd got mixed up with the wrong people and he told dad, "It got too big and got away from me."

A customer's bankruptcy left Boyd with a $465,000 loss and sent his professional life into a tailspin. He was implicated in fraud schemes and charged with a crime.

During all this, dad met with Boyd at SEMA and convinced him to come to St. Ignace. "Right up until I saw him walk up my driveway, in his iconic Hawaiian shirt, I was worried he wasn't coming. But he did."

Dad went against the grain again, as he wanted to pay homage to possibly the most famous female motorsports hero.

Linda Vaughn returned, not as an honorary guest, but as the Guest of Honor, making her the first, and only, female to have this honor.

"I never saw anybody with her personality," dad said. "She is a delightful woman. Her mind is like a computer, she remembers everyone."

Growing up and seeing Linda in car magazines as the original Hurst Shifter Girl, dad still pinches himself that he calls Linda a friend.

Her love of all things automotive was rivaled by Mackinac Island Fudge. She demonstrated this on her first day in town when she carried bags of it out of the shops.

Her White Lincoln Hot Rod, her outsized personality, and her gregarious nature, made her the biggest hit of any celebrity to come to St. Ignace outside of Carroll Shelby.

It was during this show that Jimmy Addison, legendary street racer and driver of the world-famous 1967 Plymouth Belvedere GTX Silver Bullet street machine, knocked on my dad's front door and asked, "Is the party still on?"

The Silver Bullet's raw power fascinated everyone who saw it run quarter miles on Woodward Avenue. Its 487 cubic inch Hemi engine allegedly powered it to 130 mph between stop lights during the Woodward Dream Cruise.

Harold Sullivan, another friend of dad's, owned the car and Jimmy was apparently the only one wild enough, crazy enough, and talented enough to handle the Silver Bullet's crazy power.

In recounting his Silver Bullet story, dad laughed as he'd heard that Jimmy spent a few years driving cabs in Detroit.

"Can you imagine hailing a cab and Jimmy Addison pulling up?" dad laughed. "Man, that will blow your hair back."

Chapter 47: Excellence

A quarter-century of St. Ignace left a legacy unmatched by any show in the country. An atmosphere like no other, hall of fame builders, designers, engineers, rock and roll stars, and the finest cars the world has ever seen crossed our bridge and entered Memory Lane.

Attending a show in the 90s was an experience for everyone in the family. Pure Michigan indeed. Cruise Night was known worldwide, the Straits Area Antique Auto Show had ceased to be, replaced with only one word, "St. Ignace" (and in some locales only 'Ignace).

Titans in the industry, from Carroll Shelby to Jerry Palmer, told all they met that St. Ignace was the place to be on the last Saturday in June. Book it.

Car magazines dad had read as a child and adult; Hot Rod, Rod and Journal, Hot Rodder, and all mainstream magazines had St. Ignace on the cover, inside, and on the back.

Dad's newest shows, On the Waterfront, and The Richard Crane Memorial Truck Show, celebrated 10 and 5 years, respectively. St. Ignace was the place for "shows within the show" and Corvette Clubs, Street Machine, and Hot Rod clubs, all had a show within their own corral on the streets of St. Ignace

Keith Crain, a friend of dads and former honorary chairman, headlined the 25th show as Guest of Honor.

"Jon Milner" (Paul LeMat) was there in his yellow coupe and added to the list of actors from American Graffiti that not only appeared at dad's show, but sat in his living room, talked about the movie and his love for cruisin' and car culture.

I communicated via Facebook with Mr. LeMat several times, but he was not feeling well and unable to commit to an interview.

Dad inaugurated an Elvis Impersonator contest and, in a bizarre twist, ended up on the same flight with them as he was leaving town.

"It was the most bizarre thing ever," he said. "Some looked great and others, well, it was time to go home and do something else."

One thing that shocked me regarding all the superstars that came to town was that he never paid them to come. He was his best salesperson for the vision. His passion was legendary. His chili ran hot 24/7 but he got things done.

"I never wanted people to know I didn't pay for people to come," dad said. "If they needed help with rooms, I cut deals with the hotels. They came because they wanted to come. They knew what I had and so did I."

Dad had a chip on his shoulder. As a kid, he was skinny, nerdy, and never included or chosen to play with the other kids, often fighting amongst themselves as the captain of one team claimed they had to take him last time and the other team had to pick him this time. He carried that rejection with him his entire life and strived to create something nobody else could; to be the very best at something.

After 25 years, he didn't rest on his success. He accepted that the show got top heavy and had to streamline to survive but worked with law enforcement and city officials to make his show safe and to bring back the family dynamic that originally built it.

Dad was not a fan of committees but would listen to people with expertise in areas he didn't have, and that made his show great.

Is he stubborn? Again, ask my sister. He is, and even frustrates me, the king of frustrating people, yet, when the show got out of control, he listened to solutions and the show got much better as a result.

Chapter 48: Turn of the Century

The 2000s rolled in with Keith Crain headlining the 25th annual St. Ignace Car Show. Chrysler Design chief Tom Gale kept the momentum going in 2001 and Larry Wood had his turn in 2002.

With more than 2.1 billion units of Larry Wood's designs sold in the last 50 years, enough to circle the earth 3.5 times, Mr. Wood is the most prolific designer of cars in the world.

As Chief of Design for Hot Wheels, there is not a kid in America that did not play with, collect, blow up with firecrackers, and stack in shoeboxes, Hot Wheels cars.

Full disclosure, I not only blew them up, I lit the fuse and rolled them down a plank into Danielle's Barbie tea party. She got mad.

It can also be said, every parent in the world stepped on one of those cars in the middle of the night and cursed those little metal beasts the likes of which were not seen again until Legos hit the scene.

With 800,000 Hot Wheels selling each week, there is no chance that his cars won't stand the test of time here long after we are gone. Such is his legacy.

Chapter 49: Talking Hot Wheels with Mr. Larry Wood

Mr. Hot Wheels and 2002 Guest of Honor

Talking to the man responsible for happy parts of my childhood was a thrill. Mr. Wood said that, even as we talked, he was working on seven different cars inside his garage.

"How is that for retirement?" he laughed. When I told him, it sounded pretty standard for car guys he said, "I should have collected stamps. Geez."

With all my interviews, talking to Mr. Woods was as easy as talking to friends and family who I've known my entire life. Car guys are different that way.

He told me he would take a break from welding to chat, then I tossed in, "How big of a welder does it take to build a Hot Wheels? Laughing, Mr. Woods said, "That would be a pencil."

Before we talked, Mr. Woods told me he still had his Guest of Honor magnet on his front door and it is the first thing he sees.

As a reader, you can't know that, just the day before I talked with Mr. Wood, I spoke to Mr. Ken Gross who told me he still has his Guest of Honor magnet in a special place in his incredible two-story garage.

To hear two men of such regard, who were guests of honor in 2003 and 2009, STILL have that memento, means the world to me and when I called dad to tell him he said, "Not bad for a guy nobody wanted on their team.

St. Ignace was so well covered in the National car media that Mr. Wood heard all about the amazing promotor and show in the far reaches of Michigan's Upper Peninsula.

Mr. Wood lived in Detroit at the time and knew that St. Ignace was "someplace different and that is why I went there. What can you say? It's such a beautiful area."

In another small world moment, Mr. Wood told me that Ken Ebberts, longtime artist for the St. Ignace show, was his roommate in college.

Mr. Wood heard that St. Ignace was still going strong, and said, "That is great. I loved going there. The Bridge, the views, the nature. It was special."

Working with Ed Reavie was impactful.

"The way he did it was fantastic. He did a hell of a job. I've done car shows, I know how difficult it is."

I told Mr. Wood how this book started, with that story dad told of Carroll Shelby concerning the State Police and a certain credit card (which you now know whose card Mr. Wood), and that is in this book, Mr. Wood laughed and said, "That sounds like Carroll."

Mr. Wood said he worked on a Shelby Mustang for Mr. Shelby while eating McDonalds French Fries and talking cars.

"That was a highlight of my life," he said.

Mr. Wood described St. Ignace and said the location of the show is what made St. Ignace what it was.

"When I came into town and drove down that hill and the town unfolded in front of me, I said to myself WOW this is where the show is held?"

Car Shows normally meant going to one location, isolated from the host town, and sitting there all day with nothing to do.

Not the case with St. Ignace.

"There was so much to do," he told me. "You could shop downtown, hop a boat and go to the Island, and always have something to see and do. To me, that made it one of the best shows I have ever attended."

During his visit, he went to Sault Ste. Marie to see the legendary Sault Locks which, depending on the direction of the freighter, raises or lowers the water level through the St. Mary's River, so the freighters can continue into Lake Superior or Lake Huron.

I appreciated Mr. Wood's praise of my efforts to document the St. Ignace show. When I told him of the men and women to whom I spoke for this book, he said, "Wow, you are doing very well."

"Retiring" 12 years ago, I asked him what projects he had going on in his garage. He was presently lowering a Model A, dropping an LS engine into a '52 Jag, a '52 Woodie (his daily driver) and '32 Nash.

"My wife kicks me out in the morning and I don't come back until about 4 p.m., which works well for the two of us." In explaining my man cave to him, we shared a laugh.

I told him I was eight years old when dad started the show and am now 55, he said, "I bet you wondered who all those people were and why your dad was so excited."

After spending 11 months writing this book, I now completely understand why my father was so excited.

"You have to get a little older to understand the significance of things in life. I am 80 so you have a long way to go. You are doing a good job."

God I love car people. Thank you, sir. This was fun.

Chapter 50: Talking American Graffiti with Ms. Candy Clark & Mr. Bo Hopkins

"This show is part of the tapestry of automotive history and culture. No question about it."
Tom Peters, *Director of Design GM Car Studio, designer of the C5-C8 Corvette and 2021 Guest of Honor.*

"American Graffiti" Stars and 2005 Guests of Honor

Talking with Candy Clark was a trip. Bo Hopkins gave me one of the best quotes of all the interviews I conducted. Wonderful people.

I caught her on the way out the door and she started by telling me that she's attended more than 500 car shows in her life and she needed a prompt to help her remember St. Ignace.

I said, "The one with the Mackinac Bridge."

Her reply was instant.

"Oh, yeah, your dad tried to get Bo and me to go up in one of those towers," she said. "I don't like heights, and plus there were a lot of stairs, tiny, and small, and claustrophobic so thank you, no."

When I spoke to Bo Hopkins, he told me something similar but there was a different result. "Yeah, he talked me into it, that I do remember," Mr. Hopkins said with that familiar South Carolina drawl. "It was a challenge because I don't like heights," he said with a laugh.

When I asked him if was afraid of heights, why did he do it? His answer was instant; "I forced myself to do it and to prove a Pharaoh ain't chicken."

The Bridge tower aside, Mr. Hopkins had great memories of working with my father and the entire car culture. When I asked him why he thinks American Graffiti still resonates with so many people nearly 50 years after the fact, he told me, "It was a feel-good movie and I think it got people back on the road again, capturing that magic they felt when they were young."

He has been in the parade and cruised amongst all the cars, so I asked him if my father and St. Ignace captured that same magic. "He sure did, we had a fantastic time there and meeting your dad was a highlight for us."

Upon hearing of dad's health issues, he said, "Give him my best love from the King of the Pharaohs to a Pharaoh. I need to make sure we Pharaohs take care of one another."

I asked him to describe the part of Joe from the movie and he compared playing Joe to being Crazy Lee in "The Wild Bunch" and wanted to make sure he portrayed Joe in a special way. "I wanted to make him cool, and I think I did."

I told him he did.

I told Candy that American Graffiti had changed dad's life and she responded, "Really? That is so cool. Thank you. Ed was very good to us. His show was a massive thing and I don't know how he did it. I admire anyone who could do that."

Although she attended hundreds of shows over the years, Candy told me she got a great feeling working for my father. "He rolled out the red carpet for us," she said. "The best hotels, the best food. He always either answered my calls or got right back to me, asking how he could help."

The experience of such a large show and the huge amount of American Graffiti fans that wanted to meet them was sensational.

She apologized because the only thing she recalled was the Bridge tower, the size of the show, and spending time with my father. But I told Ms. Clark she made a huge impact on both my dad and me.

She asked about dad, his health and what became of the show, and I told her dad sold the show and retired after the 40th in 2015.

Candy told me to tell the St. Ignace Visitors and Convention Bureau to invite her back in 2022. So Murray, Quincy, and the gang, give Candy a call and let's hope we all see her back soon.

Author Note: Mr. Hopkins transitioned to eternal life in May of 2022.

Chapter 51: Oh, Happy Days

"Ed Reavie is the world's best auto show promoter."
Ed Almquist, *publisher of the legendary "Speed" magazine, founder of the largest automotive direct mailing company in the country, and 2003 Guest of Honor.*

When I walked into the Guest of Honor Brunch, I was speechless for the first time in the show's 25 years. That was because of the three very recognizable people standing near the head table.

Dad brought, for the first time, my generation's television heroes. Anson Williams, Donny Most, and Cindy Williams sat there looking as they did when they hung out at Arnold's Drive-In, and it was a shock to my system.

Engaging, resonant, and blending with the crowd, the three brought an entirely new vibe to the show. Celebrities from Generation X.

Ralph Malph and Warren "Potsie" Weber were Richie's sidekicks, Fonzie's punching bags, and unrivaled cultural icons.

Cindy Williams, as Shirley Feeney, was in Happy Days before spinning off to her own iconic show, Lavern and Shirley. She also starred as Laurie Henderson in American Graffiti. Her appearance gave dad yet another signature on the American Graffiti Movie poster that George Lucas had sent to him and is covered with autographs from all cast members, minus Ron Howard and Harrison Ford. The three held court all weekend, engaged with the massive downtown crowds who wanted a peek at the legends of their youth.

For dad, it was an amazing time on multiple fronts. As a kid, he'd ordered from magazines published by legendary car guy Ed Almquist who just happened to make his first trip to St. Ignace and later returned as Guest of Honor.

In dad's house, Ed was handed copies of books he'd published as far back as 1946, the same ones my father read as a six-year-old and kept. And Ed autographed them.

Another hero, Daryl Starbird, "The King of the Bubble Tops" headlined a show. Dad had tried for years to get Mr. Starbird to attend, but always responded that he didn't need another plaque or trophy. Dad responded, "I am not giving you a plaque, I am giving you the entire weekend."

That sealed the deal. I wonder if Mr. Starbird had any "Key to the City" presentations made in his honor, as Mayor Dodson always did, and proclaimed the weekend in honor of Mr. Starbird and every Guest of Honor.

One of my favorite personalities to come to St. Ignace was John Jenza, AKA Top Hat John. John first arrived in 1991 and captivated everyone with his humor, unrivaled knowledge, and incredible singing voice.

It was common for show guests to become long term friends, but John and Victoria transcended that. It was John with whom I consulted about writing this book on my way home to Phoenix.

I didn't tell dad; I called John, who I never actually address with his first name. It's always "Top Hat" or as I answer his phone calls, "Hello to one of the greatest living Americans."

John's response was felt through the phone. He told me it was a glorious idea to tell my father's story. His validation inspired me to start working.

Once I hit 50 pages with Dad's interviews, I sent it to Top Hat and implored him to please tell me if I was on the right track with the storytelling.

My goal in writing this book was to have people sit back and feel as if they are having a conversation with a friend. To relive the last 46 years of this amazing show, to think of the moments I've written about, and smile.

Top Hat's talents were many, including being one of the top karaoke singers I've ever heard. Dad first saw him in a karaoke bar, where he perfectly hit all the notes to Jay and the American's "Kara Mia".

Top Hat became an advocate through GM and spread the word to everyone, everywhere, about this mystical, magical show across the Mighty Mackinac Bridge.

The most important thing John gave to dad and me was his non-sugar-coated vision of what the show needed to continue its success. He told dad that his event needed to change to move forward and, for the first time in recorded history, dad listened to someone from the outside and made the changes.

The changes were the Top 40 cars award, to streamline the award process, and enjoin professional judges to determine the top cars so the awards are sought-after in car culture.

John was the first person to be Guest of Honor for both the St. Ignace Show and Antiques on the Bay. Possessing a sharp mind, deep intellect, and nearly instant recall, he is a historian with no equal and the quintessential car guy.

John held court adorned in his trademark Top Hat, told stories, talked about the winning cars as if they were his own, and lent the show a huge shot of credibility among serious car guys.

He had deep roots within GM and was at the forefront of getting GM Performance to participate in the show. He brought a parking lot of iconic performance cars to their space on Dock One.

Big Block Chevy engines were raffled, the top brass at GM came to town, gave beautiful awards, and made St. Ignace a showcase of their new concept cars.

Another man who changed the show, was a big, gruff, loud, silver haired titan who walked and spoke with a purpose.

Before Linda Vaughn, Jack "Doc" Watson was the face of Hurst Corporation, appearing at races dressed in medical garb to fix broken down cars.

Doc was involved with the creation of the iconic 1968 Hurst Olds. A visionary responsible for 87 specialty designed cars, Motor

Trend put Doc in the same class as Larry Shinoda, John DeLorean, and Vince Piggins.

Doc had a way about him that didn't need a lot of introduction. He was a commanding presence with a beautiful shock of silver hair, large glasses, and a baritone voice that could slice through the din of any room.

Such was his amazing creativity and eye for opportunity that Doc was instrumental in the creation of the "Jaws of Life;" a device used to save people hopelessly trapped in automobiles. As a first responder, myself, to see that device work was astonishing. I often told firefighters I knew the man who designed it.

Doc headlined the 32nd Annual St. Ignace Show, He was already a longtime family friend. His daughter Whitney celebrated her sweet 16 during one of the VIP cruises.

Years later, Doc became more than a friend. He hired me to help with a new division of his company. I sat with him in an Auburn Hills Restaurant and sought his counsel regarding my life that, up to that point, had not amounted to much. I had just been fired for the first time in my life and my then fiancé decided the grass was greener on the other side of her life's fence. Yes, the black hole took out another one and sadly, not the last. I was dead inside.

As he listened to me talk about my education, experience, and thirst to do something great, Doc slammed his meaty hand down on the table hard enough to send the silverware flying and exclaimed, "Come work with me! I have an idea."

And I did. It was cool. It was fun. It was the second chance I needed to point my life. I can safely say that I am the only person to have worked for two past St. Ignace Car Shows Guests of Honor. Any takers?

Chapter 52: Father Viper and Bo Duke

"The best thing about St. Ignace is you could sit and talk about your heroes and legends, turn around, and see them sitting at the next table. There was nothing like it."

Roy Sjoberg, *"Father Viper" head of Chrysler's Viper Project and 2008 Guest of Honor.*

The Dodge Viper had a massive impact on the consciousness of the automotive world and gear heads everywhere.

Chrysler President Bob Lutz suggested to Tom Gale (a past guest of honor) the company needed to produce a modern "Cobra" and Mr. Gale, head of Chrysler Design Center, had a clay model presented to him within a few months.

So enthusiastic was public reaction that Chief Engineer Roy Sjoberg was directed to develop the Viper as a standard production car. Head of "Team Viper," Mr. Sjoberg assembled 85 engineers to make the high-performance car a reality.

When I met Mr. Sjoberg, I determined that he was one of the nicest, most learned men I had ever met. As Guest of Honor, he enthralled the crowd with stories of the Viper and battles with Lee Iacocca to bring the $70 million vehicle to fruition.

Viper clubs across the country showed up as a tribute and lined both sides of Main Street with every variant.

Mr. Sjoberg was a close friend of Zora Arkus-Duntov, had heard of St. Ignace and brought his cars to our little town in previous years.

John Schneider was the most amazing guest we had for dad's 40 years of car show production. He launched his career at age 18 as Bo Duke and stayed in the public eye for decades. His appearance in St. Ignace was legendary, as he held court the entire day signing autographs, taking photos, shaking hands, took no breaks and met anyone who wanted to shake his hand and talk with him.

"It's not fair. That is one of the most handsome men I've ever seen," dad laughed. "I mean, come on, blonde hair, blue eyes, 6' 3" and that personality?"

John was an incredible talent, charting multiple songs on the country charts and founded, with Marie Osmond, the Children's Miracle Network.

Once he secured John, dad started placing ads in car magazines looking for the "General Lee" in pristine condition. Dad dangled the carrot for the General's owner to come to St. Ignace, drive with John Schneider in it, and stay a night in St. Ignace during the show.

And he got just that. The car was exceptional, drew huge crowds and thousands of photos were taken with John, his fans, and the car.

The caliber of people who came to town was incredible during dad's tenure. Hot Rod legends like Ed Almquist and Paul Hatton (2011 Guest of Honor) routinely came to St. Ignace. "If you had a car striped by Paul Hatton, you had the best," Dad said. "He was incredible."

He'd always wanted to publish a book about his 50 years on main street, so, in 2010, he did. "St. Ignace Car Culture" was more a pictorial history and not the type contained in this work.

It was a cool book that he dedicated to me and added "published author" to his growing list of accomplishments. It is that book from which I drew a lot of insight into the cars dad owned.

The year the "Great Race" came to St. Ignace, longtime supporter of the show and one of the finest automotive minds in the world "Top Hat" John Jenzda was Guest of Honor.

The "Great Race" is a competitive, controlled-speed endurance road rally on public highways specifically for antique, vintage, and collector cars. Starting at various points, it can be West to East, North to South, etc. It is a test of a driver's ability to endure a cross country trip driving at, or below, the posted speed limit.

After 32 years, and getting better each year, the success of St. Ignace was a testament to my father's tenacity and the chip on his shoulder from being an outcast and never picked to play on a team when he was a child.

His way of living was by design. The way he ate was by design. Everything had a purpose. Life without purpose was not worth living for my father. Write it down. Work it. Change course if it's not working. Write down a new way, do it, rinse, repeat.

A purpose-driven life was something I never found until one of the worst moments in my life, when I was 39 years old. Foreshadowing at its best.

Chapter 53: Talking Cars with Mr. Roy Sjoberg

Executive Engineer Viper Project and 2008 Guest of Honor

Known by the colorful nickname of "Father Viper", Guest of Honor Roy Sjoberg started coming to St. Ignace in the late 1970's. With a summer home in nearby Indian River, it was a nice early summer diversion for the yet to be named father viper.

He rose to Executive Engineer-Viper Project in February 1989 and created a legacy high-performance car with mass appeal. In that position, he created and managed the Project Team for the development & production of the Dodge Viper.

So cutting edge was Mr. Sjoberg's design of the "Platform Team" (created to produce the Viper) it became the corporate-wide organizational structure for Chrysler.

With dozens of shows already attended, St. Ignace was no secret to Mr. Sjoberg. It was the Guest of Honor luncheon that was Mr. Sjoberg's favorite as he knew many of the people being honored.

"They all took pride in what they created and loved what they did," Mr. Sjoberg said of the many luminaries attending the show. "That is why I loved the St. Ignace Car Show. You had people who loved what they did and loved to talk about it and share their stories. It was always fun."

Mr. Sjoberg traveled the country to various car shows, so coming to such a small town to see such big-name people, he loved the fact the car owners were people who did all their own restorations. You could touch the cars and they "were not trailer queens," meaning the cars were driven there.

His love for the 1951 Mercury, one of his personal favorites, was indulged, as there were typically several in attendance. Mr. Sjoberg also enjoyed talking to the car owners, who never strayed far from their machine. "If you go to Amelia Island or Pebble Beach, the owner will introduce you to his restorer because what he knows about the car is what it costs," Mr. Sjoberg said. "St. Ignace was always the exception to that."

The one component St. Ignace had, the venue, was the draw for many people. "Was the venue special? Hell yes," Mr. Sjoberg said. "It was terrific. There is not a lot of politics or bullshit going on. People came because they loved cars and wanted to see them."

Mr. Sjoberg said the Friday night Down Memory Lane Parade was incredible, from the people on the street, watching, to the floats, to the cars.

When dad asked Mr. Sjoberg about coming as Guest of Honor he called it a "Pleasure and a privilege."

Longtime friends with Zora Arkus-Duntov, Mr. Sjoberg said he was proud to be included with him on the Guest of Honor list. The year Mr. Sjoberg was Guest of Honor, dad had dozens of Viper Clubs in attendance and they lined up and down the street to honor Mr. Sjoberg as "Father Viper".

Of all the people Mr. Sjoberg met in St. Ignace, and this list is a Who's Who Worldwide, it was Linda Vaughn who was the most impactful. Ironically, it was the same thing that impressed me most about Linda, her mind.

She was magical in her ability to recall the name of every person she met, from the person in charge, to the car parkers, the gatekeepers, and stage hands.

"She remembers everybody and that impacted my wife as Linda called her by name and even knew the names of our children," Mr. Sjoberg said. "She knew how to do it, she was a real marketer."

During a Barret-Jackson event, Mr. Sjoberg was in the crowd when Linda approached and asked why he was not up on the stage. When he told her nobody had invited him, she quickly waved that away and told him to follow her.

When the security guard came to question him, Linda interjected, "Hi, Joe. How's the wife?" and we were let right in." Approaching the camera man, Linda, of course, knew his name too, and told him to make sure he focused on Mr. Sjoberg.

"I ended up on the podium speaking," Mr. Sjoberg said with a chuckle.

Working with my father was a great experience, Mr. Sjoberg told me. "Getting invited to his house and to see the museum he has in there was a thrill and a lot of fun." Mr. Sjoberg told me that coming to St. Ignace was always a pleasure because dad always made sure he had everything he needed.

St. Ignace was unique for Mr. Sjoberg because it was not politically statured like Pebble Beach. "It was not uppity in St. Ignace, not about who you were seen with or your attire. It was just fun. It was a ball to walk around and see cars you just don't see every day."

It wasn't enough that dad brought working cars to town, driven by the owner, restored by the owner, and having the owner there to talk about his car, so then dad started the truck show.

"To see all those working trucks lined up downtown like that was incredible," Mr. Sjoberg told me. "I ran into the owner of one of the rigs as he was putting Armor All on all 18 wheels of his truck. I asked him how long it took him to do all that. He'd started at 3 a.m. and it was 7 a.m. and he was almost done."

The major thing about St. Ignace that Father Viper loved more than anything else was the grassroots, all-American car owners who loved their cars, loved talking about their cars, and wanted to hear about your car.

"There were no trailer queens in St. Ignace," Mr. Sjoberg said with a laugh.

I was glad to speak to Mr. Sjoberg as he truly is one of the nicest men I've meet. Gregarious, happy, and always extending his hand to me with a smile on his face, he was a huge asset to St. Ignace. One of the best things Mr. Sjoberg did for dad was to introduce him to the top automotive people at GM, Ford, and Chrysler to appear at the show.

Through all the years and memories, Mr. Sjoberg was steadfast to what was the best experience; The Guest of Honor Brunch.

Attending this event over the years enabled him to see old friends, and to sit and talk about cars and their heroes.

"The greatest thing was you just didn't talk about your heroes, you turned around and they were sitting at the next table. The automotive royalty in one room was mind blowing."

Chapter 54: Talking Cars with Mr. Ken Gross

"Ed Reavie is in the top two show promoters of all time."

Chuck Miller, *1966 Ridler Award Winner, renowned car builder, and 2010 Guest of Honor.*

Former Director, Petersen Automotive Museum, Celebrated Automotive Journalist, and Guest of Honor 2009

To list all the accomplishments of Mr. Ken Gross, I would need an appendix in the back of this book.

Mr. Gross is a distinguished author, historian, judge, collector, and art enthusiast. With more than 30 years as Chief Class Judge at the Pebble Beach Concours D'elegance, Mr. Gross authored dozens of books, is head automotive writer for Playboy Magazine, contributes to more than 40 other publications, and received the Automotive Hall of Fame Distinguished Service Citation in 2014.

It is from that experience and pedigree that I listened in awe as he talked about my father's show and, truth be told, I got emotional at the praise he lavished upon my ailing father.

Mr. Gross attended the show once prior to his Guest of Honor turn. "Keith Crain (Guest of Honor in 2000) told me this was the one show I did not want to miss," he said.

He'd heard of St. Ignace and thought it was more of a regional show, so he told me he'd underestimated the reach and depth of what St. Ignace was.

"It's a happening, it's very special," he said. "It gave me an understanding of where all my Michigan friends went in the summertime. This show was a big deal, and it made people feel they were part of a tradition and something special."

When my father called him to offer the Guest of Honor role, Mr. Gross told me it was an honor and he was delighted to attend.

"St. Ignace had national cache," Mr. Gross said. "It exceeded my expectations and I usually don't go into anything with expectations, but St. Ignace was so much more than that."

When the conversation turned to the total package that was St. Ignace; the parade, the cruise nights, and the show, all with that backdrop, is when Mr. Gross spoke very highly of St. Ignace.

For a man so well-traveled, a man who has judged Concours events in North America and Europe in all the exotic locations he's seen, it was important for me to know just how incredible was the show that my father started. So I flat out asked Mr. Gross this question.

Mr. Gross made a pensive pause, then said he started a Concourse event in Chattanooga where he tried extremely hard to give participants the full car show experience; not all in one big day, but over three days.

"I don't think I planned it this way, I think St. Ignace was a big influence on how it came together, "Mr. Gross said. "St. Ignace will never be a toney car show, but your dad's formula for success was to make sure everybody had something to do, to give people as much as you can for the time and money, and St. Ignace does that."

After we'd discussed the show, I asked Mr. Gross to rank Edward Reavie in the world of auto show promoters.

"I compare your father to Bill Warner (founder of the Amelia Island Concours D'elegance)", Mr. Gross said without hesitation. "Bill, with his enthusiasm and energy, started a small show and was able to get Sterling Moss and Roger Penske and great collectors to bring their cars to his show."

Mr. Gross also praised me when he told me it takes something like this book to honor a person for their lifetime of work.

When St. Ignace started, there was no local or regional show that had the fame and reputation of the St. Ignace show, Mr Gross said. "That is the achievement, he put St. Ignace on the car gathering map. He did that and more."

Before our talk ended, he told me the story of when one of the two Guest of Honor signs blew off the car as they went over the Mackinac Bridge. He stopped the car and gathered the other sign, not wanting to lose both. Thirteen years later, he knows right where it is.

"It's in my garage, on my tool box," Mr. Gross said. "I was proud to attend. It was fun all around, I have been to shows all over the world, Italy, Belgium, France and England. I look back at St. Ignace as being one of the fun events I was fortunate to attend."

I called dad after the interview and asked him to tell me about Bill Warner. Dad gushed about Mr. Warner and called him one of the finest show promoters in the world.

He then asked me why I asked. I told him it was because Ken Gross had just compared him to Bill Warner. Dad was shocked to silence before simply saying, "Wow."

Thank you, Mr. Gross.

Chapter 55: Talking Cars with Mr. Chuck Miller

"You will never find a nicer show. There is no better setting on State Street along the water when other shows are on concrete and football fields."

Dana Decoster, *Founder Cruising News 2014 Guest of Honor*

1966 Ridler Award Winner and 2010 Guest of Honor

Chuck Miller first opened Styline Customs in River Rouge, MI in 1963, and is legendary in the world of custom cars. His 1966 Ridler Award winning Fire Truck and the Red Baron are just two examples of his amazing body of work.

When I called him for this interview, it was nearly 7 p.m. Michigan time and he was still in the shop working on a car. I'd met Mr. Miller when he came to St. Ignace in 1986, so we caught up on each other's lives.

During the conversation, it was, to me, like opening up a photo album to my past and we both reflected on the amazing years spent at the show. (In fact, Mr. Miller, our conversation gave me the idea as to how to end this book so thank you.)

When I asked him how he first heard about the show in St. Ignace, I got a great answer. He has a home in Grayling (90 minutes South of St. Ignace), on Lake Marguerite.

"I would always see all these great cars heading North on I-75 and wondered where they were going," he said. "Someone I knew in town asked me if I had ever been to St. Ignace."

As the years went by, Mr. Miller went to the overpass and watched the automotive cavalcade rolling north. "After a few years I decided it was time to check out this show."

Bob Larivee, Sr., was the guest of honor in 1986, was friends with Mr. Miller, and encouraged him to attend the show. Mr. Miller did make the trip to St. Ignace and it was there he met Jack Walker, and the two are fast friends to this day.

Ever the champion for my dad's show, Mr. Larivee told dad that Mr. Miller was coming, and dad made him "Honorary Chairman" and invited him to the famous Guest of Honor brunch.

"Dave Bell, Jack Walker, Dan Webb, and many others were at the K Royale Hotel," Mr. Miller said. "And we all decided to go on the boat ride together. And that is when it started. We became friends and those friendships still exist to this day."

The friendships made, and heroes met in St. Ignace was a running thread with all my interviews and Mr. Miller got more excited the longer we talked.

"We came every year and one particular year, who do we see? Ed Roth and then, further down the road, Buffalo Bob. Wow. Am I right? My childhood hero was Buffalo Bob. How do you meet people like that? Each year it was something different."

The fun of St. Ignace had a lot to do with St. Ignace itself.

"St. Ignace? Where is that?" Mr. Miller said. "Pull out a map and there it is. You met new people, met your heroes. These were people right out of the magazines and I never thought I would meet them. George Barris, Jerry Palmer, Linda Vaughn, I met them all there."

Meeting them was one thing, he told me, but sharing experiences, getting to know them, and then staying friends with them was the ultimate as, each year, they came back.

I asked him about Cruise Night and got an instant reaction. "Oh, I really liked that," he said. "Cruising, listening to Dick Biondi play the songs, it instantly took me back to high school. I really enjoyed that." Hearing his reactions to the memories as he recalled them, made me smile. It was the show. It was the complete experience being re-lived.

He also partook in the Mackinac Bridge tower climb and shared that he thinks Jack Walker's hand grips are still indented into the ladder rungs going to the top.

"I would do that again in a heartbeat," he said. "Walter North was an amazing guy. He took us up there. That was something you will never forget. It was a great experience."

One event flowed into the other; the boat cruise, the guest of honor lunch, cruising, the parade, Cruise Night, and then, very little sleep until it was time to get downtown to park the cars.

"We got up E-A-R-L-Y," Mr. Miller laughed. "It was a ridiculous early time but we got up, got down there, and got into position."

After the amazing show was dinner with friends, checking out the concerts, and cruising around.

"Your dad figured out early that, to get people to a little town nobody really heard of, you needed to entertain them," Mr. Miller said. "He did a super job. He couldn't have done it any better."

Of course, no trip to the show was complete without visiting dad's auto museum within his house, "I don't think he could have fit anything else into that room," Mr. Miller said with a laugh. I told him not only did dad fit more, he built another room to hold more.

He's been involved in the industry since 1963, when he was 20 years old, and traveled the country, so I asked him to rank St. Ignace for the total experience.

"Top 10. Maybe even higher. It is something everyone needs to do. St. Ignace is right up there with Oakland, Louisvlille, and Detroit."

He was last in St. Ignace in 2017 to see his friend Jack Walker as Guest of Honor, and I asked Mr. Miller to rank Ed Reavie as a show promoter.

"He is in the top two," he said without hesitation. "The reason being, how can this guy, in a little town nobody heard of, be able to have the people he had as Guest of Honor? Barris, Buehrig, Roth, Shelby? No way, it just can't happen. He did it. There are not a lot of people who can pull off the amazing talent your dad did."

The thing with my father, Mr. Miller said, was he did things himself and it was a personal invitation from him, not a secretary.

"Your dad had the perfect personality for what he did and he did things as a friend."

Another common thread was meeting heroes and the same happened for Mr. Miller.

"Dave Bell, I followed him for a long time and there he was. Linda Vaughn, there she was and then I turn around and see George Barris? He was a California guy. It was incredible. They were right out of the magazine. My heroes. Wow."

I asked him if he plans on returning, he said, "In fact, Jack Walker and I talked about it, coming back this year. What your dad has done for his city and our state, wow. He is near the top and you should be very proud of him."

I am sir, I am.

PART 16

The Time Has Come

Chapter 56: The next 40 years

Time and age were unkind to my father.

Men like Gene Winfield continued to create masterpieces well into their 90's. Bob Larivee, Sr., is in his 90's, and is still a big part of the industry, and Chuck Miller is still in his shop working long hours. Dad is relegated to having others drive him around.

He began suffering a series of cognitive issues that affected his legs which made walking and depth perception tricky. During the 2012 Barrett-Jackson event we attended, he started having issues with his legs.

After Super Saturday, he stopped, grabbed my shoulder, and told me he didn't think he could walk down the grassy slope of the parking lot, so a golf cart was summoned. Sunday morning was the same.

It was difficult for him to watch the 85-year-old legendary car designer Mr. Winfied walk down the street looking as if he were a man in his 50's while he was relegated to sitting in a golf cart with me watching over him. That was hard.

He suffered a massive heart attack on Christmas Day of 2004, and then had a quintuple bypass. His days of hoarding the double Big Mac coupons and eating like a college student were over.

I recall him taking me to lunch at our McDonalds. He had a two-for-one Big Mac coupon and after he ordered, asked me what I wanted.

I looked at him incredulously and asked about the second Big Mac on his tray. Laughing, he said, "Get your own coupon, this one is mine."

Seeing him in the hospital, struggling to survive, crushed me. That event set into motion a series of illnesses that, with proper care from his live-in girlfriend, could have been avoided.

I helped him stand and held him tight when he wobbled, and my heart broke. I had to have heart-to-heart talks with him about limitations. My sister, as she struggled to deal with him, called me and asked for my intervention nearly every other week as the strong-willed Rebel gave her the business for trying to help.

But, as the legends grow, the show must go on. And it did, bringing some serious muscle both automotive and personal.

Gene Winfield was a master painter and designer and brought his "Golden Sunrise" 1958 Chrysler to town. Shaking hands with Gene was amazing, his grip was like iron, having worked a wrench for decades. A nicer man you cannot meet.

Mr. Winfield had a great charisma about him and his work, not only in the world of automobiles, but in television and the movies.

Al Bergler, the first Ridler Award winner, came to town with the "Motown Shaker" among others and I vividly recall Al lighting up those engines and having a "cackle fest''. Talk about blowing your hair back.

"Cruise News" publisher Dana Decoster, who covered nearly every St. Ignace show, and gave dad so much publicity over the years, came as Guest of Honor.

"I was surprised when Ed Reavie called and offered me a "Guest of Honor" Dana said. "It really freaked me out."

Chapter 57: Talking Cars with Mr. Gene Winfield

"The King of Kustoms" and Guest of Honor 2014

Gene Winfield is legendary in all things automotive. In 1951, he entered "The Thing", a custom Ford Model T, at Bonneville Speedway, hitting 135 MPH.

He worked with Detroit auto manufacturers to help them customize their cars and, along the way, developed incredible cars. One of which was known as The Reactor, and it appeared on the television show "Bewitched." His creations appeared in movies The Last Starfighter, Blade, and Robo Cop. Television shows with his creations included Get Smart, Bewitched, Star Trek, Batman, and Mission Impossible.

Mr. Winfield hailed from the California coast and turned down my father's invitation; twice. After finally accepting and arriving in St. Ignace, he was shocked at the beauty of the area and quickly accepted when asked to climb the bridge tower.

"I loved the boat cruise when we went under the bridge," he said. "It was beautiful and I remembered when you got married during one of the trips.

He has traveled the world attending car shows, and said my father stood out as a promoter for his sheer love of the genre.

"Ed Reavie did a great job," Mr. Winfield said. "He was a fantastic man and was great at everything he was doing."

Mr. Winfield said his greatest memories revolved around meeting new people who became friends for life.

He attended every event for many years, including the parade, Cruise Night, the brunch, and the big show. He has lasting memories.

"I met Linda Vaughn there and that was great," he said. "Each event was incredible. It was very good. So many people, so many events, and everything worked great."

Now 95 years old, Mr. Winfield still works in his shop, "Winfield's Custom Shop" (where this interview took place over the phone) and told me to have the organizers give him a call as he would love to come to St. Ignace again.

I sent Quincy a message with just that information.

Gene Winfield, another legend who came to our little town.

Chapter 58: Save The last Dance

Looking back on the list of Guests of Honor, I still am in shocked at the men and one woman who were so honored by my father. What can you say about that list?

However, all great things must end and so did dad's run as promoter and producer of this incredible show. For the 40th St. Ignace show, dad's last, he brought back legendary General Motors man Jon Moss as his final Guest of Honor.

Their first meeting was less than happy and caused dad to wonder if Mr. Moss was going to be an advocate or an antagonist. Dad remembered Mr. Moss telling him, "It is not my fault I am 6' 9" and not very smiley."

Speaking with both dad and Mr. Moss, the story is the same. Two large men, both with huge reputations, squared off in a verbal tussle that, had traffic not already been parked, would have stopped traffic.

I think Seagulls stopped flying and dove into Lake Huron when Mr. Moss lit into my father over what he thought was an intentional slight.

Mr. Moss started his career in 1963 working the Oldsmobile assembly line before he enlisted in the United States Army. In the 1980's, he rose to the Director of GM's Specialty Vehicle Group.

When he arrived in St. Ignace and went to the General Motors display that was set up and waiting for him, he was thunderstruck.

While dad had provided them with a prime location right on the water, the car parkers inexplicably parked a Dodge car club right in front of it.

To say this did not go over well with Mr. Moss would be akin to shaving one's head with a cheese grater while chewing on tin foil.

"BRING ME ED REAVIE!!!" he boomed.

When dad arrived, the towering Mr. Moss thundered at him for the indiscretion. If you have met Mr. Moss, you would know how this went over.

Dad told me "When Jon Moss enters a room, there is no question on earth who is in charge. People stop talking and break away eye contact. He has a powerful personality."

I remember dad came back to the main show area looking as if he'd been beaten with a bag of oranges. He was flustered, looked like he'd lost his best friend, and was worried that he just blew it with what was his biggest corporate supporter.

Lee Orton, head of the parking valets, is an old school car guy who kept things under control with his no nonsense attitude and was the road general from 4 a.m. to 9 a.m., when thousands of cars rolled into the show area. Controlling nearly two miles of roadway, he conducted the symphony of American metal with an orange-tipped paint stick and made sure the cars were parked in such a way as to help with the flow of tens of thousands of people as they came into the show.

Sometimes, and it was rare, a Dodge car club got parked in front of the show's biggest sponsor and caused a clash of titans to take place. When I asked Lee if he remembered such a thing, he responded dryly, "Yes, I do. Yes, I do."

Chapter 59: Talking Cars, with Mr. Jon Moss

2015 Guest of Honor

In speaking with Mr. Moss, he told me Jerry Palmer and other members of his design staff had visited St. Ignace for years prior to his arrival.

He visited St. Ignace in early April 1990, to get an idea of what awaited him and his team. He laughed about the ice chunks still floating under the Mackinac Bridge.

It was all set. The biggest, baddest car company on the planet, with Jim Perkins, the Head of the Chevrolet Division leading the team from GM Performance, they had a prime spot right in the middle of the Marina Dock; show HQ for 40 years.

Mr. Moss arrived the Thursday before the show to ensure everything was accounted for, in place, and ready to go. He was excited to be a part of this amazing, legendary show, but he soon found out all was not well.

Mr. Moss was immediately beset upon by an enraged Jim Perkins, red faced, fists balled, and screaming.

"Who in the hell parked DODGE in front of GM?!?! Mr. Perkins roared upon seeing Mr. Moss.

"I said 'What the hell? Ed has us parked behind DODGE! Bullshit!"

"I learned that day, shit does indeed roll downhill," dad deadpanned telling me the story.

Yes, it happened. Through some miscommunication, "The MOPAR Roadshow" display blocked the front of the GM Performance Display. The metaphorical gauntlet was tossed at the feet of MOPAR legend John Greer and GM Legend Jon Moss. You can't believe such a thing could be true, I dare you to even try.

"And that was when I first met Ed," Mr. Moss said with a laugh as he recalled the less than pleasant encounter with dad.

He thought he was getting second billing behind a competitor, and called my dad and asked him in a slightly aggressive tone, what was going on?

Dad replied they indeed had a great spot, right on the lake and right in the middle of the show, as promised.

"Yeah, behind Dodge!" Mr. Moss said laughing as he recounted the moment. "Your dad was terrified of me for a while after that."

For those that know Mr. Moss. He is a towering presence simply based on his personality. Add to it he is, in fact, 6' 9" tall, and you have a recipe for intimidation.

Dad found Rich Woodmansee (Chevy Creative Services) and they walked over to see Mr. Greer and Mr. Moss giving each other the business about who needed to move.

Dad credits Mr. Woodmansee for defusing the situation, recalling that Mr. Woodmansee reminded the two titans that both of their spots were comped. so it was not worth it to continue such debate and they should work out a solution for everyone. It was finally agreed upon by all parties to move GM to the empty lot between the main Arnold Line Boat dock and the Galley Restaurant. Mr. Moss noted it wasn't paved, had pot holes, and was a mess, but was still better than "being parked behind Dodge."

With only two days before the show, Dad called in a favor from local contractor Tim Huskey who worked his magic to make the lot usable. It turned out to be perfect.

Mr. Moss was so impressed with the show and the lot's location that, in later years, he contacted the Arnold Line Boat Company (owners of the great spot) and offered them a deal; Chevrolet would pave the dirt lot to get a break on the rent. Problem solved.

In subsequent years, The GM Performance Lot became the premier place for tens of thousands of persons to gather. GM Performance brought multiple tractor trailers and an incredible array of automobiles every year. Dad and I had the chance to drive these amazing cars in the Down Memory Lane Parade.

"The setting was absolutely spectacular," Mr. Moss told me of his impression of the show. "We were ten feet from the water. It was a great show."

As I interviewed people for this book, there was one thread of concern with all of them regarding how businesses in St. Ignace played a huge part in hurting the very show that brought hundreds of thousands of persons to their door.

Mr. Moss recounted the concerns he had with the hotel owners raising their prices for rooms that had no amenities other than a place to sleep, and he didn't sugarcoat it.

"A lot of people got ticked off about that," he rightly opined. "Add that to the minimum three night stay and the high prices in the restaurants, the city lost a golden opportunity."

He said that, because of the limited cuisine choices and large crowds, his wife decided GM should hold a catered dinner.

Dad introduced him to a caterer, and Mr. Moss called Chevy Creative Services to bring up tables and chairs. They charged $10 a person to eat, sit and watch the parade on those Friday nights.

One thing my father did to shift the paradigm in the auto show business, was to incorporate his show into the city instead of the other way around. The City of St. Ignace was the centerpiece, not a football field, campground, parking lot, or dusty fair ground. I asked Mr. Moss if he ever saw anything like that concept in all his travels.

"For such a small town, no, I didn't," your dad built this to be one of the top shows in Michigan."

Other towns and cities followed Dad's template in ensuing years and gave people the chance to walk through the town, stop into the shops, and enjoy the atmosphere.

The City of Frankenmuth is a prime example of how a city followed dad's template. "The difference was the attitude of the city, Ed had to bow down to them sometimes. The city did not realize what they had," Mr. Moss said.

Mr. Moss was astounded at the lack of foresight. He remembered the huge crowds being frustrated with stores being closed or out of product,

"The foot traffic (during the show) was beyond comprehension," he said. "And some businesses were closed. They wouldn't listen to Ed."

I remember one business, right in the middle of the show area, closed their doors and blamed the car show for bringing so many people to town they couldn't get to the business to open up.

During the years of CLOSED BECAUSE OF CAR SHOW signs in their window, it is not farfetched to say nearly a million people walked past their doors with nothing to show for it. If they just sold water, sun screen, and ice, imagine the money they would have made. But yes, blame the car show.

Mr. Moss echoed a lot of feedback received over the years as long-time participants could no longer afford the three-night minimum and went elsewhere.

Communities around St. Ignace, like Mackinaw City, reaped the benefits of sticker-shocked show goers. New hotels sprang up on the shoreline of Mackinaw City with no three-night minimum to stay and restaurants followed suit by not doubling their prices.

"I felt sad for Ed, he tried so hard to make that city better, but he was fighting against a brick wall," Mr. Moss said.

As we continued, he laughed as he said dad and he eventually buried the hatchet over the Dodge mishap and developed a strong relationship. To make sure all was well, dad set up Mr. Moss and his wife on a private carriage tour of Mackinac Island.

"Ed was so gracious, he invited us to his home, he saw to it we got front row billing in our own spot," Mr. Moss said. "He just couldn't have been better to work with."

He said it was an honor to be Dad's final Guest of Honor; the 40th show was dad's last.

"Looking back at all the years we were there, we accomplished a lot," he told me. "We supported Ed and did all we could to help that show continue on."

Dad was so grateful for him, and later Craig Shantz, who took over the role after Mr. Moss retired. Working with GM was one of dad's crowning achievements as it was the biggest company on earth and responsible for so many great cars in history.

Dad not only worked with them but created a friendship with his fellow gear heads that lasted more than 20 years. Having Jon Moss as his final guest of honor was one of the best things dad did. Once GM invested in St. Ignace, Ford and Chrysler followed.

Such was their investment that GM hosted a golf tournament on Mackinac Island along with Peterson Publishing who brought their family of automotive magazines to the show and helped promote the town to the outside world.

"It was an honor and a culmination of all the years we came up there," Mr. Moss said.

Now retired after nearly 41 years at GM and the director of all specialty vehicles for GM in North America, Mr. Moss continues to be a vocal supporter of the show and dad's legacy.

"There were some unbelievable cars in St. Ignace, we participated in the charities Ed championed," Mr. Moss said. "St. Ignace was a neat, neat show."

The impact of General Motors and the philanthropic endeavors they created for St. Ignace can never truly be measured.

As he recalled the vast number of cars stretching from the Highway all the way to the Napa Car Parts store, parked up side streets, and in the lawns of hotels that could not even get into the show, Mr. Moss had one word to describe St. Ignace in its heyday.

"It was insane."

Yes sir, it really was.

PART 17

The Golden Jubilee
and Beyond

Chapter 60: Speeding Forward

The 2015 show, the 40th anniversary, was dad's last as promoter and owner. He vacillated for years regarding the how and when to say goodbye and enjoy what he created.

He spoke at length about what he wanted and how he wanted to go out. It was a process that took a lot out of him. His tenure as show promoter was as legendary as his stories about Carroll Shelby and others. He created something that, looking back, is nearly impossible to comprehend.

Speaking with other legends, "Top Hat" John Jenza in particular, who asked the constant rhetorical question, "How did you do this" still rings true.

The greatest cruisers, engineers, designers, minds, legends, and creators of the genre, came to St. Ignace, Michigan.

A town that didn't, and still doesn't, have traffic lights. How does a drag racer even want to come here? Don Garlits, the greatest drag racer of them all, not only came here, but he was also a convert. "I've never seen anything like it," he told me when I interviewed him.

The Batmobile and Munster Coach drove down Memory Lane. The Hirohata Mercury Clone, String of Pearls, The California Kid, Shelby Cobras, the 3rd ever built Corvette, Vipers, Packards,

Duesenbergs, Cords, Auburn Boat Tail Speedsters, The Bugatti Royale, Rat Rods, slammed, nosed, decked, scooped, and every other single variation of automobiles lined the streets spanning four generations.

Oh, and let's not forget thousands of antique farm tractors, pedal cars, big rigs, model cars, Posie specials, and Barris originals and clones. Add to that multiple Ridler Award winners, and you have the alchemy of a nearly perfect Auto Show experience.

I decided to turn that rhetorical question into an open ended one. When Top Hat John asked dad that Sunday, over ice cream, "how in the hell did you get Carroll Shelby to come here?" I heard the answer from my father. That answer was one that will ever be his legacy. "I never stopped asking him."

But, what now? Covid wreaked havoc on the world and on the continuity of the show. I was worried the show would be canceled for the second year in a row, but the community and new organizers made sure that didn't happen, and 2021 was sensational.

Shelby, Murray, Top Hat, you not only saved the show, you made it better and designed it to fit seamlessly into a new generation.

The previous chapters spoke of the history. The following addresses the future. I spoke with those entrusted to move the show forward to a new generation of gear heads. The new driving forces behind the small-town show known globally as, "St. Ignace."

Before going forward, it is important to understand the economic impact this show had, and continues to have, on St. Ignace.

Chapter 61: Economic Impact

The Local Heroes: First National Bank President James North

Jim North, the son of local legend, Mackinac Bridge Authority President, and State Senator Walt North, ascended to the top job as President at dad's bank in 1998.

A lifelong St. Ignace resident, Jim grew up watching the car show grow from a cool event to "the" event. The day before we'd planned our interview, I ran into a situation at work and had to delay our conversation. As a School Resource Officer, I was needed to speak to a child who had gotten himself into trouble.

When I told Jim this over text, he replied, "Summon your inner Kress."

I had to laugh as Jim did not know my grandfather well but man, he knew his reputation.

"I only heard of Kress from Edward, but I was told it was something to behold," Jim laughed when we finally connected.

A natural leader, Jim became dad's boss for the last 17 years of his bank career and again, received support above and beyond to do whatever he needed to make the show a success.

Dad heaped praise on Jim's leadership style and ability to understand the needs of not only the bank, but the car show.

As president at the bank, Jim devised a formula to show the impact of "the big car show".

Jim knew that the last Saturday in June was historically the slowest weekend in the city, thus it would be easy to track revenue as nothing had started to show the economic impact.

Keeping well in mind that 1998 to 2015 (when dad retired), paled in comparison to 1980-1998 when the show took the state, city, and nation, by storm.

Using this formula every year to give him a baseline, Jim took the bank's market share and other variables such as money being deposited in other financial institutions, into ATMs, and through the drive-thru, into account.

In just pure deposits alone, at its peak during Jim's tenure, the St. Ignace Car Show averaged $3,500,000 in economic impact annually. Annually.

Just the car show. Not considering the Richard Crane Memorial Truck Show, On the Waterfront, Antiques on the Bay, the tractor show, etc.

In just those 17 years, the "Big Car Show" brought $59,500,000 into the First National Bank. The number is staggering.

If the years previous were considered, with the record for one week being $9,000,000 in the early 90's, and if you want to meet in the middle and say the First National Bank, and the First National Bank alone, averaged $5,500,000 during those shows, that is $93,500,000 for a total of $147,000,000 in economic impact.

Just. One. Show. Just. One. Bank.

Let's hypothetically include the Richard Crane Truck Show, Antiques on the Bay, Tractor shows, On the Waterfront, AND potential deposits in banks other than First National covering the 25 year history of those shows.

It's safe to say, Edward K. Reavie and his show brought $250,000,000 into his community.

"It was a big number for such a small town," Jim said. "I hit the scene in 1998, past the peak of revenue for the show."

The impact was noticeable to those who came to the show for years. "You could see it in the new park benches downtown, the boardwalk, the restoration of the buildings, and the hotels, "said 2010 Guest of Honor Chuck Miller. "The town thrived during that show and all who came over those years saw it all change from year-to-year."

Being dad's boss was a bit daunting, so Jim spoke with board Chairman Prentiss M. Brown Jr. (Moie) about how to balance the two.

"I am a community banker, I get this," Jim said. "What is good for the community is good for the bank."

Worried about perception of dad working car show business at work, Jim quickly made the call what was good for the show was good for the customer and the city itself.

Be it an important phone call, say from Zora Arkus-Duntov, Carroll Shelby, Bill Mitchell, and even Jay Leno, who all called the bank wanting to speak with dad, it was something the entire chain-of-command was going to support.

"Ed never abused it. If he went to a trade show, he burned his vacation time, not bank time," Jim said. "It was a year-round production and your dad never made it a problem, he knew how to juggle it."

One of the keys to dad's success, Jim felt, was his uncanny ability to get the right people in the right places to get things done.

"It's like a NASCAR pit team," Jim said. "Your dad had that ability to get everyone to work perfectly together." During his years with dad, Jim said dad and he enjoyed, and still enjoy, a great personal relationship.

"He has a great sense of humor," Jim said. "Your dad sees life through a little different filter than some of the rest of us. It was often humorous."

I learned something else about my father that I share as Jim told me some stories.

"Even if he didn't have anyone to talk to, that man could carry on the greatest conversations with himself like I never saw anyone else do before."

One of my many flaws is that I do the same thing. My wife of 12 years, Melissa, learned many years ago to tune me out as I ranted in my office, when nobody else was in the room. "When you actually talk to me, let me know," she famously said. "That way, I can stop tuning you out."

When I transferred to the Child Crimes Unit and sat across from a 33-year veteran, I had one of my talks with myself, and got his attention.

The befuddled detective yelled out to me asking if I was talking to him. When I said no, he said with a deep emphasis, "Then shut the f**k up, my God man, seek help."

Jim laughed as he told me about hearing all the incredible conversations coming out of dad's office. When he went in to see to whom dad was speaking, he learned something new about dad.

"It was just him and boy, was he carrying on. He wasn't on the phone; it was just him."

Agreeing with me about dad's almost superhuman ability to organize, Jim laughed again, "Although you would never realize it by looking at his workstation."

I brought up dad's magnificent office/museum at home and the epic mess of it all. Somehow, he knows where everything is located, be it a story in a Japanese show car magazine, or a letter from Willard Scott he received.

"Ed ranks high when he has a passion for it, he gives a thousand percent. It's in his character."

As chief loan officer of the bank, dad often had to repossess items from those who failed to make their payments. Depending on the task, he was thrilled or, not so much.

I shared my favorite dad repossession story with Jim, one he had not heard. A local took out a loan to purchase a big, beautiful pick-up truck and defaulted. The man knew dad's ability to locate items and repossess them, so he decided to try and outsmart dad and the wrecker he had with him to take his truck.

Instead of hiding it, the man snaked a thick, long chain through both windows, and secured the ends around a large oak tree in his front yard.

Not one to shy away from a challenge, dad went to ACE Hardware to solve this problem. A normal person, who my father is not, had multiple options to include bolt cutters, or a lock pick.

Dad bought a chainsaw.

After he cut down the tree, he hopped into the truck, and drove off in great haste honking the horn and waving as he peeled out of the driveway. This is my dad.

Chapter 62: Talking St. Ignace with Wesley Mauer Jr.

Owner-St. Ignace News

Wes Maurer Jr. came to St. Ignace in 1981 and is a fixture in the community. Along with his wife, Mary, he worked tirelessly next to my father, often pulling all-nighters to complete the show supplements.

Wes, to my father and me, is family. He gave me my first real job at the age of 16 and formed my career as a writer. His father, Wes Sr., was the most learned man I ever met, a true newspaper man and former Dean of the University of Michigan School of Journalism.

When I returned from college, I made a point to visit Mr. Maurer and his wife. I never saw him without a shirt and tie. Since I left for Phoenix in 2006, no trip home was complete without stopping at the St. Ignace News to see Wes and Mary.

We talked for at least an hour. I always told Wes and Mary of my successes because it was important to me to be seen as successful in their eyes.

At first, it was a running joke and then Wes made sure to run stories about me and the successes in not only my career (two state of Arizona Police Officer of the Year Awards) and then my Foundation.

My stories were very nice, with color photos, but always were inside the paper. Why? "The front is still reserved for your father," he said with a laugh. "One day, keep going."

Wes was in charge of the Mackinac Island Town Crier and his father hand-picked me to work as a reporter, making me the only undergraduate and non University of Michigan student to do so. I returned for three summers, rising to editor my last year.

I remember one happy summer night, Jed Boals and Kevin Vineys, fellow reporters from UM's Grad School, were just a bit tipsy from our fun and frivolity to include making pyramids out of our empty Stroh's cans.

And what do our bleary, bloodshot eyes, and beer goggles see? Wes Jr. walking down the sidewalk. Talk about an instant sobering up moment.

We pushed the cans into the corner and tried to compose ourselves as best we could. Wes walked into the office, one more sheet to the wind than we were, produced a 12-pack, and the party was on. That is how cool Wes is.

I was devastated when Mary died from cancer. It crushed my heart and soul. Wes and Mary were a team. When dad was at his sickest, Wes and Mary made dinner and brought it to him and we talked for hours. It was a crushing loss to our town. During the 2021 show, I made three attempts to find Wes at the paper for our annual chat. I was told he didn't come in much anymore.

On my last day, just hours before having to drive to Grand Rapids to catch my ride home, I stopped by the house. I knocked. And knocked. And knocked. Dad could not move well and was in the car.

I was sad and turned to leave when I heard "DON'T LEAVE" and then footsteps. Wes was upstairs and saw me on his camera. We talked in the yard for a long time. I hugged him and told him I loved Mary and him, which I did and do. Great people.

The first thing Wes told me when I called him for this book was, he didn't know how much help he could be but would give it a try.

It was the best interview I did because I asked one question and Wes laid out a perfect tapestry of history, covering everything I wanted him to cover. We talked for an hour. We shared stories and memories of a time that newspapers were handmade "key line and design" Google it.

Wes worked side-by-side with my dad for more than 30 years, so he was a perfect person to tell and validate the stories dad told me about the long nights, and most notably, the difficulty working with George Barris.

I remember the stress this put on my dad as he feared George Barris would not come to the show. This caused dad to reach out to Bob Laravee who famously "smartened" George Barris up to the smallness of the town and that only two people were doing this. George dropped the request and had the time of his life in St. Ignace.

"We were used to staying up, but this was never ending, and he was never satisfied," Wes said. "He sure could find a lot of photos of his cars."

Back in 1976, Wes Sr. assigned reporter Greg Means to write the first newspaper edition for the first car show, prepared by hand, by the staff at the newspaper.

Wes and Mary moved to St. Ignace from Cedarville in 1980 or 1981, went full-in with dad. Mary handled the mailings and Wes worked with dad.

When Greg started, Wes opined with humor, "I am sure your dad was hanging over his shoulder." As time moved forward, Dad became the ad salesman, Wes wrote the stories, created the ads, and did the proofs.

Sending the final product to dad was always interesting. "He would rip them up and we would start over," Wes said with his dry sense of humor delivery. "It was never done until we told your dad we needed to get it to the printer in time for the show. He was a fantastic proofreader."

Wes and Mary always gave it their all and quickly fell in favor with my perfectionist father for the same "do it right or don't do it at all" view of life.

"That is how we ran our newspaper," Wes said. "We served a constituency and we went to any length to make it as good as we could."

Spending some, "awful long nights" working with dad, Mary sorted the mailing labels by zip codes and enlisted several local community members, like Cheryl Schlehuber (starting her professional career as my father's incredible executive assistant) Carol Lorente (my kindergarten teacher and longtime family friend) and others to come in and hand address the envelopes.

This was the way of the show in those days. Things were done this way. Peeling labels, sticking them on envelopes by their zip codes. Thousands of them.

To thank the crew for their hours of long nights working on the tedious doings of the show, dad always had pizza in hand on the last night. For the workers.

"When everyone was gone and it was just your dad and me, we had Big Macs," Wes said laughing. "Those were pretty good at 11 o'clock at night. They were fun to eat."

Through the years, I recall many times when dad sent me to Wes and Mary to make a new name plate for a guest dad wanted to include at the luncheon. Again, this was before digital and it was a grueling task to get things done in the short amount of time we had. Sometimes, it was the day before. Sometimes, it was hours before.

Wes talked about the growth of Cruise Night and touched on something that, to this day, makes my dad hit the roof. After Bootsie's Drive-in closed, dad reached out to the other drive-in on West US2.

"They turned him down," Wes said. "They told him they were too busy that weekend as it was. It made your dad furious."

Sadly, Wes recalled more than one example of people dismissing the show saying they were too busy that weekend to deal with helping.

"What they never realized," Wes said. "Is that they were busy because of the car show."

Moving the Cruise Night to the Big Boy was a game changer, as it closed the entire highway to accommodate the growing crowd, cars, and off-the-hook tomfoolery.

"The police were very concerned about something touching an incident off because they lacked the manpower to handle it," Wes said. "One year, a bunch of drunks confronted kids on one of the floats during the parade and cursed them out. Later, someone spread feces on a church sign."

Alcohol fueled cars? Yes. Alcohol fueled idiocy? Not so much. This all led to the zero tolerance the city enacted as people without show cars posted about the huge party in St. Ignace, which brought an element that threatened the show and its purpose.

"It got mammoth," Wes said. "It turned into one big drunken party." Once the alcohol was removed, the show shrank in size as people were just tired of the foolishness."

Wes recalled my father's disdain for committees and shared a fun story about him dealing with that very thing after the first few years and the show's success.

"I have a sign in my office," Wes said. "It says committees should be composed of not more than three people, two of whom are absent."

This is how my father saw things. I follow his lead. Groupthink cannot work when people sit back passively and opine on all the hard work that goes into building anything when they do none of the work. Conviction is a luxury of those on the sidelines. When the hard decisions must be made, it takes a strong leader to weigh out the options.

I changed out nearly my entire board of directors this year for this reason. Lots of ideas from people who didn't do anything to grow the foundation except complain about things or be contrary to things I wanted to do and then complain how I did it, not realizing I did it because they didn't. Weird how things never change.

Wes told me that the biggest element of dad's success was to make everything he did, free to the public. When General Motors raffled their engines, dad gave the proceeds from the raffle to various groups in town.

"Your dad spoke their language," Wes said of the car executives and hobbyists. "He talked the talk, he knew as much as they did about the industry and hobby."

Being free and family oriented is the foundation on which dad built his show, Wes said. "People who put on events here don't understand that," Wes said. "The thing that made the car show grow, other than your father's personality and enthusiasm, was this concept he would entertain the car show people and make it free and entertaining for families."

A natural showman, dad always came up with ways to entertain the people who came to the show. Small cocktail parties grew to sunset cruises on three-deck boats, but he always kept one thing universal.

"He always invited the locals," Wes said. "He invited Mary and me, other business owners, locals, and he never charged them. They never paid anything. Your father had a great sense of what was important to people."

Sharing the wealth was a huge part of what made the show successful.

"I don't think your father ever had in mind the show was going to be a profit-making thing for him and he would get rich," Wes said. "I don't know if he did as I never kept his books but, just so you know, he was slow to pay, I'll tell you that."

This set me into a fit of laughter. My father is a bit tight with his own money. A clam with lockjaw isn't as tight and he has been accused of being so tight that he has to screw his socks on in the morning. Allegedly. And Wes and I allegedly shared a belly laugh over those comments.

"We loved Ed because he did it all," Wes said. "He made a good living and making money from the show was never the point for him. He shared the wealth and made it that much more fun for everyone."

Wes has a sharp mind and recalled dad's "official entries" was no more than sending me out with a clicker to count any car on the side streets "that looked to be painted or in any way customized" to help grow the event that much more.

It's all about the marketing, hyperbole and creative license aside.

"Every year, like the Mackinac Bridge Walk, the event got bigger," Wes said with his wonderful dry humor. "There was never any gate so there was really no way to know for either one of them."

I literally giggled recalling all the years I walked for MILES finding any car that wasn't on the show stage. I thought playing guitar caused callouses but using that clicker for hours ground my thumb to a nub.

The network of car people dad built was something to behold. "Your dad was so enthusiastic, that when people came and experienced him and the show, they came back."

To think that Gordon Buehrig, Carroll Shelby, and Zora Arkus-Duntov came back multiple times was mind blowing. That was the show in a nutshell.

"He had the best attitude and the best venue," Wes said. "He had them out on the street, not in a field somewhere. That brought the casual car fan to the show time and again."

Through the years, Wes worked seven days a week. The only time he took a day off was the Saturday car show. He got up early, had friends over for coffee on his large front porch, walked down the street, saw dad and me parking cars, had breakfast, met friends, and saw the cars before the show officially opened. It was damn near a rite of passage as the years ticked past.

Also remembering those morning "coffee" clutches on the Maurer porch, I helpfully reminded him that the main drinks, in my memory, were the amazing Bloody Mary's he made for his guests.

"Alcohol figured into our lifestyle," Wes said flatly.

"Your dad's insights into what people liked and what was successful always amazed me," Wes said. "He had the vision. He liked working with people who 'got it' and got things done. He had a fantastic way of getting people excited about his projects. We were all young and had energy and we were able to get it done. We had great senses of humor and made fun of everything which helped."

Wes said it took him a lot of years to learn the secret of hiring people smarter than him. "Unfortunately, when I got to that decision, I realized just about the entire world was smarter than me."

While my father never utilized committees, he found people who shared his vision and could count on to get his vision spread and take care of things.

"I learned a lot from watching your father," Wes said. "We lost sleep and worked our asses off to make things work right and I think that is why your dad liked Mary and me so much. For one Big Mac a year, it was all worth it for us."

Correction Wes, dad loved you both.

Wes also offered to digitize dad's photographs you see in this book. He asked me when I planned on getting the photos to his office, I told him as soon as possible.

"Just don't wait until the day before," he chimed in as we both laughed.

Chapter 63: Talking with Debbie Evashevski

Director Downtown Development Authority

As with most St. Ignace residents Debbie and my family have a long history. I attended K-12 with Debbie's brother, Jeff. Debbie is married to the former attorney for Nostalgia Productions Inc, Tom Evashevski and just happens to be dad's neighbor.

"I watched our little town go from shooting a cannon down Main Street and not hitting anyone to all those incredible activities," Debbie told me. "That began with the car show."

The show was a catalyst during Debbie's 22 years as director. During this time, she was on the event committee that helped construct the boardwalk in town, and never once thought our sleepy little town would be the host to such a renowned event as the car show.

"It was amazing," Debbie said. "The organizers, your dad, and the people who took over when he got older, did so much. I have so many memories."

She laughed when her young daughter, Erin, first met dad during the time he had let his hair and beard grow, and said, "I don't like Ed. He is a bad guy." Erin, now an attorney working with her father, still gets teased about it.

Speaking of teasing, it was a running tease with dad and Tom over one thing. "I think Erin said what she said because her dad doesn't have a lot of hair."

We both laughed at that one.

Taking the director job in 1995, Debbie attended a workshop my father gave on tourism and she still has a lasting memory.

"He was so dynamic, what a speaker," she said. "He captivated everyone in the room and did a fantastic job."

Dad's relentless ways in regard to the promotion of the show also had a lasting impact on her. "I don't think people really appreciate what he was doing, but people who did know all he was doing, really appreciated him. People know."

Chapter 64: Talking with Janet Peterson

Director, St. Ignace Chamber of Commerce 1985-2017

Starting as director of the St. Ignace Chamber of Commerce in 1985, Janet Peterson had the advantage of working with my father for years at the First National Bank.

She worked her first car show in 1986 and knew dad as, "First National Bank Ed, and I didn't have a problem talking with him at all." Her husband, Steve, also did work on dad's 1955 Chevy.

"It was an easy transition working with your dad," Janet said. "When I started with the chamber, it had yet to do a lot within the community."

Once the chamber was fully on board, the first office for the chamber was located on Dock #2 and became the show headquarters for a long time. Volunteers came in to work the registration lines, award process, and be part of the welcome wagon for people coming to the show for the first time.

Janet had to laugh as cars are not her thing. "The show is my very favorite Edward thing," she said laughing. "How many thousands of times I had to remind him I know absolutely nothing about cars or car people."

Addressing Janet as "Mother Peterson," dad would ask in exasperation, "Mother Peterson, how can you not care about cars?"

Linda Vaughn was the most impressive person Janet met. "She was a pretty amazing and impressive person," Janet said. "But for someone like Linda to come here to St. Ignace all those years says a lot about the show your dad built."

The show began to resonate when Janet met true automotive royalty who kept coming to our lakeside town. Asked by my father to pick up a VIP from one of the hotels, Janet learned later who it was and it stunned her.

"I picked him up and had a conversation with him and he was so nice and normal," She said. "Here I was, driving him around and just talking, having no idea who it was. It was amazing."

Her passenger? Zora Arkus-Duntov.

"How did all this evolve for the St. Ignace Car Show and our Community to be this important to all those people who came back here time and again?" she asked rhetorically. "Just how that all transpired and evolved through the years to become such a big deal."

Knowing my father since she was a little kid, she always knew him as "St. Ignace Ed" the banker and community leader.

"In the car show world, his knowledge, his persistence, his personality, whatever combination it took, it was the right mixture of skills and people," Janet said. "This could not have happened anywhere else in the country."

From the beginning, there was one common denominator. "It was his show, like it or not," Janet said. "He made things happen. To us, he was Ed Reavie of St. Ignace or Ed Reavie of the First National Bank. To all those incredible people who came here, he was Ed Reavie of the St. Ignace Car Show. He is really a big deal."

Addressing the long-held rumor or gossip that my father made millions of dollars from the show (he didn't), Janet defends dad. "If he made millions, he deserved it. He worked 365 days a year on this show, to make this city better," Janet said. "He is responsible for tens of millions of dollars coming to this city."

When the Chamber took over registrations, I told Janet the best part of the day for dad and me was when her team arrived at 5am to deal with the already-long line of car owners wanting their pre-registration packs or to register their cars.

That early morning chaos is hard to describe to people, but when I became a police officer and was first on scene to a chaotic event, I was able to stay cool and handle it.

A favorite moment for Janet was when Linda Vaughn came into the chamber to say hello to all the ladies working there. Janet's six-year-old niece, Meredith, whom she described as a "little prissy thing" was there.

"Meredith looked at Linda, who was wearing a black-and-white checkered jumpsuit, and told her she dressed funny," Janet said. "Linda, without missing a beat, got down at her eye level and said, 'you know what? I bet people say the same thing about you.'"

Linda was Janet's favorite and looked forward to her visits. "She was Linda Vaughn, she was very busy, yet she always had time for people," Janet said.

Janet did registrations for so many years that she had memories and stories to go with that, too. When the show was at its height, and traffic made movement nearly impossible, the registration team met at the Big Boy for breakfast; at midnight.

We got to the registration site between 3 and 4 in the morning," Janet said. "And by that time, the line was out of the parking lot."

The days were so long and so fast paced, counting ballots, in the trailer, trying to go through the boxes of ballots, everyone, including dad, were in deep discussion. Janet turned to look at dad and ask him a question and she was in shock.

"He was sitting there, not moving, and he was sound asleep," Janet said. "He was sound asleep, sitting straight up, and didn't hear a word we were saying."

As Parade Director Merv Wyse's sister-in-law, she always helped with setup. "The great thing about the parade was it brought people to town a day earlier," Janet said. "Merv loved organization and loved parades and had a relationship with your dad so it's been a great thing."

Through the years, Janet realized the importance of the vision that my father had. "Love him or hate him, Ed Reavie IS this show," Janet said.

Janet was a key component to the show's success. "My fondest memories are of bugging your dad," Janet said. "But I feel most accomplished because I felt I could talk to your dad, and make suggestions, and I knew I could make decisions that would help him, and I loved it."

She started working with my father in 1976, and has a long history of Ed Reavie stories and shenanigans. Asking what my dad is like, Janet did not pause before giving her answer.

"He is crazy."

I couldn't disagree.

Chapter 65: Talking with Cheryl Schlehuber

Owner, Mackinac Properties

Starting her professional relationship with my father as his executive assistant at the First National Bank, Cheryl Schlehuber is a successful businesswoman, badass champion golfer, and the only person who gets away with calling me "Junior," for the incredible amount of similarities between dad and me.

When she asked how dad was doing, I told her and then mentioned he was being stubborn about it. "No, really? That is so surprising," Cheryl said laughing. "It was a fun ride working with him."

She started out as a bartender at the new Zodiac Bar (the same place that Carroll Shelby and dad got their hamburger), then applied to be a Teller at the First National Bank and ended up working with my father.

"It was a different life," Cheryl said. "It was fun, it was so much fun working with Ed, Merv Wyse, Debbie Garcia, and others. It was separate from the big wigs at the main bank. It was our own club."

Cheryl said she never felt as if she worked for my dad, but with him. It was the way he treated people and made them feel part of what he was doing.

She often wondered why dad went into banking, as his love for automobiles and automotive history was well known, and if there had been a subject matter expert in such a genre, it would be him.

When the show started, Cheryl helped by putting on roller skates and being part of the first Cruise Nights at Bootsie's drive-in. Her father was a designer at American Motors Corporation, and she was able to relate with dad as he shared the same passion as her father.

"Your dad is a marketing genius," Cheryl said. "He was so far above anyone else and thank God the bank supported him. He drove this market and made this town what it is today."

Now, as a business owner, Cheryl looks at what dad brought into the town. "He changed the face of St. Ignace. He generated so much for this town."

As Owner of Mackinac Properties for 24 years, Cheryl saw an incredible impact because "The show opened so many people's eyes to the Straits of Mackinac. People saw this was one of the most beautiful places to live. It was a no brainer. They came here and fell in love."

Before the show, Mackinac Island was the draw for people to come to St. Ignace, but once they were here, they jumped a boat and left for the Island, spent their money there and not in St. Ignace.

Once the show got its footing, that changed.

"People came for St. Ignace events. Not the Island. St. Ignace," Cheryl said. "For the first time, they came across the Bridge, saw the Straits, and were in awe. It's a given they come to the real estate office and want to buy property and a home here."

One word that most people used when they talked about my father is passion. "He did it well and he did it with a passion you could feel," Cheryl said. "Over the years, that evolved into a huge fanbase for Ed because people knew he was in charge and who he was. The show became so well known that Cheryl said she gets surprised when she goes places and people don't know about St. Ignace.

"Your dad is a regular guy with a zany sense of humor," Cheryl said. "He is so off the wall and you never knew what he was going to say. He is very easy to be around."

I reminded Cheryl of dad always claiming to be a shy, humble country boy and she laughed.

"People respected him because he knew what he was doing, he knew the industry and he attracted the right kind of people to the show," she said. "People want to be around people they like, and he was that guy. He knew so much about the history of the auto industry and how to get that history here. He knew what he did well but knew what other people did better and deferred to that."

When Cheryl saw "Ford vs. Ferrari" and saw the kind of person Carroll Shelby was, she said everything about my dad and his passion for men like Carroll Shelby fell into place.

"Your dad was crazy for people like that and now I know why. They came here multiple times because of who your dad was. He is genuine, and he is real, and people see that."

PART 18

The Future of "St. Ignace"

Chapter 66: Show Talk with Mr. Murray Pfaff

President Pfaff Designs, and 2018 Guest of Honor

I met Murray Pfaff for the first time in 2021. He is the strong willed, highly energetic, creatively gifted man behind turning St. Ignace back into a destination show via new and exciting awards, community spirit, and generational participation.

I was impressed. He did not know me, but I quickly liked the look in his eye regarding my father's legacy. He moved fast, shook hands, shared ideas, and loved everything automotive.

A renowned designer and car builder, Murray has created more than 400 car designs since starting Pfaff Designs in Royal Oak, Michigan. He created everything from a 140 mile-per-hour speed boat to a jet-powered VW. His signature design is the "Imperial Speedster," a Hot Rod concept car that won the Daryl Starbird "Go for the Gold" award.

"Moving forward, I am trying to build excitement and to get people coming back to St. Ignace," Murray said. "In 2021, it was Tom Peters with the new Corvette which we hope leads to new buyers and new people coming to the show."

Murray is working with the St. Ignace Visitors and Convention Bureau and understands the direction he is moving must be approved and fruitful for their interests.

"They are very helpful and approved of all the changes I wanted to make to include The St. Ignace Six and Muscle on the Mac, " Murray said of his incredible new additions to the show culture. "I hope they continue to approve of what I want to do to make the show relevant for years to come."

A big change Murray wants to make is the name. St. Ignace Car Show Weekend is not only long as a name, but also a "snoozer," he said in comparison to other shows that are gaining traction around the country and using catchy names to do it. "I still haven't worked it out yet but it's something I want to do and feel we need to work on."

One main goal is to bring in corporate sponsors for naming rights to the overall event and the secondary ones to include Muscle on the Mac. One thing I know well is to attach naming rights to my events to give more credibility and ease costs.

The greatest change Murray made, and one that certainly will carry forward an incredible tradition, is "The St. Ignace Cup."

"People want to get recognized," Murray said. "I don't want to be a judge, as I am a picker of great cars, so that is when I go to my peers to take care of that."

Murray and team find six cars to represent "The St. Ignace Six" which leads to the final "St. Ignace Cup" winner. Having the awards on Sunday, with all six finalists being told Saturday to come on Sunday morning, was a stroke of brilliance in many ways.

The first is that it extends the show and peoples' stay in the area. Second, it makes those six car owners appreciative of the intensive judging process that goes into selecting the winner.

Murray has a specific five-year plan to make the St. Ignace Cup coveted among car owners. Knowing this, he is careful with the cars he selects to attend the show and wants a gradual buildup of top-grade cars to come and compete instead of the other way around.

"Some of these cars, if they came now, is akin to bringing a machine gun to a knife fight," Murray said with a laugh. "I have to allow the competition to grow organically so I can still invite 25 cars and, as with The Ridler, have them just be happy to be included."

With" The Gordon Beuhrig Run" going across the Mackinac Bridge, it opened up the bridge to so many similar events. Murray wanted to give people another chance to see cars on Saturday night for "Muscle on the Mac" to give the show a much-needed element after years and years of concerts and cruise nights on Saturday simply slowed to the point of disappearing.

As Murray learned, there are two types of people who come to St. Ignace; those who want to see cars and those who want to hang out. "One we definitely want, and one we welcome, but they still have to behave themselves," Murray said. "The discussion we are having now is to make sure we can keep people safe. As long as they don't get out of control."

Not making the past prologue is a great first step and I say that from experience.

Approaching the show's 50th anniversary, rare air in the show world, Murray envisions the show gaining it's old stature by bringing in top industry names as Guests of Honor and to make the St. Ignace Cup a nationally sought award.

Murray credits Top Hat John and the amazing Chuck Leighton for his status as 2018 Guest of Honor and sees great things ahead.

Murray is now firmly involved in giving St. Ignace a much-needed re-tool, vision, and energy, and has reached out to his colleagues in the industry to make sure the top minds are working with him.

"Ed learned fast what it was to be a promoter," Murray said. "It's just not the product, it's the kid with his first hotrod to the builder who's built dozens of cars to the legends and heroes everyone wants to meet. How do you attract all those aspects of the industry? Your dad did that."

Going forward, Murray wants to embrace the same ideology and atmosphere wherein dad created that "vibe." The vibe must embrace all the people to make their experience the best it can be, Murray told me.

"The car owner that can take the time to invite the kid to sit in his hot rod, to answer the questions they hear time and again, is about treating people with respect," Murray said.

As such, with the creation of the "St.Ignace Cup," certain variables must be met to be considered; stewardship is a big one. "Can this person have that vibe, to draw people to them and their car to take the time to explain to you how they did something to link to that next generation."

"Attitude and weakness kill the hobby," Murray said. "We want to be a show that attracts all those aspects to St. Ignace and have something for everyone, not just for the present, but for many generations to come."

Speaking on behalf of my father, he could not be happier with Murray and his vision. Being protective of my father's legacy falls to me. I agree with my father; Murray is the man to lead this show into its 5th decade and bring with it the excellence for which St. Ignace is known around the world.

Chapter 67: Talking Public Safety with Tony Brown

St. Ignace Chief of Police

Public safety is paramount to the future of the St. Ignace Car Show. I lived through the insanity of "Cruise Night" and saw the show teeter on the abyss of being shut down.

Then-Chief Tim Matelski took the zero-tolerance policy to heart, law enforcement embraced it, and created a new era for the show that brought back the sponsors and families.

"Your father changed the roadmap for St. Ignace," Chief Tony Brown said. "Once that history is gone, it's gone. I am so glad you are taking all those memories and putting pen to paper."

Appointed Police Chief in 2019, Tony came to the show when he was a kid, and hasn't missed a show since 2000, a streak of 21 years.

With all that experience, Tony brings a wealth of knowledge learned over the years and recalls the campers in the highway cloverleaf and the endless drag racing.

"There was organized chaos outside the city because, quite frankly, you couldn't move in town because of the traffic," he told me. "Those were the days and 1998-2001 was the busiest I ever saw it from walking on the streets, the businesses, the cars, and the trouble."

The energy in town was neither good nor bad, it was a car energy and it "just felt different." Drinking was rampant, and now, with the zero-tolerance policy, Tony says the family atmosphere has returned due to the lack of alcohol on the street.

A police officer since 1999, Tony wore the badge for multiple jurisdictions before being picked to replace the retiring chief, Mark Wilk. His appointment caused incredible controversy in the city.

"This is the first time in a long time the department is up-to-date in our training, has new patrol cars, and is out doing police work," Tony told me. "Yet, at the same time, we are the most criticized generation of police officers here."

Looking into the future, Tony wants a brand of police officer to come to St. Ignace with experience in bigger departments and who wants to put their roots down in St. Ignace and be part of the future.

The 2019 show was Tony's first as Chief. Meeting with the Visitors and Convention Bureau went well, as did the show.

Then, Covid hit, and the show was canceled. Tony had to laugh at the canceled show aspect. "People still came. The hotels reported they were not down business for this time of year," Tony said. "We still had the show, not sanctioned by anybody, but there are still going to be people in town."

Record numbers of people still showed up with their cars, still rented the rooms, still cruised, and still spent their money.

"People who couldn't make it because of Covid, came later and we had a secondary show," Tony said in disbelief. "They still met at the airport, they still drove through town, they moved parking lot to parking lot and you know what? We didn't have any problems. People took care of themselves."

Restaurants were full, sidewalks were overflowing, and even though record numbers of tourists did not come, Tony was hit with an indisputable truth.

"The momentum of the car show did not stop," he said matter-of-factly. "Not only did it not stop, but they also didn't get enough during the last Saturday in June, they came back over Labor Day with another 300 to 400 cars and did it all over again. It was amazing."

The show, such a vibrant part of keeping St. Ignace alive, was still alive itself. People embraced it and took care of it. The one year that life stopped moving forward, the car show did not.

"Everyone misses Ed Reavie, the food trucks, the GM Booth, Carroll Shelby, the Ice Road Truckers, these huge people," Tony said. "While we will still be bringing in big names and great cars, the Ed Reavie era is always going to be remembered for the greatness it brought here."

He laughed at the memory of how dad ran the show. He said he parked his car on one of the docks in 1999 and when he came back, his car was towed.

"Your dad needed space for vendors," he said laughing. "He towed every car in that parking lot. I came back and instead of my truck, there was a pickle vendor there or something like that."

When he approached my father, he got the classic Ed Reavie response. "I am running a car show here, I am not worried about your truck." This sent Tony into laughter at the memory of it all.

When 2021 looked to fall to the Covid hysteria, Tony gave his opinion on the Visitor Bureau wanting to hold five smaller events in other towns, and only one meet up in St. Ignace.

"The whole purpose of the car show is to have everybody in town (St. Ignace)," he said. "We want people here and we want to be safe.

One thing Tony did not like, that started again last year, was the "pro stock" style burnouts near the hotel row area. They dug into the new black top and left rubber all over the roadway.

"Sure, it makes a great TikTok video, but that is the black eye. That guy comes here to visit, and does that, and then leaves. It's that recklessness that bothers me. It puts a black eye on the show."

The "Spirit of Car Show" needs to live on, Tony said. The willful disregard for the show, by those who "get juiced up" and sit in their juiced-up cars to create potential danger for everyone," can't continue.

Chapter 68: Talking Car Show with Quincy Ranville

St. Ignace Visitors and Convention Bureau Director

The year after the show was sold, Quincy Ranville took the helm of the Visitors Bureau in March of 2016.

Quincy had a full plate, what with the daunting task of driving the event forward and the single hardest task still not achieved; making people who had "St. Ignace" memories happy with the new direction. A car show participant since she was a child, Quincy came with her father in the 1990's until Woodstock/Armageddon, AKA Cruise Night, got so wild that her father no longer felt comfortable bringing her.

Quincy fell in love with the Upper Peninsula as she attended St. Ignace and the Hessel Boat Show. She told her father that she wanted to work in this beautiful part of the world.

"He laughed and told me I would never find a job in the Upper Peninsula," Quincy told me. "All the time now I say, HA! I did it."

The first year, with Mindy Rutgers at the helm, and going into year two, were "intense," as it was a huge undertaking.

"We didn't really know how well we did compare to how it used to be in the previous years," Quincy told me. "We are really starting to get things on track. I really didn't know what I was doing but Top Hat John and your dad were extremely helpful."

When dad's health stabilized, Quincy made trips to dad's house, "and sat in that cool room of his and picked his brain on how to do this."

Once dad told her the multilayers of how his mind worked and how he brought all these things together, it was a shock to her system.

"It was astonishing, unbelievable really, how he was able to do all those things," Quincy said. "I knew event planning, but did not know car culture at all, but I am really learning."

Amazed at how Top Hat John can identify a car and know every bolt it took to make it go; Quincy is forever thankful for Top Hat bringing on Murray Pfaff.

"His role has expanded dramatically since he first came on," Quincy said. "The St. Ignace Cup is going to be a staple of the show going forward."

When I first learned that the awards were moved to Sunday, and not knowing about the new award procedures, I was confused. The awards were always part of the nightmares dad and I had as there was so little time to put it all together and make sure they started on time.

The first big change was Top Hat's changing the awards to a Top 40 Show Car award. In no order, each award could have been the top award and people left happy.

In previous years, there were literally 100 awards, as every time people complained about the lack of a certain category, dad told them to find a sponsor for that award and he would present it. It was suffocating, overwrought, stressful, and often, went way past closing time.

"Moving them to Sunday, strictly from a business perspective of the hotels and restaurants, it helped," Quincy told me. "But it also gave us time to give proper attention to the cars and give the sponsors a dedicated space and time for their specialty awards."

As Top Hat told me, Chuck Leighton and his team of judges view the cars Saturday and inform the owners they are going to be part of the award ceremony on Sunday, ensuring full participation.

After the chaotic first year, the changes started to manifest. Antiques on the Bay was removed from the show schedule after 2019 as the younger generations are big into hot rods and want to show their cool cars.

"We have not fully abandoned the idea of having a dedicated antique section within the show," Quincy said. "The issue is there are not a lot of those car owners around anymore to bring them."

As this book has documented, the biggest change causing unrest was removing the Guest of Honor Brunch from the schedule.

"We changed it into a Friday evening party which is still evolving," Quincy said. "The plan this year is to do an event after the parade, open it to the public, and have it in a nice location on the water and make it new, fun, and hip."

After the cancellation of the 2020 show, Quincy said a lot of the "St. Ignace" staples are returning.

"Cruise Night and the (Down Memory Lane) Parade are coming back," she said. "Looking back at the last five years, I wonder are we doing this wrong or changing it too much?"

In the Reavie years, the show changed yearly with dad creating something new, changing something old, or flat out not doing an event again as it ran its course; Muscle Car Mania comes to mind. "That is what events do, they change," Quincy said, "They get different, they get better, and that is the nature of events, so that makes me feel better."

The biggest change for 2021 was having the event in St. Ignace again. Restrictions in the State had the show broken off into multiple cruises going to different cities, which was a lot of work.

"People were going to come to St. Ignace anyway," Quincy said. "When the restrictions were lifted, we still had the time to change the plans and we had to do it."

The 2021 show, although put together at the last minute, still came off well and successfully; except for the rain. It reminded me of the great Parade "Float" rain burst that nearly swept people and dogs into the lake, such was the power and amount that fell.

The biggest difference? The rain burst in 2021 did not stop and forced people off the streets as early as 2 p.m.

"Up to that point in June," Quincy said. "We didn't have any rain at all."

Going forward, Quincy said that increasing the focus on The St. Ignace Cup and Muscle on the Mac are a priority. Rain hampered the Muscle on the Mac in 2021 but in 2019, the event showed signs of success.

"I was sitting there, completely overwhelmed with 150 people all waving money in my face to register," Quincy said. "I thought it was going to be a disaster, but it wasn't."

As in the first year of the show, the 10th, 25th, and 40th anniversaries, there is one thing that will never change.

"The view of the Bridge and the Straits of Mackinac sets our show apart," Quincy stated. "No other show has that view."

For 2022, the Feature Cars and the bulk of the vendors and food trucks are going to be at Little Bear Arena for its large parking lot, nice bathrooms, and, as happened in 2021, shelter from another biblical downpour.

"How well Little Bear works for the (Richard Crain Memorial) Truck Show makes it clear to me that it's doable, which is awesome," Quincy said. "This is going to be the future."

Quincy never met my dad prior to her hire, and was stunned by his energy and knowledge. "I talked to him on the first day," Quincy said. "I had no idea what he was talking about, he was going 100 miles an hour. That first year was scary, but it was so fun."

Chapter 69: Talking with Top Hat John

"When I get this question regarding people asking me to tell them about good shows to attend. St. Ignace is one I mention. Ed Reavie has a presence, is a striking looking guy, and his mustache is pretty good too."
Dennis Gage, host of *"My Classic Car"* and 2019 Guest of Honor.

Automotive Historian, St. Ignace Show Consultant, and Guest of Honor 2012

Before getting into my conversation with Top Hat, who is, to me, one of the greatest living Americans, it would be a mistake to not be upfront about how dad and I feel about this man.

In 2021, John celebrated THIRTY YEARS coming to St. Ignace. In those 30 years, John has impacted the show in ways many don't know.

John saw the disaster of the awards handling (my words) and made a simple suggestion to my father that changed the course of the show.

By introducing the "Top 40" award, it solved a lot of problems. Not presented numerically, a participant receiving one could rightly think their car was #1. It streamlined the awards, made the plaques sought after by car owners, and gave St. Ignace a new direction.

John and his partner, Victoria, quickly became not only part of the show, but part of the family. His wit, depth of knowledge, and giving heart was apparent from the beginning.

Tearing up whenever he asked for a moment of silence for military and first responders, John represents the best of American values. His love for pie became a rallying cry for us over the last few decades. It wasn't, "where are we going for dinner?" it became, "Pie?"

I am unsure when the tradition started, but Dad, John, Victoria, my wife Melissa, and I, always met for dinner after the show, joined by a host of friends in the circle of the ever-growing family that was Car Show.

John was the one who asked dad the question that became this book. It was John, not my father, whom I called as soon as I got into my car to drive home after coming back from St. Ignace 2021.

I wanted to know if this idea, this book, was something to pursue. He quickly said yes it was. I called him several times to ask if the direction I was taking would resonate with automotive minds. His answer was an emphatic, "Yes."

My father's knowledge of the automotive industry and culture was extraordinary. I truly never met another person who had the depth of knowledge about all things automotive; until I met John.

Imagine my surprise, in March of 2021, when John came to my second-ever car show as a judge. He helped me with the flow of the show, and even recommended that my DJ tone down his music.

When my father sold his show in 2015, it came with the caveat that John be retained as a consultant for five years. His genius and management skills are apparent to all who work with him.

Now, teamed with Murray Pfaff, John and Murray are helping form St. Ignace for the next generation.

"I always wanted to go to St. Ignace," John told me. For years, John was invited but for one reason or another, couldn't go. Jon Moss, a very good friend personally and professionally, invited Top Hat to go. "He said he couldn't pay me but told me he had a room and told me to go."

That was in 1991 and Top Hat has only missed one show (after serious health issues) since. His first year, at the behest of Mr. Moss, Top Hat picked cars to receive some of the amazing GM awards.

Taking Jim Perkins, Vice President and General Manager of Chevrolet division, to show him the cars he chose for the awards, Top Hat was flattered that Mr. Perkins went with his suggestions and those cars received the awards.

In subsequent years, Top Hat was given a Chevrolet to drive during the week of the St. Ignace show, wrote a review on that car, and continued to be heavily involved in General Motors business during St. Ignace.

"When I first got there, I was amazed at the amount of foot traffic and car traffic in town, Top Hat told me. "Moreso, I was amazed with the quality of the cars in town and the multitudes of famous names in town. Not one or two, but dozens."

He'd already heard that St. Ignace was the best show in Michigan and agrees with that.

"The way the show was run, the way your father put it together, it was a friendly, kind show," Top Hat told me. "Lots of crazy stuff going on, lots of people having fun."

The Guest of Honor brunch was one of the most amazing parts of the show, with hundreds of people in attendance. "It was a who's who of car culture," Top Hat said. "I was enamored with your father and what he did and how he did it. I learned so much by coming up there and watching your father."

Sitting in the Guest of Honor Brunch was an incredible time for Top Hat. "Look at this, I said, all the people I write about, are in this room," Top Hat said. "Your father had the best of the best there, from all genres. It was incredible."

The big thing about the show I learned from interviewing so many people, was simply how much dad put into one weekend.

"I could not believe the festivities never stopped," Top Hat said. "From the show, the parade, to the cruise nights, to the concerts, there were people dancing in the streets, it was beautiful. This show set the stage for so many shows happening across the country."

Top Hat credited dad for moving car shows to the next level of evolution and marveled that everything dad did, worked.

"To see this kid, who helped his grandfather build cabins on the beach, work at the grocery store, then to the bank, and put on a show on the weakest financial weekend in St. Ignace, to build the biggest show in the state. It's historic."

Once Top Hat's run with General Motors came to an end during the bankruptcy and Jon Moss's retirement, Top Hat called my father to tell him he was no longer with General Motors but that would not stop him coming to the show.

"He told me I was NOT coming to his show," Top Hat said. "He told me you are working with me now. I was very flattered by that."

The show was so, "Sensibly streetwise structured," it took Top Hat very little time to bring the Top 40 award structure to the event. That award structure is still part of the show.

During this run, Top Hat became the only person to be Guest of Honor for Antiques on the Bay and the St. Ignace Car Show.

Antiques on the Bay was a significant event in my father's catalog. It lasted 20 years and brought an incredible amount of Brass Era cars back to St. Ignace.

And a credit to Merv Wyse, the parade was an event that made everyone take notice, Top Hat said. During one parade, Top Hat added another element that still occurs to this day.

John took to the street with a microphone and, with his God-given ability to verbally mesmerize a crowd, announced VIPs, luminaries, and historical information about the incredible cars that rolled past Gary Engle's announcing booth on Dock Two.

He interviewed people, gave mad props to car builders and the cars themselves, Top Hat became the voice of the parade, bringing the human element to the event.

When Bobby Lewis (singer of Tossing and Turning) came, most didn't know who he was until Top Hat announced him to the crowd, interviewed him, and gave him the respect that an early star of rock and roll deserved. The crowd responded with wild applause.

"What a blast for me to do that," Top Hat said, describing a similar story introducing Ed "Big Daddy" Roth. "It helped the show and that was an amazing experience for me."

Top Hat learned from legendary announcer Dave McClellan at drag races around the country and brought that experience to life in St. Ignace.

He was all in to help the show. One year, when Candy Clark and Bo Hopkins were downtown signing autographs, Top Hat asked, and was told, they both loved vanilla milkshakes and he made sure both of them had one.

During his 30 years, Top Hat was proud to meet, and befriend, Gene Winfield, Keith Crain, and Ed Roth among others.

"Getting to know your father, he was the biggest one," Top Hat said. "He was the gentle general that made everything happen. Watching him function was an artform."

Once Top Hat informed dad that he was going to be part of the show going forward, he started looking at things and how they functioned to see if tweaks or changes were the best course of action.

"Janet Peterson and Eileen Evers were wonderful people," Top Hat said about both of them and their work with the registration and awards. "There were no real problems with things, but some situations could be simplified, so that is what we did."

The structure and strategy of the show was changed to keep its integrity, design, and to look the same as it always did, Top Hat said.

Top Hat came during the height of Cruise Night and was astonished at how many people and cars were involved in that one event. Through the chaos, there was one thing that stood out to him. "Everyone was happy," he said. "Nobody got hurt, the police were great, the crowd was great, Mayor Dodson, and the chief of police did everything right."

To Top Hat, the function of the show was fascinating. "It was so smooth, everyone worked together, and one thing led to the next with military precision."

Even after dad sold the show, Top Hat made sure to include dad in the planning. "He kept contributing to it," Top Hat said. "And then we had ice cream and I asked him that question and it turned into this book. And that is what makes life good."

The simple formula for success, be at the right place, at the right time, recognize it, do something with it, and finally, "just do it!" Top Hat told me.

When dad sold the show in 2015, The Visitors Bureau brought Top Hat on as a consultant to help take the show to the next step.

"Once we got to the point to simplify the show to take it to the next step, things happened," Top Hat said. One of those things was Chuck Leighton asking Top Hat if he could shadow him while Top Hat judged cars and later, he made a suggestion that told Top Hat it was time to bring Chuck on board.

"He told me about a restaurant that had great Lemon Meringue pie," Top Hat said with a laugh. "But it was time to make him an embodied part of the show and we were able to do that."

Now that a new direction arose, Top Hat began the search for someone who held the same values, ideals, and most importantly, work ethic to endear themselves to the Visitors Bureau to help drive forward even further.

"It's a new society, we need to get younger people and ideas into the show," Top Hat said. "We were at the point where the older generation was slowly going away, and we needed change."

One of the biggest changes was going from my father's relentless use of yellow legal pads and Sharpies, mass mailings, and advertisements in magazines. Social Media was the new wave of information sharing and promotion, and Top Hat wanted to make sure they made use of it.

"The guy who came to mind, who I was following for years, was Murray Pfaff," Top Hat said. "He was dedicated to what he was doing, had a passion for it, like your father did, and he knew how to work with people, top to bottom. He knew how to do it. He knew how to feature people and listen to them."

Murray was invited to the show as the Guest of Honor. He met with the team and Top Hat proffered up Murray's name to take the show into the future. The vote was unanimous.

"To his credit, Murray came up with the St. Ignace Six, got a healthy sponsor, and now we have a mini Ridler Award with a $5,000 check to the winner," Top Hat said. "With his social media credentials, his ability to work with people, and his stature, Murray is helping bring the status back to the show that it began with and continuing what St. Ignace is supposed to be."

When I came home for the show and learned that the awards were on a Sunday, it hit me that we had, after more than 40 years, a paradigm shift. Going in with an open mind, I was blown away with the professionalism of the event and the building expectations of the car owners as they awaited their names to be called.

Working with my dad, there was a verbal agreement between the two. When dad sold, he insisted Top Hat be included in the new direction of the show.

"The biggest thing now, is Quincy and it was a windfall to get in that spot or the Visitors Bureau," Top Hat said. "And the biggest rule we have about working together is communication."

Communication is the key to the success of the new team, Top Hat said. "The communication skills with this team are perfect," Top Hat said. "Reverence for history is so important," Top Hat said. "You rely on that to keep the status quo."

I asked Top Hat where he sees the show at the 50th Anniversary. "It will still be going, and the way things are now, we will probably have an award for an electric car," he said laughing. "We will see about that down the road."

The management team for St. Ignace is crucial. "St. Ignace is one of the top shows in the country; still," he said. "Michigan has another show that is right there, in Frankenmuth."

The shows succeed because of the management making it available for the public. Shows may become smaller or larger, but it's important to keep them alive.

"This is why we have Murray Pfaff and the entire team," Top Hat said. "There are going to be changes. You can count on that."

With Top Hat's decades of traveling the country to shows and meeting the genre's legends, I asked where my dad and his show rank.

"First of all, you have to understand that St. Ignace is known across the United States," Top Hat said. "People came from all over the United States. Ed Reavie as a person, as a celebrity, as a manager, is known around the world."

For Top Hat, it is important to keep my father's name attached to the show. "We need a bust of your father downtown," Top Hat said. "His name always has to be on this show because one day, someone will ask who he is and someone can tell that person all about him and what he did. That way, he is always alive."

The City of St. Ignace, Top Hat pointed out, is alive for what it is; a perfect tourist destination. The St. Ignace Car Show will keep it that way forever.

"All the guests that came to St. Ignace, the list of people, I always go back to it, to bring back the memories of those people and what they did to make that a part of what we are doing now."

The totality of "St. Ignace" is something that is hard to believe, Top Hat said. The Richard Crane Memorial Truck show was also top three. Having Bill Mitchell, "One of the men who made automotive history for the entire world" and guests like George Barris, Carroll Shelby, Gordon Buerhig, made dad's show one of a kind.

"I am comparing Ed to Abraham Lincoln in their characteristics and philosophies," Top Hat said. "Your dad, in the way he works with people, is a natural. He masters handling people in such a flawless way it is beautiful to watch."

PART 19

The next 40 Years

Chapter 70: Legends Are Still Coming

"Ed Reavie puts on one great show. He really rolls out the red carpet."
Candy Clarke, *"Debbie" from American Graffiti 2005 Guest of Honor.*

The greatest quote from my father is why he started this show and is included in the beginning of the book. To him, he had too many heroes and there was not a chance he could travel to meet all of them.

His plan? Create such an incredible event, one with so many amazing attractions, one with so many cool people and cars, that his heroes would travel to meet him.

And that is exactly what happened.

My goal in this book was to speak with all the Guests of Honor and top automotive minds in the industry who attended. I missed several and it was in no way intentional. I had many people working with me to contact as many as I could to create a book many people would read to see what they had to say.

When the Visitors and Convention Bureau took the reins, the legend of the show allowed them to still attract some serious royalty to our little town.

I was blessed to speak with so many of them and learned so much about the car culture's history and why people are so successful. The passion came through the phone when speaking with Dennis Gage, Brian Baker, Murray Pfaff, and Tom Peters. It made our "interviews" more like conversations between old friends. Exactly my goal for presenting this book to the public.

We begin with the first Guest of Honor of the Visitors and Convention Bureau era and, man, did they hit a homerun with Mr. Brian Baker.

Chapter 71: Talking History with Mr. Brian Baker

Brian Baker, Director National Corvette Museum, Bowling Green KY, and former VP Education & Principal Historian at the Automotive Hall of Fame, and 2016 Guest of Honor

One universal thing in this process is just how fun and cool "car guys" are to interview. Brian Baker is in that class.

I reached out to Tom Peters to make our virtual introduction, and within five minutes I had a text from Mr. Baker to set up a time to speak.

"St. Ignace is an institution," Mr. Baker told me in regard to my efforts with this book. "Dick Teague took me under his wing at a very young age and, when kids were writing book reports about Bart Starr and Joe Namath, I wrote mine on Bill Mitchell."

I appreciated Mr. Baker's candor in his appraisal of this book after I explained what I was doing. Upon hearing that I had 60 photos, he told me flatly, "That seems pretty light for a 500-page book." So, thank Mr. Brian Baker for the several dozen more photos appearing here to make this a 600-page odyssey.

As Principal Historian for the Automotive Hall of Fame, Mr. Baker offered his insight to the finished manuscript prior to publishing. An offer I quickly accepted.

"My greatest challenge to you, friend," he said in teacher mode, "How do you help someone who was never there, understand the magnitude of this show?"

He asked me directly if I could make a parallel to the St. Ignace show for comparison's sake. I could not and directed the question back to him.

As the son of disc jockeys, (Bouncing Bill Baker) Mr. Baker shared a memory of meeting the Beatles when he was five years old and terrified by the screaming girls at the show. With the Peter Jackson "Get Back" retrospective on Disney Plus, Mr. Baker feels that a book like this, harkening back on so many great memories, is destined to do well.

"Sitting on the back of a Camaro riding through the St.Ignace and having people shout out my name gave me chills because it reminded me of riding through parades with my dad."

The concentration of the crowd as the parade goes on is like no other, he told me. "It's an amazing event for such a small town."

I know that Mr. Baker has traveled the world to not only car events but visited 350 automobile museums and is a teacher of car culture history. So, I asked him if he ever saw an event, in totality, like St. Ignace.

Listening to such a learned, experienced man in the world of automobilia struggle to draw a comparison to the show my father built, made me smile inside.

"I've been to India, Korea, and Japan, and I am trying to think of car events that, you know what? Let me get back to you on that, okay. Let me ponder this, would you? I want to sleep on this one."

I loved it.

"Part of the beauty of St. Ignace is it's a family event," Mr. Baker said. "That is what makes it so cool."

He first came to St. Ignace in the late 1980's, so I asked him about his view of the Cruise Nights. "Overwhelming," he said flatly.

He spoke so highly of Mr. Jerry Palmer and his passion and advocacy for St. Ignace, and said he worked for Mr. Palmer for years. Mr. Palmer was a relentless promoter for the St. Ignace Car Show. I told him I agreed and told him Mr. Palmer asked me to call him "JP" now.

"You are in the inner circle now pal," Mr. Baker told me.

As an author himself, I asked if this book, nearly 600 pages in this standard 6 x 9 format, would create reader fatigue. He didn't hesitate before saying, "I will get through it the first night."

The new direction of the show inspires him. "Murray (Pfaff) is a great guy with great energy and is keeping the hobby and the vision alive," he said.

Being the 2016 Guest of Honor was "One of the highs of my life," Mr. Baker said. "It was a significant experience, I was so flattered. They made me feel like a king for a day. I felt like one of the family. It's a magical place."

Before we ended the interview, Mr. Baker had the comparison he was searching for earlier.

"Main Street USA at Disney World or Disney Land," he said with excitement. "You have throngs of people around you are going down that main drag of the city. That is the magic I felt in St. Ignace."

Chapter 72: Classic Car Talk with Mr. Dennis Gage

Host "My Classic Car" and 2019 Guest of Honor

Dennis Gage has a PhD in Chemistry, holds multiple patents from his time working at Procter and Gamble (you might see his image on a can of Pringles) but is more known for his amazing television series and glorious mustache than his incredible academic and professional achievements.

He first attended the show in 1996 and filmed the first two episodes of a new television show called, "My Classic Car" which is still in production today.

Celebrating 25 years, Dennis and I had a fantastic interview and I soon realized why he is so successful; he makes you feel like his best friend and carries on a conversation with a fluid ease that made me glad I record and don't take notes, as I legitimately felt as though I was just shooting the breeze with an old friend.

Talking to Dennis was fun. Seriously fun. He was out walking as we spoke and we spoke as if we were lifelong friends. It was the first time we spoke. His enthusiasm and depth of knowledge for the car industry was palpable through the phone.

For 25-years, Dennis Gage has traveled the world with his incredible show, "My Classic Car" seeing and experiencing everything an automotive enthusiast could hope for.

"It's about 24-and-a-half years longer than I thought it would be when I started," Dennis told me. "It refuses to die. I can't believe it. It was lightning in a jar. Some things work, some things don't, and this one just did."

Dennis told me something profound after analyzing his own show, something my father did with his show, and something I do with my Foundation.

"We do the same thing every time and it's always different. Somehow, those two things always work."

Suddenly, the call dropped, and the line went dead with the dreaded three beeps. I feared perhaps he slipped, was beset upon by a wild pack of Chihuahuas and carried away or met some other nefarious fate worse than being carried away by a wild pack of Chihuahuas.

I called Dennis back and he answered, "Yeah, that was a thumb malfunction. The phone slipped out of my hand and then I didn't hear you anymore," he said with a laugh. "Turns out, I grabbed the phone real fast and my thumb hit the off button."

Unbeknownst to me, "My Classic Car" filmed two of its first episodes in 1996 at the St. Ignace Car show. He had just begun his show with a 13-episode run, said he was breaking and didn't have the working knowledge he does now. "Turns out, we shot two episodes of the show in 1996, something we haven't done again," Dennis said. "We milked it for two shows."

That year, Ed "Big Daddy" Roth, of Rat Fink fame, was the Guest of Honor. "I had never met him, I was new to all this, I was a car guy, but my background was as a PhD. chemist."

Dennis had no footprint in the automobile industry and said he had "No freaking idea what I was doing." When he saw Mr. Roth, he exclaimed, "Oh my God, that is Big Daddy Ed Roth."

I shared with Dennis the story of Mr. Roth being late to his own Guest of Honor Luncheon and the grand entrance he made, while the crowd erupted in applause as he strolled in wearing a pair of paint-spackled jeans, a light blue sport coat, and a Rat Fink top hat.

He opened the coat to show his Rat Fink T-shirt and soaked in the applause. "There's a shock," Dennis said with a laugh. "That's him."

Dennis told me his own story with Mr. Roth, and said the legendary Rat Fink was pinstriping a toilet seat (which I forgot to mention Dennis, was for my father and still hangs in his office).

Dennis interrupted him, introduced himself and asked for an interview, to which he agreed once he completed the toilet seat. Upon finishing, Mr. Roth got mic'd up, the prompts were given, and they were ready for the shoot.

In a moment of Rat Fink Legend, Mr. Roth told the crew to wait, and dipped his fingers into a paint palette several times.

"He dotted the paint on his face, all these different colors," Dennis said. "And when he was done, announced to us he was ready to go."

I have memories of seeing Mr. Roth with that paint on his face. That year's show was celebrating 20 years. Dennis knew of it from stories he'd read and heard while attending other shows. "At that time, St. Ignace was around for a long time and people had heard of it," he said. "Iola, Hot August Nights, St. Ignace, and Du Quoin, IL, were all doing great shows," Mr. Gage said. "It was on the radar for us when we launched the TV Show."

As one of the biggest shows of the time, St. Ignace was in the "lore of automotive culture," Dennis said. "We came the year the city really clamped down on the wildness that took place in past years."

He used only freelancers his first year and one member of his production team (the shooter) lived in Grand Rapids, close enough to drive to St. Ignace. This made it practical to see.

"It was a great show in a great location," Dennis said. "St. Ignace was maybe in the first five shoots we ever did and when we got there, well said, wow, what a cool event."

Both episodes shot that year turned out fantastic, Dennis said. "Back then none of the segments were really that long," he told me. "We had only 22 minutes and 30 seconds of air to fill, with the show being part of the three segments we shot for the shows then."

With no money, no experience, and few sponsors, Dennis realized that cutting the shoot into two separate episodes would work great for their first season.

That's not the case anymore. "My Classic Car" has since traveled to all 50 states and around the world, filming and documenting shows in such places as Puerto Rico, eight Canadian Provinces, seven European countries, Trinidad and Tobago, and many other fantastic locales.

"As my show evolved, it became as much a travel show as a car show," Dennis said. "I was always looking for events in places that were destinations all by themselves. St. Ignace fits nicely into that mold."

The first shoot in St. Ignace was random, done for convenience and to save money, Dennis told me. Working with my father, he said, "He is just a great guy and so easy to work with and it's amazing the dedication he had for that show," he said, noting that dad had a full-time job and still maintained his passion for cars and his city. "All the cool things he did to create this thing for St. Ignace was just cool."

Dennis told me his impressions of my father, "He struck me as very bright, articulate, and a very interesting person." He floored me when he remembered talking to me on the phone about his appearance in 2008 as we worked out some logistics for his stay.

"St. Ignace is a great destination that happens to have a really great car show," Dennis said. "It shoots well, it shows well, and if you get a good day, man, you can get some shots. The Island boats are going back and forth in the background. You can't beat it."

Normally, Dennis said his show is hard work with a lot of travel, and as such, his wife does not come with him on his road trips. But she came to St. Ignace because of the attractions.

They spent two days on Mackinac Island and it was a wonderful experience for the both. "You can go to St. Ignace for the show and take a couple days to go to the Island and see other incredible destinations in the area.

One of those destinations was Whitefish Point, in the Northernmost part of the Upper Peninsula. For students of shipwreck history, Whitefish Point was the area where the iron ore freighter Edmund Fitzgerald sought shelter, when it sank during a "Perfect Storm" on Lake Superior.

"We got there, and someone was mowing the area and he had on a helmet with netting on it," Dennis said, thinking nothing of it. "When we got out of the car, we were instantly attacked by mosquitoes to the point we jumped back into the car wondering if we really wanted to do this. It was a squadron of mosquitoes and I've never seen the likes of it before."

That might be worse than a wild pack of Chihuahuas.

He has traveled the world and seen every destination and show the country has to offer, so I asked him to rank the St. Ignace shows on his list of great destinations.

"It's interesting," he said. "I get this question a lot regarding people asking me to tell them about good shows to attend. St. Ignace is one I mention."

Being such a cool place, Dennis is happy to promote it. "It's a cool area, with a great show, and cool things to do," he said. "People ask me all the time and St. Ignace is one of the shows I mention to them."

When I talk to men and women like Dennis, legends in this genre, I always ask them to talk about dad in relation to other promoters they meet in their travels.

"Your dad has a presence, is a striking looking guy, and his presence is a welcoming one," Dennis said. "And his mustache is pretty good too."

I told Dennis about my plans for the book and he told me, "It's a great tribute to your father. He is a great human being and has left his mark. It's really cool and what more can you ask for in life?"

Thanks again Dennis, it was fun. Hope to meet you again one day.

Chapter 73: The Corvette Legend Grows

I returned to the show in 2021 and was amazed at the changes implemented by Murray, Top Hat, Quincy and the rest of the dedicated team.

I was impressed when they told me that the Guest of Honor, Tom Peters, was in the same line of legends as Jerry Palmer, Larry Shinoda, and Zora, with his incredible designs of the new generation Corvette. I met him and he agreed to come to see dad's museum, and that's when I realized, like all car guys, that he is just a cool car nut like the rest of us.

When I told him how incredible the new C8 was, he smiled and said, "You haven't seen anything yet."

Watching "Barrett-Jackson" when the 2023 zo6 sold for $3.6 million, I knew exactly what he meant by that statement. In a later conversation, I asked him that question and he confirmed it and said again, "You still haven't seen anything yet."

Well done sir, well done.

Chapter 74: Talking Corvettes with Mr. Tom Peters

Director of Design (retired), General Motors Car Studio, and 2021 Guest of Honor

Tom Peters is a legend in his own right, having built his legend designing the Corvette, Camaro, Cadillac XLR, Corvette Indy show car, Chevrolet Silverado, and many more to include the radical, bitchin', glorious C8 Corvette. I first met Mr. Peters during the Sunday award ceremony of the 2021 show. He had sketched a drop-dead perfect version of the C8 Corvette on a napkin, signed it, and gave it to a fan. There was a line of them with books, photos, and posters, and he graciously signed them all.

My father was having a bad day, was not walking well, nearly fell twice, and had to be helped into his chair. I approached Mr. Peters, explained Dad's condition to him, motioned to where dad was sitting and asked him if he would meet with him and sign the books and posters, he had with him. Keep in mind, he knew not who I was, not that he should. Without hesitation, he walked to dad, shook his hand, and happily signed dad's memorabilia.

"Your dad is full of creativity and I love that it sees the light of day, for him to share that with people, with kids, it locks into the power of what cars are all about and the people, it gives it life and soul and the synergy is world changing," he told me when we spoke on the phone. "It's fun to see the younger generation be so excited about not only the newer designs but appreciate the classics."

Mr. Peters was no stranger to St. Ignace, as so many of his peers had attended or were Guests of Honor or special guests. He remembers his first show in 1990 when he met Norm Grabowski and the show made a major impact.

"I could not believe all those incredible cars so far away in such an exotic location such as St. Ignace," he said. "You could walk to docks, take a boat ride to see the (Mackinac) Bridge, go to the Island, and see cars from all over the country and Canada."

The impression St. Ignace made on him "was an impression that was unforgettable" he told me. "General Motors participated with a huge display, there were thousands of cars, legends of the industry who came, and car enthusiasts were everywhere. It was an incredible thing for a young designer to see and take in."

His 2021 trip was his third time in St. Ignace and he told me he had yet to meet my father before I introduced them. The weather that year was frightful, and a torrential downpour ended the show early. By 2 p.m., the sky was pitch black and streets were flooding, such was the power of that storm.

"People were anticipating the weather and the hockey arena worked out great," Mr. Peters said, speaking on the awards being presented inside the Little Bear Arena. All the award winners were notified Saturday and, as such, all were there.

"Talking to people who built these cars, the ones who wrench on the cars, who know them inside and out, were there and it was awesome talking with them."

The St. Ignace car show has an appeal unlike any other show, Mr. Peters said. "It's like you are at a resort, right on the water, decks at restaurants are on the water. Everyone is friendly, the sky is blue with puffy clouds," Mr. Peters said. "You never met these folks before and they were so friendly and happy to see you. Add that to the people you already know, and it makes for an amazing weekend."

He recalled his dinner at a restaurant named MI Patio as he sat on the deck and looked over the marina. "The water was blue and sparkling, it was so beautiful," he said. "We had a table for 8, had a burger and beer and looked at the cars and the water and the boats. Everyone is in a great mood, happy to see you, having fun with cars. It was fantastic."

He was already in love with the spirit of the show, but had no idea what awaited him when he met the heart of the show, my father's office museum.

"I was overwhelmed with the creativity, the history, and the passion of the artwork, the wide range of automotive representation in that room," he said concerning what he saw.

I remember when dad asked Mr. Peters to come over and see the space. He was busy packing up his truck but looked at his watch and said he could take 30 minutes to come take a look.

He spent three awestruck hours there.

"Not taking away from professional museums, but this was a family museum," he told me. "The Corvette is a family and I saw Larry Shinoda, Zora Arkus-Duntov, and Jerry Palmer on the wall and the stories are generations deep. To have that in a private home is like the soul of the automotive industry coming alive. I felt very comfortable there."

He briefly met the legendary Bill Mitchell and said the stories about him run deep, and people still use euphemisms that Bill used, his one-liners, his passion and demeanor. They still express themselves that way.

"Your dad touched lives and inspired so many people," Mr. Peters said. "What is more important than impacting, in a positive way, another human being? If you leave a lasting impression on them, you've really done something."

During his visit, I learned that Mr. Peters shared my passion for Bruce Springsteen and guitars, and we spoke at length about both. I showed him photos of my custom made 1967 replica Telecaster I named "Hot Rod" because of the authentic Candy Apple red paint, handmade red ionized switches and knobs, and an authentic Joe Bailon medallion placed in the body. He was amazed by it.

"When I first came up for the Guest of Honor role, it was just another town, just another show to me and it was fantastic to see so many enthusiastic people. When he toured the office, his view of the show changed drastically.

"Jerry Palmer was here? He is my mentor. All those people, all that history in this small town, wow," Mr. Peters said. "This show is part of the tapestry of the automotive industry and culture. No question about it."

I thank Jerry Palmer, "JP," for getting me Mr. Peter's phone number. When I asked him to write the foreword for this book, he gave an immediate positive reaction. "I am honored to even be asked," he told me, agreeing to do just that.

It was my pleasure to meet you sir. I look forward to your autographing the book with the rest of the legends who appear again during the 2022 show.

Letter from a Legend – Spot Edward

And what is this book without a letter from Mr. Reavie himself to his then six-year-old son after the loss of their family pet? This is a small glimpse into the mind and rugged humor of my father.

Dear Sean.
I have left to retire to the farm. The years with you were the best of my life, but now, I need to rest. Please honor my memory by promising to never come looking for me and to never, ever, get another dog.
All my love,

Spot Edward

Author's note: It took many years for me to realize Spot never wrote this letter. It wasn't until Herbie the Hamster left behind a cleaned-out cage and a similar letter, that it dawned on me. Coming during the same year I learned Santa wasn't real, this was a rough thing for a 14-year-old to deal with I tell you that. Spot was hit by a snowplow and Herbie escaped his cage, never to be seen again. When I called dad to remind him of this, he laughed so hard, had there been a false tooth in his mouth, no doubt a spry younger person would be looking for it in the sewer. He then denied the events ever took place.

PART 20

46-years Later

Chapter 75: Goodnight Sweetheart, It's Time to Go

While selling the show had to happen, it wasn't easy. Dad's physical health had declined since his Christmas day heart attack 11 years earlier.

"Health took this away. If my health was better, I would still be full steam ahead but it's not and I'm not."

He thought for years about when to pull the ripcord. New people were in city politics. When he started, there was no competition for his show. Now? "There are probably five shows in Detroit today as we are talking."

A creator of proud moments, one of his was that he never allowed a beer tent at his show and was never seen drinking in public, not that he drank much. Perception is everything. As Homer Simpson eloquently stated, "Alcohol, the cause of, and solution to, all of life's problems."

"The drunkenness and rowdy behavior hurt this show. It hurt my relationship with my sponsors and even my supporters with the city."

Zero tolerance meant for anything against the law. Even leaving rubber behind. Tickets and bookings and fines.

The fines from all the tickets did not go to the city or my father's pockets. They went to fund and build the beautiful St. Ignace Library.

"That's what people don't understand," dad said. "For years I had to hear how much money I made from the show and nobody realized what I did with that money. The biggest problem with people? They don't know. They don't care to know. They just think Ed Reavie made millions from the show."

Truth be told, he did make money from his 40 years, and made it look easy. Please see the definition for free enterprise and/or capitalism if you are confused about the concept.

"Working on the show 24/7, weekends, holidays, it's all I did. Go ahead and ask my kids if they saw their father or spent time with their father."

Ask my sister and you will get a narrative worthy of "the old man" from a Christmas Story, with a colorful tapestry of expletives woven so tightly you would be shocked as it strangled you.

As I said, her emotions not only run hot, but she lacks the filter to care. Oh, and the Reavie way of holding a grudge? Ask her about Dave Bell. Just once. I triple dog dare you.

The "Henry Hirise" cartoonist forever documented my sister's struggle with quitting smoking; something of which (smoking) Mr. Bell did not approve.

In one of his national cartoons about the St. Ignace show, he had a town crier hold up a newspaper and bark, "Danielle Reavie quits smoking. St. Ignace Cheers!" This was 30 years ago and Danielle is still so pissed about it she may take a swing at you.

It is odd for me, a fellow creator, organizer, and philanthropist, how people think. We live in a constitutional republic fueled by free enterprise and the free thinking of men and women interviewed here and men like my father.

I have found, and dad learned this lesson long before I did, that people are simply upset that they didn't create it themselves. Instead of being advocates and helping, they stand in the way with arms crossed saying how dare you benefit. The stress and backlash I received from starting my children's foundation will shock you when that book is written. People are petty.

Dad traveled coast-to-coast, was guest of honor at many shows and sat on panels with men he only read about at the Oakland Roadster show.

His body faltered but his mind was sharp, and he drew from his vast memories of creating this show and the incredible events surrounding it. Legends of the genre now call him just that; a legend.

Looking around the car world, 40 years into something is the time to draw the line in the sand. "I was on top and that is the best time to stop," dad said. "But the problem is, you are on the top and don't want to quit."

He and I never spoke of his diagnosis, of the thief that was going to steal his mind. During the entirety of our conversations, which spanned more than 100 hours, we never spoke of it.

The closest he came was when he told me the biggest reason for selling his show. "I wanted to get out while I still knew my own name. Who I was. What I created. So, I made up my mind to do just that."

It was heartbreaking to hear him say this. It was his first acknowledgment of what was happening to him. It hurts but reality and truth are often painful.

A lesson in life he'd told me all my life came into play. Whenever I had a major decision to make, he told me to get a yellow legal pad and put two columns on it; Pro and Con.

Whichever side has the most, is the way you need to go. Taking out his legal pad, he did this; Do I retire after the 40th show?

The pros won.

"It was time to go," he said, voice full of emotion. "People still recognize me. Still come up to me and talk to me about what I did. I wanted to be remembered for what this show meant to so many people. I left on a high note and don't think anyone can touch what we did," dad said.

Before St. Ignace, cities did not embrace the sprawling displays of cars, flowing through the streets making the town the center piece.

The St. Ignace show was a living, breathing entity that did not shut down the town as detractors pissed and moaned about for decades. Rather, it revealed it to the world and made St. Ignace a part of automotive lore for as long as men and women cruise in their cars with windows down and music blasting.

Local, state, and national political figures visited St. Ignace and presented him with plaques of appreciation. "I'm glad I did what I did when I did it but I miss it. Maybe one day, I can get back into a car and drive again. Maybe."

When the time came to sell, he "went to where the money was," that being the St. Ignace Visitors and Convention Bureau, as they had cash flow from all the hotels and restaurants.

There was controversy when dad tried to sell the show. He gave them a number which they rejected so he took his ball and went home. He told a newspaper reporter to show up at a meeting that dad essentially did just that. Told them the show was over and walked out in full view of the camera from the TV 9 & 10 Team.

"I wanted to test the waters and see what was out there," he said. "I wanted a number, and nobody wanted to meet that number, so I gave them something to talk about."

He wanted nothing to do with committees, group think, or anyone to tell him how his vision should play out. I recall as a teenager, a wanna-be show promoter called the house and asked for advice on how to be a successful show promoter.

When dad learned the young man was the vision and driving force behind it, he asked him if there was anyone else working with him. He told dad two other people had formed a committee with him to start the show.

Dad offered him one piece of advice; "Get rid of the other two people."

I learned a lot from watching him work with a scorched earth, single-minded purpose. I took a lot of that drive into building my own foundation and made enemies along the way. Like my father, I was successful.

After he sold it to the Bureau, he watched as they "immediately took the meat off the bone," and did away with Antiques on the Bay, shrunk the parade, and ended the Guest of Honor Brunch, his signature event that allowed people to meet and mingle with the superstars of the car world.

"It will make it," dad said. "The problem is, they have few car and truck people working with them to put together car and truck shows. With Murray, Quincy, and John there, it will work just fine."

He praised the local newspaper (The St. Ignace News) and its hard charging editor, Wes Mauer Jr., and superstar reporter Erich Doerr, who gave him wall-to-wall coverage for 40 years. He said Wes embraced the show and gave it incredible space in the paper.

I remember Wes and dad working until after midnight in the legendary years of the show. They worked on supplements, flyers, stories, and advertisements. I ran back and forth to the paper to get items for the brunch 30 minutes before it started.

I heard the melancholy in dad's voice as he recalled the selling process, waxing nostalgic on what he created; a worldwide phenomenon that transformed our sleepy little town with no traffic lights into the Mecca of automotive shows.

"It was a heck of a run. I hope people never forget it. I am still amazed at the names of the people who came here and came back, wrote letters. These are people who went all over the world and they came to St. Ignace."

A defining moment was being announced from the podium of the Oakland Roadster Show.

"That is as big as you get, it's the show that defined them all for me and here they were applauding me for an incredible show in St. Ignace."

He applauded the efforts of Murray Pfaff who is taking St. Ignace to the next level with the St. Ignace Cup, and awards that will rank up there with The Ridler, America's Most Beautiful Roadster, and the SEMA Express Award.

"When I started this show in 1976, I had one goal," he said proudly. "And that was to create the single greatest show in the country with the legends in the automotive world seeking me out. For my heroes to come here and meet me. And, that is exactly what I did."

Spirit of '76, Dad and Me

"St. Ignace is the best car show ever."
Pat Ganahl- *Rod and Custom Magazine, Founder of Rodder Journal*

Thirty-three years after our father-and-son trip to the U.S. Nationals, so many things had changed.

A life-changing event happened to me in September of 2006 when I found out everything I had worked for was gone.

I had nowhere to go, so I called dad and drove the longest five hours of my life to St. Ignace. I had lost my house, savings, and had nothing but a Jeep Liberty. I was 39 with no job, no prospects, no place to call home, and nothing left. Not the ideal situation nearing 40.

We had a long talk after he found me sitting in the garage, crying. He sat down on the step and told me the following; If I wanted to feel sorry for myself, that was fine. He told me to take 15 minutes and get it out, "throw up, break something, cry, whatever you need to do." He was clear that at the end of that 15 minutes, I was to come inside, get a yellow legal pad, and he would help me make a plan.

I was in my hometown as a failure. Defeated, broken, stressed beyond all belief, and honestly didn't know what to do.

Sitting in the beautiful St. Ignace Library, the very space that dad and General Motors helped build, I signed up for a job search site and went to work looking for a new life when the new life found me.

There was an email from my friend Bart who had suffered a similar fate when the Michigan housing market collapsed. Now living with family in Phoenix, Arizona and living with family, he asked if I still had the dream of becoming a police officer.

He told me that, while driving around Phoenix, he saw billboards from the Phoenix Police Department recruiting. Those who knew me, knew the one thing I wanted to do with my life; become a police officer.

When I checked, the department had no age restrictions. Suddenly, I was alive again. I found out the next testing date and booked a flight to Phoenix.

Upon returning home, dad and I went through the requirements to pass the physical fitness test and I started training. I ran daily, and dad held my feet for sit-ups and counted pushups, I hit it hard.

Three weeks later, I crossed the finish line on the Arizona Law Enforcement Academy track (it was 106 degrees) well ahead of my target time. I passed the written test, easily knocked out the push-ups and sit-ups, and I called dad and told him I did it.

I flew back home and awaited the call from Phoenix PD for the interview process. Dad and I ate dinner together every night, watched Curb your Enthusiasm, Seinfeld, Judge Judy (our new favorite) and laughed ourselves stupid for four weeks.

This was the longest period of time we ever spent together. We stayed up late talking, watching movies, eating popcorn, and laughing a lot. It was wonderful during a gut-wrenching time in my life.

I had not yet been contacted by Phoenix Police, and it was the end of October. We sat down and discussed what I had to lose by heading out the Phoenix anyway, to start over, whether I was hired.

With November right around the corner, and winter storms brewing, the yellow legal pad told me to pack up and head out. My Jeep was idling in the driveway with everything I owned inside, the exhaust curled into the air and dissipated into the inky blackness as sleet pelted the windshield.

It was 9 p.m. I was to drive to Detroit, meet my friend Andrea, stay at her sister's and then we'd drive out to Phoenix together.

In the kitchen, dad was leaning against the stove and me the sink. We faced each other and knew this was goodbye and, with me being so far away, with no job or place to live, I was taking the biggest chance of my life. I truly had no idea when I would see him again.

Thirty-three years later, the same awkward silence between us was back. This time, my disdain and his desperation were replaced with a palpable, heartfelt sadness.

"Before you go," he said, his voice quivering, he reached into his pocket and produced a bridge fare coin, "This is for your trip there."

I swallowed hard and took it from him. Both of us were crying, tears streaming down our faces. He reached into his other pocket, took out another coin and held it out. "And this is for when you come back."

We hugged and cried for several minutes, gasping and weeping, wrapped in a hug, the emotion of which I had never felt from my dad. He stood in the driveway and waved until I was out of sight. I began the three-day trip from my tiny hometown to the 5th largest city in the country.

I arrived in Phoenix on November 1, 2006. I had no job and no home. On November 16, 2007, my father arrived in Phoenix and pinned my Phoenix Police Badge on my chest at my academy graduation. I was elected by my class as speaker and began my law enforcement career with 30 people, friends I made along the way, including Bart and his wife, Jennifer, in the crowd cheering for me.

I still have the Bridge tokens, right next to my favorite photo of the two of us. (Which appears later in this book). Symbols of our journey as father and son.

The two of us did not end up with a song lyric. We ended up as father and son. The nearly one year it took to finish this book required at least four phone calls a week for information and more stories.

Not everything I wanted included in the book, was, for one reason or another. I hope I told my father's story in a manner befitting such an unbelievable tale.

I hope the reader was catapulted back to those great summer days and nights in Northern Michigan when time slowed down just enough to remember when and ensure that my father's story was heard by future generations of gear heads.

PART 21

Thank you for the Memories Mr. Reavie

Chapter 77: Still No Traffic Lights

In 1976, I was eight years old when the Straits Area Antique Auto Show began. This being Chapter 76 took a lot of work to make sure the last chapter reflected back on the first event.

When my father sold his show and production company "Nostalgia Productions" in 2015, I was far past a grown man and nearing my 50s.

To the "old timers" who watched me grow up, it was a pleasure to get to know all of you. My life was shaped by your presence in our town.

Now 55 and producing at least two car shows a year, I am proud to be a second generation auto show promoter. Growing up, watching this show grow with me, it became a part of who I am. The people I met and those we lost along the way are always a part of this amazing car show family.

Ed Reavie created something more than notable; he created generational change, opened old memories and paved the way for new ones. Ed Reavie was the paradigm shift and changed how car shows were produced, structured, and managed.

He saw a need to expand his show into the city itself and created a living, breathing synergy that changed how show promoters looked at their shows and venues.

His success led to other towns and cities creating shows, some of which grew into legendary shows in their own right; Frankenmuth comes to mind. The Woodward Dream Cruise may, or may not, have come about after the founders attended Cruise Night in St. Ignace.

Through the years, dad's stature and identity as a "local banker" was changed to "car show promoter" and finally, "Legend."

When men like Big Daddy Ed Roth write in their books, "Ed Reavie is an artist of auto show promotion," and legendary, world traveled car builder Chuck Miller said dad is "top two" regarding promotion, it's not hyperbole.

Pat Ganahl, one of the greatest automotive writers, called St. Ignace the "Best Run Ever" on the cover of Rod and Journal. The accolades came from across the globe about the small town in Michigan's Upper Peninsula.

Dad was inducted into "Who's Who World Wide" in the automotive genre. The shy, humble, country boy was a peer to his heroes.

To those I interviewed, thank you. Each time I completed one, I called dad and told him what you said about him. How much praise you gave him. I could hear him smile. Yes, you can hear a smile.

Dad is not aging well. Rumors of his health are widespread. The 13-year-old hellion who was driving a 1939 er, sorry Bucky, 1940 pickup truck all over Silver Sands and at 16, had the nicest car in town, and blew away State Troopers in his GTO, can no longer drive.

I call it a privilege to drive him. He was embarrassed at first, but I told him, like all automotive royalty, he deserved a driver so he could spend his time looking at what he created.

The early part of this book talked about my father's relationship with his father.

After Papa suffered his first heart attack, Papa and Dad had their relationship change. They had their, "what are you trying to tell me?" Moment.

From that point on, they became father and son. Kress told my father that he was proud of him. They took drives, they took walks, they had coffee together.

Every Saturday when I was home from college and working in Mr. Law's drug store, Kress came in to see me. He waited with his arms open for me to come around and he hugged me.

Now aware of his own mortality, Kress was a different person. He was iconic in our town. He was a giant. Dad and Kress became close, making up for time they lost.

They smiled when they saw each other. We walked the Mackinac Bridge together for years. Three generations of Reavie men walking across the world's longest suspension bridge dividing Lake Michigan and Lake Huron.

I remember on a warm Spring day, April 22, 1988, I was sitting in the living room of 1024 University Street on the campus of Central Michigan University when dad called.

This was well before the call dad made to me that changed our relationship, so I knew something was wrong.

Enjoying the spring weather, Papa went to my aunt and uncle's cottage that shared the same shoreline with Silver Sands Resort. He shoveled off their walk and porch, raked up the wet and molding leaves, bagged them, put his rake and shovel in the trunk, and set off for home.

On his way home, just past Silver Sands Resort, Kress Archibald Reavie suffered a fatal heart attack. His car left the roadway and went into the woods.

Trooper Chris Magraw and Paramedic Mark Wilk were first on scene and tried to save my grandfather. At the age of 81, Kress Reavie left us.

The news shattered the town. His obituary was one of the first to include a photograph. His funeral was the first time his church held a funeral on a Sunday.

At his funeral, I remember my reading teacher and junior varsity basketball coach, Charles Fowler, coming up to me and telling me Kress was his Christian example in life.

Grandpa's friends told me how proud he was of me. My father was shattered. He told me, "I just got to know my father and now he is gone," echoing words you have read about me getting to know my father.

I firmly believe dad understood what was going to happen with us and didn't want to wait anymore. Although it took him another 18 months, he knew he needed to bridge the huge gap between us.

Dad has two reminders of his father; the old Detroit Tiger baseball hat Kress wore everywhere, and his eyeglasses. I know right where they are. To honor his father, he started giving "The Kress Reavie Memorial" award during the car show.

This award went to a car Kress would love. So, that meant, a "nice sedan" a Buick Roadmaster, or a work truck to be used at Silver Sands. Dad and I pick this award and, every year, we both zero in on the same one. Every year.

How about dad and me?

The nearly one year of writing this book meant we talked several times a week. I gave him homework each time. Find me this person, look up this car or fact. He was ready and waiting.

It's been a hard year for my sister trying to take care of our father. I am far away. Coming home is difficult or next to impossible. She refused to quit on him. Everyone with this book in their hands needs to find a way to thank her. Dad would be dead and this book wouldn't exist.

The Car Show is part of my life. I do not have a memory of this show NOT being in my life. The greatest part of the show for me, after we got the avalanche of cars parked from 0400 to 0600 hours, I drove dad to get coffee and donuts when we had a bakery in town.

The downtown was so still and quiet with happy car owners talking, drinking coffee, and getting their cars ready. California Car Mops in hand, the proud drivers pulled out their chairs, their displays, talked with friends, and excitedly waited for the day to unfold.

Dad and I sat on the dock nearest the marina, put our feet up, drank coffee, and watched the sun rise out of Lake Huron as it sent streaks of bright reds, pinks, purples, and yellows across the sky and reflected on the mirror-still waters of Lake Huron.

It was peaceful. It was our time. We just talked. About the show, about life, about the great day ahead.

Gary Engle boomed over the PA, welcoming everyone to St. Ignace. Dad looked at me and said, "Are you ready?"

We entered the roadway in our golf cart.

It was show time.

Epilogue

Down Memory Lane

After the brief intro to "Almost Grown" comes and stops, dad says, "Let's go" and the song kicks in and I slowly press the pedal and coast past show headquarters on dock two.

We made our way into the show area, the scenes opened like pages in a photo album and the golf cart transformed into our DeLorean time machine.

As I drove him down Memory Lane, the show came alive and the soundtrack of his life started playing.

"Fannie Mae" came over the speakers as men and women shined up their '55 Chevys, GTOs, Convertibles, Cobras, Corvettes, Mercurys, and Nomads under other earthly blue skies, cool breezes, and smiling people.

"Love Potion #9" started rocking as we entered the main show area. The shouts of "Hey Ed," are everywhere and we stop for all of them.

We see "Big Daddy" Ed Roth painting a photo or is it a toilet seat? top hat on, sly grin on his face (which is covered in paint) as he spins tales about the "Rat Fink."

"96 Tears" plays. Under a tent is Dave Bell autographing a "Henry Hirise" page, creating a St. Ignace masterpiece for my dad. As he works, he keeps one eye open looking for my sister, as the crowds streamed into the show area; filled with two miles of cars snaking along the shoreline of Lake Huron.

Tom Gale wants to say hello and he walks past a Prowler, Viper, and Lamborghini, laughing at the memory of how dad got his PT Cruiser; allegedly.

Zora Arkus-Duntov, talking to members of a Corvette Club, tips his martini glass in our direction, curls of smoke from his unfiltered Camel circle his head.

Across the street from the First National Bank, Jon Moss waves dad over to show him the new display and the bitchin production cars GM brought up this year. Thankfully, there is not a Dodge Car Club in sight. We share stories with Craig Shantz and have a laugh about a certain burned out clutch. A whitefish dinner is planned.

Heading back toward the Feature Car area, George Barris yells, "HEY ED!" as we take photos in front of the Batmobile. Across the way, Roy Sjoberg waves and smiles as he stands near a row of Vipers; menacing even as they sit still.

Del Shannon's "Runaway" plays as we pass an astonishing display containing a Duesenberg, Auburn Boattail Speedster, and a perfect 1936 Cord 810 Cabriolet.

Dad gets out to shake hands with Gordon Buehrig and they talk about the bridge climb. Dad thanked him for opening the door to automotive royalty that came to our town because he came first. Gordon tells dad the pleasure was his.

"Come go with Me" by the Del Vikings plays, but we can't hear it well because Dick Biondi has dad's ear, talking a mile a minute about Cruise Night and takes dad's requests.

The crowd swells and we pull off to the side. Sitting in the golf cart as the show unfolds, Candy Clark comes over and strokes the leather seats and laments its lack of being tuck and roll. Bo Hopkins does the secret handshake with dad, one only known to those lucky enough to be a "Pharaoh".

We make our way back into the show as the crowd parts; whispers of "Wow, that's Ed" are heard. Stagger Lee plays as Pete Chapouris drives past in the "California Kid."

Don Garlits, surrounded by fans he never thought would come to see him, waves as he can't make his way to us as the crowd grows, all smiling, all opening pages of their own memories.

The Shirelles sing "Dedicated to the One I love" acapella as the crowd applauds, remembering when as Herman's Hermits walk past anything but silhouettes in the shade. "There is that nice bloke" is uttered as their manager slaps me on the back.

The crowd gasps as a helicopter lands on the dock and dad takes a Domino's Pizza from Tom Monaghan before Mr. Monaghan steps into his $8 million-dollar Bugatti Royale and his driver takes him away.

"Personality," fills the air as Linda Vaughn, in a checker flag designer jumpsuit, surrounded by her fans, shouts to dad, "Thank you for shifting my gears all of these years, Ed Reavie."

Bill Haley and his Comets belt out "Rock Round the Clock" as Ralph Malph, Potsie Weber, and Shirley Feeney sit and sign autographs in front of us. All three smile in gratitude for dad bringing the past to the present.

The Hirohata Clone has a huge crowd around it as George Barris, Doug Thompson, and Jack Walker pose for photos. A collection of Rat Rods wait for Rat Fink to stop and say hi.

Hearing the telltale horn from "The General Lee" John Schneider asks dad for a photo and asks me if he can play dad in the movie once the rights to his book are purchased.

"Little Deuce Coupe" plays as I pull up to a bright yellow '32 3-window Deuce Coupe parked near the Thunderbird. I rev the pathetically underpowered engine of the golf cart. Paul LeMat, cigarette hanging off his lips, white t-shirt clinging to him and in his best Jon Milner, tells me, "Go win a few races first kid."

"Hey Ed" is now replaced by "Thanks Ed," as Wally Parks, Ernest Hemmings, Chuck Jordan, Gene Bordinat II, Larry Wood, Doc Watson, and Darryl Starbird walk past, each holding their custom-made Guest of Honor plaques. All ask dad to sign them.

Dennis Gage asks me if I can get dad out for an interview about who has the better mustache. Driving on, Bill Mitchell is seen looking at one of his designs and sees in the paint reflection all the engineers and builders that made it come to life.

Pat Ganahl, used to being the interviewer, must settle for me interviewing him for the St. Ignace News, as he tells me St. Ignace is the best car show ever. Ed Almquist hands dad his latest mailer in case dad didn't get it yet.

"All Summer Long" by the Beach Boys is drowned out by Dave McClelland, ice cream cone in hand, raising his touched-by-God voice over the din to say hello to dad.

We drive past Boyd Coddington showing off his wheels to Chip Foose. Keith Crain puffs his cigar as he sits on the bench with Franklin Q. Hershey and Pat Chappel, and they talk about the 1955-56-57 versions of the Thunderbird versus the Chevy.

Paul Hatten takes time from his pinstripe demonstration to smile at us as dad waves.

Larry Shinoda, Jerry Palmer, and Tom Peters, Chevant Clay in hand, stand around the 1953 Corvette #003, sitting behind red velvet ropes in Feature Car Row. Zora walks toward his inspiration to join them and tells them all to amaze him. Tom says standby as they haven't seen anything yet.

A Tucker Torpedo, flanked by Designer Alex Tremulis, sits behind velvet ropes sent to dad by George Lucas. The card was signed, "Ed, may the Force be with you."

Freddy Cannon sings "Take where the Action is" as we wind our way out to the "Y" and run into Top Hat John and Chuck Leighton, clip boards in hand, finishing up their work and giving their picks for the Top 40. John tells me about a new place that has some serious pie. Plans are made.

Feeling strong, dad steps out of the cart. His legs mysteriously come to life as, for the first time in more than a decade, he stands to his full 6' 3", and rises above me again.

"Good to see you, Junior," dad says with a smile.

We look down the hill at a scene shimmering with life. Cars of all colors, styles, and makes in perfect harmony with 100,000 persons staring at them in awe. Heat waves from the midday sun rise off the road, giving everything an otherworldly glow.

The sparkle from Lake Huron makes us shield our eyes as "I did it my Way" by Frank Sinatra echoes up the hill, and we look at each other and smile.

As he did everytime we arrived here the last 30 years, he looked at me and said, "WOW. Would you look at that? This is my favorite view."

This view is recreated in countless magazines around the globe, from San Francisco and Detroit, to Japan, Sweden, France, and Australia.

I tell dad all of this will make a good book one day. He laughs and says, "If that happens, make sure the title is Rebel without a Clue because I have no idea how I did all this."

A Star Line Boat, with a water "rooster tail" behind it, zooms by in the bay, "The Crystals" with dad's friend Dee Dee, sing "He's a Rebel" as the most famous show promoter of them all, Bob Laravee Sr., yells, "Hey Ed, great show."

Slowly making our way back, Bryan Hyland sings, "Sealed with a Kiss," the wind blows back dad's glorious hair and he says, "I wonder what Bucky feels when it's windy?"

We see a handsome, muscled man in a white t-shirt and jeans talking cars with Frank Livingston and Dana Decoster. Gene Winfield looks at dad and smiles.

Making the final approach to Feature Car Row, Dick Teague, standing by an AMX, sees dad and doffs his driving cap. Only able to nod as his hands are full of souvenirs, Curtis Fischbach thanks dad for all the years he gave the hobby.

As we get closer to the main show area, people ask for dad's photo. One-man approaches, "remember me? I was the guy with the Aston Martin from ten years ago" to which dad says, "Of course, you had your wife Jamie with you and we loved having you. I hope the room we found for you worked out."

"One Fine Day" fills the air as we pass the Alexander Brothers talking to Chuck Miller, Al Bergler, Troy Trepania, John Greer, and Dan Webb, about their Ridler Awards and new projects they are putting together.

In the Feature Car area, Doug Thompson and Joe Bailon talk about proper application of candy apple red paint to one of Doug's builds as Jack Walker leans in to hear the conversation.

I point out to dad that Phil Hill, Art Arfons, Roger Guston, E.J. Potter, and Gordon Johncock, joined by Don Garlits, are waving to him from the race car driver section of the dock, as Jimmy Addison hops into The Silver Bullet.

Sonny Geraci, Jim Gold, Jack Scott, Ronnie Dove, Lou Christie, Gary Lewis and his Playboys, Bobby Lewis, and Gary US Bonds hang out together singing their songs.

Leslie Gore, Little Eva, the Shirelles, and the Contours listen, clapping and cheering. Danny and the Jrs. in matching varsity jackets, talk about going to the Hop later that night.

We park in front of show headquarters where there is a large crowd on the dock, screaming in sync with roaring Cobra and Super Snake engines. The crowd parts and a man in a black cowboy hat strides up to the cart and gives my father a firm handshake, thanking him for being the most persistent son of a bitch in the world. Handing dad a cold Budweiser longneck, they toast the other and Carroll Shelby turns back into the large crowd to talk cars.

Dad and his son get out of the cart. He looks at me and smiles. We embrace and he asks how on earth all these legends are in St. Ignace.

Carroll, Zora, and Bill Mitchell have a crowd gather as they talk about their designs just as "The Angels Listened In" by the Crests plays.

Off in the distance, I swear I see grandpa Kress looking at the mess of his 1940 Chevy Pickup truck with missing bumpers and white paint all over the tires. Instead of scowling, he is smiling.

Jumping into the triple black Cadillac Eldorado that carried Carroll Shelby, Zora Arkus-Duntov, and Bill Mitchell, dad takes the passenger seat that is reserved for legends.

We drove just outside of town to a part of the I-75 closed by the Michigan State Police just for dad. *"Whiter Shade of Pale"* fills both our eyes with tears.

Waiting for us is Bucky and Kyle. There are two identical 1965 Nightwatch Blue GTOs side-by-side idling. Kyle and I hold open the doors and hug our dads as they get into the cars.

Looking at each other, each nod their heads with cheshire cat grins as they make that engine roar. The blast from their engines rattles our sternum as Kyle and I watch two rebels with 75 years of history together, roar down the asphalt.

"I got next," I tell Kyle.

My father recreated the best years of his life for not only me to experience it, but millions of people. People in Japan, Australia, and Sweden know about Ed Reavie's car show.

Ed Reavie grew up a rebel, a high school pushout who never fit into the world around him. He stocked shelves, raced cars, cruised endlessly, and dreamt about California and the car culture.

For 40 endless summers, he created his own car culture and world that others seamlessly fit into with him and was the paradigm shift in living form.

This was his story. I lived it with him and I am nothing but a witness to history and a scribe to document ensuring that history is preserved.

If you look at the front inside of the book, pay close attention to the LLC I created to publish this book. The rights to the name expired. The day after that happened, My father's son bought and now owns it. Forever. That is my second gift to you dad. The first, is in your hand.

I hope you enjoyed this tribute to my father. Ed Reavie. Legend. His show was the stuff of dreams. But it was real. It changed the genre and the culture and made the world a better place every last Saturday of June 46 years and counting.

About the Author

Sean Reavie makes his debut as a published author with "Rebel Without a Clue."

In the epilogue, Sean included the conversation between his father and him about a potential book to tell this story. This was at least 20 years ago, and Sean remembered his father giving him the title.

Sean was born and reared in St. Ignace Michigan. He attended Lake Superior State College and Central Michigan University, and his life's dream was to be a police officer.

As an eight-year-old, he stood by his father's side and helped him with the first St. Ignace Car Show. He consequently grew up meeting legends like Carroll Shelby, Zora Arkus-Duntov, George

Barris, Gordon Buehrig, Big Daddy Ed Roth, Bill Mitchell, Don Garlits, and many more.

Sean became a police officer at the age of 40 in the 5th largest city in the country, and subsequently became a detective in the crimes against children unit of his department.

It was in that unit Sean had his own original idea and created the "Put on the Cape A Foundation for Hope," a national organization for comforting and empowering children suffering from acute physical abuse and sexual violence.

A two-time State of Arizona Police Officer of the Year, and the 2021 Who's Who in America Humanitarian of the Year, Sean has a degree in journalism and a master's degree in organizational leadership. Sean was inducted into Who's Who In America in 2021.

In addition to being a hero for those who need a hero, Sean likes to play guitar. He and his wife, Melissa, live in Phoenix, Arizona with their four dogs: chihuahuas Demon Puppy and Chucky, and two French Bulldogs; Satan's Tater Tot and Ralphie. A proud stepfather to Breann, Brittany, and Bryce, Sean has finally found peace in a family unit.

He began the interview process with his father on July 3, 2021, and their first phone call exceeded two hours.

Over the course of the summer, Sean was shocked to learn so much about his father, stories he had never heard, struggles to which he was not privy, and formed an incredible bond with his ailing father.

The goal with his book was to tell great stories about an American original rebel to the world, but it became so much more as it ended up giving Sean incredible insight into his own life and his history. The writing process became cathartic as it helped father and son come to grips with events that impacted their lives, talking about them for the first time.

Guests of Honor at the St. Ignace Show

The Edward Reavie Era

1980 Gordon M. Buehrig*
1981 Richard A. Teague*
1982 Zora Arkus-Duntov*
1983 William L. Mitchell*
1984 Carroll Shelby*
1985 George Barris
1986 Robert E. Larivee, Sr.
1987 Gene Bordinat II*
1988 "Big Daddy" Don Garlits
1989 Wally Parks*
1990 Ernest R. Hemmings*
1991 Franklin Q. Hershey*
1992 Chuck Jordan*
1993 Phil Hill*
1994 Art Afrons*
1995 Gordon Johncock
1996 Ed "Big Daddy" Roth*
1997 Dave McClelland*
1998 Boyd Coddington*
1999 Linda Vaughn

2000 Keith Crain
2001 Tom Gale
2002 Larry Wood
2003 Ed Almquist
2004 Darryl Starbird
2005 Bo Hopkins*
2005 Candy Clark
2006 Cindy Williams
2006 Donny Most
2006 Anson Williams
2007 Doc Watson*
2008 Roy Sjoberg
2009 Ken Gross
2009 John Schneider
2010 Chuck Miller
2011 Paul Hatton*
2012 Top Hat John
2013 Gene Winfield
2014 Dana DeCoster
2015 Jon Moss

The St. Ignace Visitors and Convention Era

2016 Brian Baker
2017 Jack Walker
2018 Murray Pfaff
2019 Dennis Gage
2021 Tom Peters
2022 Ken Lingenfelter
*Deceased

Suddenly It's 1958 Again Concert Performers

The concerts, a staple for 25 years, were held in the local high school gymnasium. The joint was jumping as 16 of the Billboard Top 200 groups from the 1960's performed to overflow, dancing, singing, and sometimes, crying, lovers of rock and roll.

Here is the list. All appeared. All left it on the stage. The concert was an event that could stand alone. Added to the Car Show, it became part of legend.

It was the one-time Ed Reavie let his walls down and enjoyed what he created. Sitting stage right, he smiled endlessly, clapped his hands, and when Sonny Geraci belted out "Precious and Few" he uttered, "Oh, my god."

His heroes on stage, he sat back and listened like the rest of the crowd.

Herman's Hermits- There's a Kind of Hush, Silhouettes on the Shade, Something Good."

Gary Lewis and the Playboys- "This Diamond Ring, Everyone Loves a Clown, She's Just my Style."

Gary US Bonds- "This Little Girl, Quarter to Three, Jole Blon."

Bobby Lewis- "Tossin and Turnin"

Jan and Dean- "Surf City, Little Old Lady from Pasadena, Deadman's Curve."

Leslie Gore- "It's My Party, Judy's Turn to Cry, You Don't Own Me."

The Crystals- "He's a Rebel, Da Do Run Run, Then he Kissed Me."

Lou Christie- "Lightning Strikes, Rhapsody in the Rain, I'm Going to Make you Mine."

Freddy Cannon- "Transistor Sister, Palisades Park, Where the Action is." Most American Bandstand appearances in history.

Ronnie Dove- "Right or Wrong, One Kiss for Old Times Sake, Cry."

Bobby Vee- "Rubber Ball, Devil or Angel, Take Good Care of my Baby." Filled in for Buddy Holly the day after the music died.

Jack Scott

Danny and the Jr's- "At the Hop, Rock and Roll is here to Stay."

Johnny Tillotson- "Poetry in Motion, Send me the Pillow you Dream on."

Sonny Geraci- Lead singer for The Outsiders (Time won't Let Me) and Climax (Precious and Few).

Jim Gold- Formed Gallery (Nice to Be with You, I believe in Music.)

Bryan Hyland- "Itsy Bitsy Teenie Weenie Yellow Polka Dot Bikini, Sealed with a Kiss."

The Shirelle's – 100 weeks in the top 40. "Soldier Boy, Tonight's the Night, Dedicated to the One I Love, Will You Love me Tomorrow?"

The Contours- "Do ya love me."

Little Eva- Locomotion reached #1 twice

Jerry Lee Lewis- No discography needed. It's Jerry Lee Lewis People!!! (Appeared at Kewadin Shores Casino during the show.)

The Turtles- "Happy Together" Appeared at Kewadin Shores Casino during the show.

Automotive Royalty in St. Ignace

Hall of Fame North

Michael Alexander	Larry Alexander	Joe Bailon
Bob Kaiser	Leroy "Tex" Smith	Dave Bell
Gene Winfield	Wally Parks	Dick Biondi
Pat Ganhal	Dean Jeffries	Norm Grabowski
Bill Cushenberry	Pete Chapouri	Bob Larivee Sr.
"Baggy" Bagdasarian	Bill Reasoner	Art Himsl
Rod Powell	Ed Roth	Linda Vaughn
Ken Fenicil	Frank Derosa	Dick Landy
Bill Golden	Roger Lindamood	Chuck Miller
Art Arfons	Joe Wilhelm	Jim Perkins
Tom Gale	Paul Hatton	Doc Watson
Gordon Johncock	Frank Livingston	Ed Almquist
Bill Hines	Larry Shinoda	Jack Walker
Joe Maneri	Dave McClelland	Boyd Coddington
Larry Wood	Rick Perry	Andy Di Dia
Troy Trepanier	Angelo Giampetroni	Dan Webb
Gray Baskerville	Rich Boyd	Sterling Ashby

Keith Crain

Bruce Meyer

Top Hat John

EJ Potter

Larry Wood

Jack Florence

Paul LeMat

Kay Buehrig

Daryl Starbird

Rebel Without A Clue Too?

On April 3, 2022, nine months to the day after I called my father to start this book asking, "Are you ready?" I called him again.

With "Whiter Shade of Pale" playing in the background, his dad's favorite song, Sean learned it was released on May 12, 1967 (my birthday).

I had just one thing to say to my father. "It's done."

We both became emotional. It was a short phone call.

To celebrate, my wife took this photo. We don't drink alcohol so I thought it was a perfect close to the book about my Rebel without a Clue father showing I didn't fall far from the tree.

If you want to join me in my effort to empower abused children, In 2023, I will publish the children's book, "A Frenchie Tail" and "Soul Shine" about ordinary men and women devastated by tragedy, rising and creating change for their city, state, and country.